Essentials of Psychological Assessment Supervision

Essentials of Psychological Assessment Series

Series Editors, Alan S. Kaufman and Nadeen L. Kaufman

Essentials

of Psychological

Assessment Supervision

Edited by

A. Jordan Wright

Registered Office
John Wiley & Sons, Inc., 111 River Street, Hoboken, NJ 07030, USA

Editorial Office
111 River Street, Hoboken, NJ 07030, USA

For details of our global editorial offices, customer services, and more information about Wiley products visit us at www.wiley.com.

Wiley also publishes its books in a variety of electronic formats and by print-on-demand. Some content that appears in standard print versions of this book may not be available in other formats.

Library of Congress Cataloging-in-Publication Data
Names: Wright, A. Jordan, editor.
Title: Essentials of psychological assessment supervision / edited by A. Jordan Wright.
Description: Hoboken. NJ : John Wiley and Sons, 2020. | Series: Essentials of psychological assessment | Includes bibliographical references and index.
Identifiers: LCCN 2019016570 (print) | LCCN 2019980140 (ebook) | ISBN 9781119433040 (paperback) | ISBN 9781119433019 (epub) | ISBN 9781119433002 (pdf)
Subjects: LCSH: Psychotherapists—Supervision of. | Clinical psychologists—Supervision of. | Psychotherapy—Study and teaching—Supervision. | Psychodiagnostics—Handbooks, manuals, etc.
Classification: LCC RC459 .E87 2020 (print) | LCC RC459 (ebook) | DDC 150.28/7—dc23
LC record available at https://lccn.loc.gov/2019016570
LC ebook record available at https://lccn.loc.gov/2019980140

Cover Design: Wiley
Cover Image: © Greg Kuchik/Getty Images

Set in 10.5/13pt Adobe Garamond Pro by Aptara Inc., New Delhi, India

Printed in the United States of America

V10013989_093019

CONTENTS

SERIES PREFACE

I n the *Essentials of Psychological Assessment* series, we have attempted to provide the reader with books that will deliver key practical information in the most efficient and accessible style. Many books in the series feature specific instruments in a variety of domains, such as cognition, personality, education, and neuropsychology. Other books, like *Essentials of Psychological Assessment Supervision*, focus on crucial topics for professionals who are involved in any with assessment—topics such as specific reading disabilities, evidence-based interventions, or attention deficit hyperactivity disorder (ADHD) assessment. For the experienced professional, books in the series offer a concise yet thorough review of a test instrument or a specific area of expertise, including numerous tips for best practices. Students can turn to series books for a clear and concise overview of the important assessment tools, and key topics, in which they must become proficient to practice skillfully, efficiently, and ethically in their chosen fields.

Wherever feasible, visual cues highlighting key points are utilized alongside systematic, step-by-step guidelines. Chapters are focused and succinct. Topics are organized for an easy understanding of the essential material related to a particular test or topic. Theory and research are continually woven into the fabric of each book, but always to enhance the practical application of the material, rather than to sidetrack or overwhelm readers. With this series, we aim to challenge and assist readers interested in psychological assessment to aspire to the highest level of competency by arming them with the tools they need for knowledgeable, informed practice. We have long been advocates of "intelligent" testing—the notion that numbers are meaningless unless they are brought to life by the clinical acumen and expertise of examiners. Assessment must be used to make a difference in the child's or adult's life, or why bother to test? All books in the series—whether devoted to specific tests or general topics—are consistent with this credo. We want this series to help our readers, novice and veteran alike, to benefit from the intelligent assessment approaches of the authors of each book.

Essentials of Psychological Assessment Supervision includes practical, evidence-based approaches to supervising the process of psychological assessment. All who have supervised students, trainees, and colleagues on testing and assessment know it is qualitatively different from supervising general counseling and psychotherapy. However, too little has been written to actually guide supervisors in the process of ensuring both high quality services for their supervisees' clients and adequate learning and development for the supervisees themselves. While too little empirical inquiry into this topic currently exists, this volume attempts to fill this gap, working from the literatures on assessment supervision, supervision in general, and the assessment process more broadly. Supervision is a core competency in the field of psychology, and this volume fills a salient hole in what is written about this very important aspect of many psychologists' work, notably those who supervise forensic, neuropsychological, psychoeducational, and therapeutic assessments.

Alan S. Kaufman, PhD, and Nadeen L. Kaufman, EdD,
Series Editors
Yale Child Study Center, Yale University School of Medicine

INTRODUCTION

A. Jordan Wright

Supervision has received more attention recently (and especially with the publication of the APA's Guidelines for Clinical Supervision in Health Service Psychology, 2017) as one of the core competencies for psychologists-in-training. However, the topic of clinical supervision of psychological testing and assessment has not received much attention (Iwanicki & Peterson, 2017). This book aims to provide practical, relevant information to those psychologists supervising students, trainees, and colleagues at all different developmental levels in the competent and ethical administration of psychological assessment services.

THE SUPERVISION PROCESS

The process of clinical supervision in general is one component of educating psychologists-in-training. It includes aspects of teaching and mentoring, as well as other components distinct from both (American Psychological Association [APA], 2015; 2017; Yalof & Abraham, 2009). Bernard and Goodyear (2004) highlight the role of the supervisor as not only to enhance and evaluate the professional work of the supervisee, but also to serve as a gatekeeper to the field of psychology. Many have pointed to the importance of supervised practical experience in the development of not just knowledge and skills, but actual competencies

Essentials of Psychological Assessment Supervision, First Edition.
Edited by A. Jordan Wright
© 2020 John Wiley & Sons, Inc. Published 2020 by John Wiley & Sons, Inc.

(APA, 2015; Beck et al., 2015; Finkelstein & Tuckman, 1997; Kaslow, Finklea, & Chan, 2018; Smith, 2017). How best to accomplish the goals of improving competence in assessment (and allowing supervisees "through the gate" into the field of independent practice), though, is less clear.

In the field of education, there has been an ongoing debate and line of questioning about the most effective methods for educating students. Much of the debate centers on the distinction between the teacher being a "sage on the stage" (such as in more didactic presentation, being more directive) and a "guide on the side" (such as in more experiential learning techniques, allowing students to take more responsibility for guiding the course of their learning, being less directive; King, 1993). Clinical supervision of psychotherapy most often falls solidly in the guide on the side spectrum of educational pedagogy, allowing supervisees to direct much of the flow of supervision, ask questions, bring conceptualization, and often guide themselves through a mistake-and-repair process with their clients.

Assessment, and its supervision, however, is significantly different from psychotherapy and counseling. First, it is generally much more time-limited. Assessments are usually a one-shot deal, without the luxury of open-endedness to build rapport, figure stuff out, and fix any mistakes that arise. Second, the processes in assessment are often not as reparable as those in psychotherapy. That is, procedures like the administration of tests often cannot be "fixed"; if a supervisee administers a test in an invalid manner, there's no easy way to correct it. This is in contrast to a psychotherapy intervention, which most often, if it does not work, can be corrected with another intervention later on. Finally (though obviously there are many more distinctions that can be made between therapy and assessment), while much of psychotherapy and counseling can be extremely important for the client, assessment is very often extremely high-stakes. That is, the relatively brief process of assessment most often has an extremely major and often immediate impact on the life, circumstances, or functioning of the person being assessed. Child custody decisions, learning accommodations, different trajectories of psychiatric and psychological treatment, competency, and many other high-stakes decisions hinge on assessments. Major decisions can hinge on therapeutic treatment, of course, but overall therapy tends to be less high-stakes than assessment.

The major consequence of these differences is that assessment supervision cannot as automatically fall on the side of guide on the side (non-directive), as can therapy supervision. On the continuum from sage on the stage to guide on the side, assessment supervision may fluctuate (depending on many different variables) much more than therapy supervision. The supervisor must keep many different things in mind when deciding how directive or non-directive to be in the supervision, including the general developmental level of knowledge and skills of the supervisee; the nature, severity, and gravity of the case; how the supervisee performs; and how the process unfolds.

A key component to keep in mind is that supervision takes time; a lot of time. One of the biggest obstacles found to prevent professionals from receiving adequate supervision, which in turn allows them to feel confident in their own competence in practice, is limited time and availability of supervisors (Silva, Newman, Guiney, Valley-Gray, & Varrett, 2016). Supervisors (and supervisees) need to

> **REMEMBER**
>
> When deciding how directive vs. non-directive to be, supervisors must keep in mind:
> - Developmental level of knowledge and skills of the supervisee
> - The nature, severity, and gravity of the case
> - How the supervisee performs
> - How the process unfolds

respect that this is the case, even when there is a temptation to take shortcuts in the process. Subpar supervision (either in quality or quantity) can significantly negatively impact supervisees in many ways, some obvious and perhaps some more subtle (such as their enjoyment of the process). Give supervision the time it deserves.

AN ASSESSMENT-BASED MODEL OF ASSESSMENT SUPERVISION

It is assumed that a supervisor of psychological assessment has at least proficiency (if not expertise) in the process of psychological assessment itself. As such, a supervisor should be good at both formal and informal assessment, skills that can easily be applied to the supervisory relationship. When beginning the supervisory contact between an assessment supervisor and an assessment supervisee, it is important for the supervisor to evaluate the developmental level of knowledge and skills of the supervisee. This can be accomplished in a combination of both formal and informal ways. The first step is to evaluate the general clinical and interpersonal skill of the supervisee, as this will play an important role in the assessment process. That is, the ability for the assessor to quickly build at least a baseline level of rapport and put the client at ease needs to be explicitly evaluated (though this is often an informal process of the supervisor simply interacting with the supervisee) and addressed, if necessary. Supervisors should not shy away from discussing these more subtle and nuanced interpersonal aspects with their supervisees, as they can affect test performance.

The second step is to evaluate developmental level in terms of testing. For example, a supervisee should provide for his or her supervisor a list of all coursework and experience in assessment that has been completed, including specifics of tests learned, concepts focused on, etc. It is important to remember, though, that just because a test was covered in a course or in a clinical placement does not mean that the supervisee is competent in administering, coding, scoring, interpreting, or otherwise using that test. Other methods can round out an assessment of competence in test use, such as practicing an administration on the supervisor or discussing coding and scoring rules for different measures. Ultimately, the supervisor needs to determine how much guidance (directiveness, sage-on-the-stageness) the supervisee needs in terms of test administration (usually the primary concern) and coding, scoring, and interpretation. Supervisors need to remember that test administration is one of the tasks in the assessment process that often cannot easily be "fixed" later on, so they need to be extremely confident in the ability of their supervisee to accomplish this task well.

In addition to evaluating developmental level in terms of testing, it can be extremely useful for a supervisor to see a few sample reports written by the supervisee. Evaluating these can help a supervisor gain an understanding of the level of sophistication the supervisee currently brings to the process of integrating data, integrating context and culture, and conceptualizing cases. Much like the testing process, the process of putting together data and conceptualizing may require more guidance from the supervisor when supervisees have less experience, while the supervisor of the more advanced supervisee can take a more guide-on-the-side stance.

Assessment of the supervisee and the process of the assessment should continue throughout the supervisory process. There may be tasks related to the process that the supervisee has more mastery over, and there may be later tasks that require more guidance. Further, depending on how the process unfolds, it may become clear that the supervisory stance (on the continuum between directive and non-directive) needs to shift, even within a single assessment case. The supervisor should be vigilant about maintaining his or her assessment orientation throughout the supervisory relationship, in order to meet the needs of the supervisee (and in turn the client).

DON'T FORGET

Areas to Assess to Determine How Directive to Be in Supervision

- Supervisee's interpersonal (or "soft") skills
- Knowledge and skill in test administration
- Knowledge and skill in other areas of test use (scoring, interpretation, etc.)
- Report writing (including sophistication of integration of data, culture, and context and case conceptualization)

PHASES OF SUPERVISION IN ASSESSMENT

It is important for the work of an assessment supervisee to have constant, clear, and conscientious supervision throughout each phase of the assessment process. While different sites and types of assessment services may vary in their processes, in general clinical assessments follow a relatively standard workflow. At each point in the assessment process, supervisors should evaluate the developmental level of knowledge and skills (toward evaluating how competent the supervisee will likely be at application) to determine the level of support and directiveness needed in supervision.

Assessment Planning and Context

From the moment of referral for an assessment, there is work to be done. The supervisee must think through and plan how and when to contact the client (or the parents/guardians, or whomever it is appropriate to contact) to discuss the process of assessment and plan a first session. Depending on the amount of information in the referral or application, the supervisee may already be thinking about an appropriate battery of tests to give. The supervisor should discuss the case with the supervisee, always evaluating just how much directiveness is needed in supervision, in order to ensure that the supervisee is fully prepared to engage in the beginning of the assessment relationship with the client. Some supervisees need to be told exactly how to proceed—they may need a reminder of policies of the organization where the assessment is taking place, practice with mock phone calls to be ready to answer potential questions that the client may have, practice explaining exactly what the process of the assessment will generally look like, and even support in calling the client with the supervisor present. Other, more advanced supervisees may simply need to be given the go-ahead to contact the client, if and when the supervisor is confident that the assessor can handle this beginning phase with the client.

Contextualizing the Problem and Selecting a Battery

Often, it is after a first clinical interview (whether structured, semi-structured, or completely unstructured) that an assessment begins to take form. A general question that can be asked of clients is also a good question to ask of supervisees: *What question(s) do you want answered with this assessment?* This is the beginning of understanding what the assessment can (and cannot) do for the client (or the stakeholders of the assessment), as well as situating it within a larger context. Clients and less experienced trainees often need help honing the answer to this question into something that is realistic and doable within a psychological assessment, while more advanced supervisees are generally more familiar with how to focus

RECOMMENDED

Supervisors and supervisees, regardless of level of competency, should meet at the point during an assessment when the presenting problems are being clarified and the assessment questions themselves need to be clearly articulated.

this. Supervisors should gauge exactly how much support their supervisee needs at this stage. It is recommended, though, that actual, in-person supervision occur at this point, regardless of the level of experience and competency of the supervisee. That is, every supervision process should take a moment at this point in the assessment to meet and discuss the case.

During this phase of the process, once the assessment questions have been clearly articulated (and situated within culture and context), the assessment process requires the selection of an appropriate testing battery (which may include both formal testing measures and other sources of information, such as records reviews, collateral interviews, previous reports, etc.). Again, this is when supervisors should evaluate just how much guidance their supervisees need. In some contexts and situations, the battery may be relatively straightforward and easy to select (e.g., many psychoeducational batteries, for example examining learning disabilities and/or ADHD, may look mostly consistent across assessment cases), though some may be more difficult to determine (e.g., an adult personality and psychodiagnostic evaluation may require the assessor to select appropriate measures from among many possibilities). Supervisees should be reminded, as needed, of all aspects of tests and measurement that are relevant in selecting tests for an individual assessment—these include psychometric properties of the tests (including reliability, validity, and utility); issues around culture and diversity (including understanding the normative group used for each measure); the reading level of self-report measures; and how likely each test is to contribute to the ruling out or ruling in of diagnostic and conceptual hypotheses, among other things. Of course, this may not be an immutable decision—often testing batteries need to change based on how a client performs throughout the process—but it is a start. Supervisors are ultimately responsible (regardless of how hands-on or hands-off they are at this point in the process) for ensuring that the testing battery is appropriate and sufficient to answer the referral questions.

Test Administration

This phase of the assessment process is singled out and separated from the others because of how important it is for an assessor to "get it right the first time." That is, it is often extremely difficult for an assessor or supervisor to go back and correct mistakes in the administration of tests and measures within a single assessment. This is obviously more true for some measures than others, but in general, performance-based measures (like intelligence tests, neuropsychological tests, educational tests, etc.) need to be administered correctly the first time in order to be valid and useful in the context of the assessment. Supervisors must explicitly and deliberately evaluate how competent supervisees are at administering the tests being used. As discussed previously, this may require a survey of what training the supervisee has had, a discussion of administration and coding procedures, or even a practice administration (or observed administration). It is ultimately the ethical responsibility of the supervisor to ensure that clients are receiving adequate services, spelled out in APA's (2016) ethics code, the American Educational Research Association's (AERA, 2014) standards for psychological testing, and the National Association of School Psychologists' (NASP, 2010) principles for professional ethics, as well as others. As such, supervisors should not short-cut this part of the process or assume that supervisees will always administer tests correctly.

> **DON'T FORGET!**
>
> Supervisors must explicitly and deliberately evaluate how competent supervisees are at administering the tests being used.

Test Coding, Scoring, and Interpretation

While some test item coding (applying the coding scheme of the test developers to the individual items) is required during test administration to ensure accuracy of administration, some happens after the administration phase of the tests, as do (most often) scoring (calculating the scores of scales and indices) and interpretation. Again, supervisors should explicitly (formally or informally) evaluate how much support and guidance is needed by each supervisee for this process. The amount of directive guidance needed may vary depending on supervisee competence, different measures (some are simply easier to score and interpret than others), and client performance (some configurations of performance may be more difficult to understand than others). Supervisors should again ensure that all tests are coded, scored, and interpreted in a way that is consistent with empirical literature and accepted clinical practice, as well as contextualized within culture and the client's individual situation. It bears repeating that the supervisor is ultimately responsible for ensuring that the tests are used appropriately.

Data Integration and Case Conceptualization

Different placements, types of assessments, and supervisors will have different ideas about how tests and other information should be integrated, how much integration is necessary, how much theory to integrate into the conceptualization, etc. Supervisors should not take for granted the wide variation in practice at this point in the assessment process in the field. No matter how competent or advanced a supervisee is, he or she may not have had any experience integrating data, reconciling apparent contradictions in data, contextualizing the data in culture and the client's individual situation, or formulating and conceptualizing cases in the way that the supervisor feels is adequate or appropriate. It may be best to consider the supervisory relationship as another developmental process that begins and grows, such that (no matter the level of knowledge, skill, or competence of the supervisee) the first case that is supervised in the relationship requires more directive guidance at this point, with less and less "hand-holding" as the relationship continues (as the supervisee conducts more assessments with that particular supervisor). The supervisor may have a process that is methodical and structured, or it may be more intuitively driven, but the first assessment within this supervisory relationship may be most effective if the supervisor takes the reigns at this point of the process and demonstrates how he or she tends to "put it all together." Best case, supervisees learn and grow through every exposure they have to different supervisors and how they go through this process.

Writing

Much like the conceptualization phase of the assessment, how assessments are written varies dramatically throughout the field. This is a phase of the assessment when supervisors have to make an explicit decision about how hands-on they will be, how they will structure feedback to their supervisees, and what the overall process will look like, taking into consideration the supervisory relationship (which will be addressed below). Some supervisors prefer to provide sample reports to supervisees, so that they are clear with what they expect. Others provide templates only. Others focus less on the writing style of the supervisee and more on the actual clarity of the content presented in the report. Whatever the process and focus of this phase of supervision, the supervisor should be clear with the supervisee about his or her expectations. Teaching effective report writing is perhaps one of the toughest aspects of assessment training and supervision (there is a chapter dedicated to just this in the current volume), and supervisors need to be clear with themselves and their supervisees, in order to minimize frustration, workload, and potential problems in the relationship between supervisor and supervisee. Part of this process should be a careful consideration of conclusions and (when appropriate) recommendations written into the report. Often, supervisees will need more guidance than they think to fully address the clear, specific, and reasonable recommendations that flow directly from the conclusions.

It should not be underestimated just how many mistakes end up in psychological assessment reports, even those written by competent, fully independent professionals. This has been well documented (for examples of just cognitive score data errors, see Belk, LoBello, Ray, & Zachar, 2002; Erdodi, Richard, & Hopwood, 2009; Kuentzel, Hetterscheidt, & Barnett, 2011; Loe, Kadlubek, & Marks, 2007; Oak, Viezel, Dumont, & Willis, 2018; Styck & Walsh, 2016). We as a profession need to be better than this, given both how easily fixable this problem truly is and how important and major the consequences of these errors can be. Supervisors need to be vigilant about scoring and writing errors (it should be noted that errors can occur in the coding and scoring, as previously discussed, as well as in the transfer of information into the actual report).

Feedback

Often the final phase of a traditional assessment (there are exceptions; see chapter 9 on Therapeutic Assessment for one example) is the assessor providing feedback to the client and/or the stakeholders of the process (courts, parents/legal guardians, schools, etc.). This phase of the assessment process has been conceptualized as a "hybrid session" (Wright, 2010), as it includes technical components of research/assessment (providing facts and figures) within the context of a therapeutic relationship; it is a hybrid of research and therapy. The assessor often needs to fade back and forth between being a source of information and a supportive therapist, which is not always an easy balance. Often, supervisees are better at one of these skills than the other; supervisors should figure out a way of evaluating this in order to prepare supervisees so their feedback sessions go as well as possible (one of the hard truths about psychological assessment is that there are times when the feedback is simply hard for the client to hear, and there are feedback sessions that simply will not and do not "go well" in some way). One aspect of providing feedback sessions that often goes unaddressed in training programs is how to frame the entire process/session for a client. There are many ways to do this, and one model is provided below.

☰ *Rapid Reference*

A Model for Framing Feedback to Clients

1. Warn the client that this process is a strange one. This is a way of meeting the client where he or she likely is—hearing feedback about oneself is bizarre; hearing it from someone who only just met you a few weeks ago is extra bizarre!
2. Discuss the legal and ethical parameters of the feedback session and report. This often includes a reminder that the report is the client's property, and he or she can do with it whatever he or she wants (obviously, this varies by setting and referral). It also includes the fact that the assessor can *not* do with it whatever he or she wants. For example, if the client wants the assessor to give feedback to another provider or send the report, the client will need to provide written consent for this.
3. Discuss limitations of the report/feedback. For example, it is often useful to warn a client that there may be minor factual errors in the background section, which can easily be corrected (this is a byproduct of the fact that assessors are often trying to obtain and write down a great deal of information in a short amount of time—errors can be made!). It may also include a discussion of the fact that the report may not take into account or address every single strength and weakness or dynamic that is part of the person being assessed.
4. Frame the feedback process as a whole. If this one session is it, state that clearly. If the assessor has the flexibility to offer another meeting, a phone call, etc., to the client as follow-up after the client has had time to "digest" the information, state that clearly.
5. Frame the feedback session as a whole. Tell the client what the sections are that will be addressed. For example, in a comprehensive psychodiagnostic evaluation, the assessor may preface the session by letting the client know that the assessor will first present findings around cognitive functioning, then around personality and emotional functioning, then recommendations.
6. Ask if all is clear and whether the client has any questions.

If and when it is possible, it is extremely useful for a supervisor to observe feedback sessions (in the room, live by one-way mirror or video, or delayed in a recording). It is also extremely useful whenever possible for supervisees to watch their own feedback sessions. An exercise that can be used (though this obviously adds to the time and workload of both the supervisee and the supervisor) is for the assessor to watch his or her own feedback session and write out and bring to supervision a list of strengths and areas of improvement he or she identified.

When a supervisor is observing a feedback session, there are multiple things to focus on. Some of these include: Was the information presented clearly? Did the supervisee ensure that the client (or stakeholder) understood what was being presented? Did the supervisee attend to the in-the-moment needs of the client (e.g., pausing if the client appears to be having an emotional reaction to something)? Were recommendations clearly presented? Was it clear what would happen at the end of the session (e.g., if the client needs help following up on recommendations, is it clear how that will happen and who is responsible for initiating the next contact; if the client is able to ask follow-up questions, is it clear how he or she should contact the assessor and/or supervisor)?

Closing the Loop

While this is not always possible, it is recommended that supervisors and supervisees meet after a case has been completed and closed to evaluate how it went. This is an important point in the process of supervision, as it can include feedback from supervisor to supervisee, feedback from supervisee to supervisor, coming to a mutual understanding of what worked well and what did not in the supervisory process (including what points needed more or less directive guidance), and a plan for how the next supervision may look different (if there is another case coming). As is true throughout the process, special attention should be paid to the supervisory relationship during this part of the process.

THE SUPERVISORY RELATIONSHIP

Although not unique to supervision of psychological assessment per se, it is nonetheless paramount to think critically about the role of the supervisory relationship in assessment supervision. Many guidelines on supervision in general emphasize the importance of a collaborative, positive, reciprocal relationship between supervisor and supervisee (e.g., APA, 2017; NASP, 2018). A strong working relationship is critical for supervisees to truly learn what they need to learn in supervision, especially when feedback is constructive or critical. Components of strong working relationships, of course, have a long history of being enumerated in the field of psychology, and they will not be repeated here, except for some components that are particularly difficult in assessment supervision. As

> **REMEMBER**
>
> Fostering a positive working relationship between yourself as the supervisor and your supervisees is *critical* to their professional development.

with any supervisory relationship, issues of power, trust, control, expertise, and "blind spots" (both the supervisor's and supervisee's) need to be considered, and clarity around roles and responsibilities can help immensely in navigating these issues fluidly.

Supervisor Style

The primary suggestions about the interpersonal and communication style of the supervisor are going to sound contradictory: be genuine to who you are and be flexible and adaptable to the needs of your supervisee. Supervisors should endeavor to work with supervisees the way they would work and interact with other professionals. Forcing humor, warmth, or other seemingly desirable traits that are not consistent with the supervisor's personality and style is misguided. That being said, supervisors should be flexible and adaptable in style to the needs of the supervisee (see, for example, Crespi & Fischetti, 1997). For example, it has been noted that culture can affect the interpersonal dynamics between supervisors and supervisees (e.g., Eklund, Aros-O'Malley, & Murrieta, 2014). Supervisors should make sure that they respect the culture, background, and context of the supervisees when interacting with them, working hard to consistently foster a positive relationship, even when discussing reflective feedback (Barnett, Erickson Cornish, Goodyear, & Lichtenberg, 2007; Wu, 2013).

Supervisor Communication

The key ingredients for effective supervisory communication, especially with, but not limited to, difficult feedback, have been identified in the social skills literature related to assertiveness: supervisors should be clear and honest in the information they are delivering, while respecting the rights (and feelings) of the supervisee (Lange & Jakubowski, 1976). This does not mean that supervisors should not give difficult feedback if they feel it may hurt a supervisee's feelings; rather, they should make sure that they consider how best to deliver feedback when and if it is necessary and appropriate.

> **REMEMBER**
> ....
> Communication and feedback between supervisor and supervisee should be clear/honest and respectful.

When it comes to general communication, it is extremely important for supervisors to be clear when establishing both goals for supervision and expectations for both parties in the process. Goal-setting relates to the broader knowledge, skills, and competencies that the supervisor and supervisee want the supervisee to have at the end of the supervisory process. Hass and Carriere (2008) emphasized how engaging in explicit dialogue with supervisees around their wants and needs from supervision is a respectful way of engaging them and can convey the feeling that supervisors genuinely want to understand and help their supervisees. Setting goals for assessment supervision more broadly, while they can get lost when in the weeds of the actual work of assessment, can be revisited in the closing-the-loop phase of assessment supervision, to ensure that the knowledge, skills, and competencies that the supervisee wants to gain are being adequately addressed.

Expectations for the process of assessment and assessment supervision are more granular than goals. These also tend to be more top-down from supervisor (or agency, organization, school, etc.) to supervisee. For example, it is often expected that supervisees be timely in their work (e.g., turning around assessment report drafts). Another example is that supervisees are expected to bring questions to supervision about aspects of the assessment or testing sessions that they need help with. Whatever the specific expectations are, it is extremely important for supervisors to be clear and explicit about them.

Finally, when thinking about communication between supervisors and supervisees, it is recommended that supervisors work hard to model professionalism, self-reflection, and critical thinking. Because of the power hierarchy in the supervisory relationship, supervisors set the tone of the interaction. If supervisors are often late for supervision sessions, for example, they convey that supervision is less important than it actually is, and supervisees may pick up on this and treat supervision sessions with less respect. Further, when supervisors "think aloud" about their problem-solving processes, potential blind spots, and struggles in conceptualization, they model a way of thinking that allows supervisees both to gain an understanding of the process of critical and self-reflective thinking and to maintain a humility in their work with the necessarily complex, nuanced, and unclear constructs that emerge in psychological assessment (Schön, 1983). That is, supervisees will learn the skill of thinking through problems like the supervisor does, and they will see the supervisor acknowledge that this process is difficult and rarely clear-cut.

Feedback

Perhaps most difficult in the supervisory relationship is striking the balance between maintaining high standards in the work being done by the supervisee and being supportive and respectful of them when they struggle (Guiney, 2018). As stated previously, supervisors are gatekeepers to the profession, and subpar assessment work cannot be ignored. Competence requires knowledge, skills, and application (including ethical behavior), and shortcomings in any of these areas can lead to problems in assessment services. Supervisors need, again, to practice assertiveness, being clear and honest about feedback while respecting the rights and feelings of the supervisee. Supervisees need to feel respected and empowered, while at the same time clearly guided and corrected, when necessary. The foundation of a collaborative relationship can help immensely with this. That is, when supervisees feel that constructive or critical feedback is some sort of attack on them, they can become defensive and guarded. If supervisees feel that the supervisor respects them and all feedback is offered in the spirit of helping them grow and learn, they are much more likely to be open to it. This is even true when confronting behavior on the part of the supervisee that is seemingly unethical. While providing constructive feedback is often unpleasant and often tests the strength of the supervisory relationship, it is critical. Supervisors cannot shy away from it.

CONCLUSION

Supervising psychological assessments requires all of the same skills as supervising other work delivered by practicing psychologists and trainees, such as counseling, consulting, and outreach. However, it also requires additional skills, as the process must balance the facts that assessment training in training programs is often (at best) incomplete, requiring supervision to incorporate a didactic component; that assessments are often extremely short-term and high-stakes, with little to no opportunity to correct mistakes; and that the components that make up the process of psychological assessment are quite varied and discrete, such that supervisees can be fully competent in some aspects and not in others. Supervisors should be vigilant about continually and repeatedly assessing the knowledge, skill, and competency levels of supervisees during each step of the assessment process and adapt their supervision style to meet the needs of the supervisee throughout. This process is arduous and tedious, but necessary. The ultimate goal of supervisees gaining competency across the entire process of psychological assessment hinges on good supervision.

REFERENCES

American Educational Research Association (AERA). (2014). *Standards for educational and psychological testing*. Washington, DC: Author.
American Psychological Association. (2015). Guidelines for clinical supervision in health service psychology. *The American Psychologist, 70*(1), 33–46.

American Psychological Association (APA). (2016). *Ethical principles of psychologists and code of conduct.* Washington, DC: Author. Retrieved from http://www.apa.org/ethics/code/index.aspx

American Psychological Association (APA). (2017). Guidelines for clinical supervision in health service psychology. Retrieved from https://www.apa.org/about/policy/guidelines-supervision.pdf

Barnett, J. E., Erickson Cornish, J. A., Goodyear, R. K., & Lichtenberg, J. W. (2007). Commentaries on the ethical and effective practice of clinical supervision. *Professional Psychology: Research and Practice*, 38(3), 268–275. https://doi.org/10.1037/0735-7028.38.3.268

Beck, J. G., Castonguay, L. G., Chronis-Tuscano, A., Klonsky, E. D., McGinn, L. K., & Youngstrom, E. A. (2015). Principles for training in evidence-based psychology: Recommendations for the graduate curricula in clinical psychology. *Clinical Psychology: Science and Practice*, 21, 410–424.

Belk, M. S., LoBello, S. G., Ray, G. E., & Zachar, P. (2002). WISC-III administration, clerical, and scoring errors made by student examiners. *Journal of Psychoeducational Assessment*, 20(3), 290–300. https://doi.org/10.1177/073428290202000305

Bernard, J. M., & Goodyear, R. K. (2004). *Fundamentals of clinical supervision (3).* London: Pearson.

Crespi, T. D., & Fischetti, B. A. (1997). Clinical supervision for school psychologists: Bridging theory and practice. *School Psychology International*, 18(1), 41–48. https://doi.org/10.1177/0143034397181004

Eklund, K., Aros-O'Malley, M., & Murrieta, I. (2014). Multicultural supervision: What difference does difference make? *Contemporary School Psychology*, 18(3), 195–204. https://doi.org/10.1007/s40688-014-0024-8

Erdodi, L. A., Richard, D. S., & Hopwood, C. (2009). The importance of relying on the manual: Scoring error variance in the WISC-IV Vocabulary subtest. *Journal of Psychoeducational Assessment*, 27(5), 374–385. https://doi.org/10.1177/0734282909332913

Finkelstein, H., & Tuckman, A. (1997). Supervision of psychological assessment: A developmental model. *Professional Psychology: Research and Practice*, 28, 92–95.

Guiney, M. C. (2018). Addressing problems of professional competence: Collaborating with university training programs to support struggling supervisees. *Communiqué*, 46(6), 4–7. Retrieved from https://www.nasponline.org/resources-and-publications/periodicals/communiqu%C3%A9-volume-46-number-6-(march/april-2018)/

addressing-problems-of-professional-competence-collaborating-with-university-training-programs-to-support-struggling-supervisees

Hass, M., & Carriere, J. A. (2008). Tools for working with school psychology practicum students and interns. *CASP Today*, 58(2), 8–10.

Iwanicki, S., & Peterson, C. (2017). An exploratory study examining current assessment supervisory practices in professional psychology. *Journal of Personality Assessment*, 99(2), 165–174. https://doi.org/10.1080/00223891.2 016.1228068

Kaslow, N. J., Finklea, J. T., & Chan, G. (2018). Personality assessment: A competency-capability perspective. *Journal of Personality Assessment*, 100, 176–185.

King, A. (1993). From sage on the stage to guide on the side. *College Teaching*, 41(1), 30–35.

Kuentzel, J. G., Hetterscheidt, L. A., & Barnett, D. (2011). Testing intelligently includes double-checking Wechsler IQ scores. *Journal of Psychoeducational Assessment*, 29(1). https://doi.org/10.1177/0734282910362048

Lange, A. J., & Jakubowski, P. (1976). *Responsible assertive behavior: Cognitive/ behavioral techniques for trainers.* Champaign, IL: Research Press.

Loe, S. A., Kadlubek, R. M., & Marks, W. J. (2007). Administration and scoring errors on the WISC-IV among graduate student examiners. *Journal of Psychoeducational Assessment*, 25, 237–247. https://doi.org/10.1177/0734282906296505

National Association of School Psychologists (2018). *Supervision in school psychology [position statement].* Bethesda, MD: Author. Retrieved from file:///C:/Users/ajw11/Downloads/Supervision_in_School.pdf

National Association of School Psychologists (NASP). (2010). Principles for professional ethics. Bethesda, MD: Author. Retrieved from http://www. nasponline.org/standards-and-certification/professional-ethics.

Oak, E., Viezel, K. D., Dumont, R., & Willis, J. (2018). Wechsler administration and scoring errors made by graduate students and school psychologists. *Journal of Psychoeducational Assessment.* https://doi.org/10.1177/0734282918786355

Schön, D. (1983). *The reflective practitioner. How professionals think in action.* London: Temple.

Silva, A. E., Newman, D. S., Guiney, M. C., Valley-Gray, S., & Varrett, C. A. (2016). Supervision and mentoring for early school psychologists: Availability, access, structure, and implications. *Psychology in the Schools*, 53(5), 502–516. https://doi.org/10.1002/pits.21921

Smith, J. D. (2017). Introduction to the special section on teaching, training, and supervision in personality and psychological assessment. *Journal of Personality Assessment, 99,* 113–116.

Styck, K. M., & Walsh, S. M. (2016). Evaluating the prevalence and impact of examiner errors on the Wechsler scales of intelligence: A meta-analysis. *Psychological Assessment, 28,* 3–17. https://doi.org/10.1037/pas0000157

Wright, A. J. (2010). *Conducting psychological assessment: A guide for practitioners.* Hoboken, NJ: Wiley.

Wu, T. C. (2013). Fostering self-reflection in multicultural school psychology supervision. *Communiqué, 42*(3), 14.

Yalof, J., & Abraham, P. (2009). An integrative approach to assessment supervision. *Bulletin of the Menninger Clinic, 73,* 188–202.

One

THE USE OF GUIDELINES IN ASSESSMENT SUPERVISION

A. Jordan Wright
Virginia M. Brabender
Hadas Pade

G uidelines have been developed for all sorts of different aspects of work in the field of psychology. Psychological assessment training and supervision is often a component of these sets of guidelines, but using them as a resource or tool in actual supervision is not often accomplished. This chapter presents three sets of guidelines that can be useful in the work of the supervisor during psychological assessment supervision. One set of guidelines presented, the American Psychological Association's (APA, 2015) Guidelines for Clinical Supervision in Health Service Psychology, is more broadly about supervision and needs to be adapted. The second set, the National Council of Schools and Programs of Professional Psychology's (NCSPP, 2007) Competency Developmental Achievement Levels, has specific components that are relevant to assessment. The third set, the Society for Personality Assessment's (SPA, 2015) framework, was developed specifically for the practice of psychological assessment. Supervisors are encouraged to read through each set of guidelines and determine how each of these can help them be more effective, more clear, and more deliberate in their work with supervisees.

Essentials of Psychological Assessment Supervision, First Edition.
Edited by A. Jordan Wright

APA'S SUPERVISION GUIDELINES

The American Psychological Association's (APA, 2015) Guidelines for Clinical Supervision in Health Service Psychology lay out broad areas that are relevant to supervisors across all domains of clinical work in psychology, including assessment, counseling, consulting, and more. Assessment supervisors should strive to know, understand, and meet all of the expectations spelled out in this document, without exception. However, some areas within these guidelines require even more specific knowledge and skill when supervisors are supervising assessment. Each guideline area is addressed below, focusing on what assessment supervisors need to pay attention to, even beyond what is explicitly stated in the guidelines.

Supervisor Competence

It should (hopefully) go without saying that those professionals who are supervising psychological assessment should be competent in both psychological assessment and the provision of supervision. The reality, though, is that often, because of logistical and availability constraints, assessment supervisors are either practitioners who do assessments and have limited specific training in supervision, or they are general clinical supervisors who may do some assessment but do not have specific expertise in it. Aligned with APA's guideline of supervisor competence, supervisors need to ensure that they are fully competent specifically in psychological assessment (including the types of assessment, referral questions, and populations that their supervisees will be working with) and seek out formal training in supervision practices. There are very few (if any) specific trainings on assessment supervision, but many professional

≡ Rapid Reference 1.1

APA's Supervision Guidelines Domain Areas (APA, 2015)

- Domain A: Supervision Competence
- Domain B: Diversity
- Domain C: Supervisory Relationship
- Domain D: Professionalism
- Domain E: Assessment/Evaluation/Feedback
- Domain F: Professional Competence Problems
- Domain G: Ethical, Legal, and Regulatory Considerations

development opportunities on supervision more generally can be usefully applied to assessment supervision. Because of constraints, supervisors should know their own limitations and what resources are available for consultation or additional information. Ideally, all assessment supervisors would be fully proficient (even beyond competent) in both psychological assessment and supervision practices, but supervisors should at least understand any limitations or lapses in their own competence.

Diversity

Obviously deeply ingrained within the profession of psychology is a respect for diversity (broadly defined). APA takes very seriously an understanding of and respect for diversity in every aspect of practicing psychologists' work, and assessment is no exception. As with all the guidelines, assessment supervisors should adhere to the diversity guideline as specified in APA's document. In addition to the broad "diversity competence" that is specified in the guidelines, which includes knowledge, attitudes, and skills related to diversity with regard to client relationships and the supervisory relationship, there are aspects of diversity that are specific to psychological assessment supervision.

Specifically, there are multiple "touch points" in the assessment process that need explicit consideration of diversity issues. In addition to the relationship between supervisee and client, which needs attention to interpersonal style and other cultural components, supervisees and supervisors should consider culture and diversity at multiple other stages in the process. First, when coming up with functional, dynamic, and diagnostic hypotheses about clients, assessors (and thus supervisees) must consider cultural context. Issues like minority stress, acculturative stress, and differences in the ways distress are communicated (among many, many others) should be considered when hypothesizing what may be going on with a client. Next, when deciding how best to test those hypotheses, supervisees must consider diversity issues in test selection, including whether certain tests are appropriate for clients from different backgrounds, including language, normative data availability, acculturation, and other issues. Once tests are determined to be appropriate and are administered and scored, culture and diversity need again to be considered in the interpretation of each individual test. Careful consideration should be given to the normative sample to which the client is being compared, the cultural assumptions for performance on the test, and alternative hypotheses for why test results emerged as they did.

Once tests have been interpreted, the tougher work of the psychological assessment process begins. When integrating all the data together into a case

REMEMBER

Some of the Most Important Diversity "Touch Points" in the Assessment Process

1. The relationship between assessor and client, including ways of communicating
2. Hypothesis development about client functioning and diagnosis
3. Test selection
4. Test interpretation
5. Data integration and case formulation/conceptualization
6. Diagnosis
7. Recommendations
8. Feedback

formulation/conceptualization, supervisors and supervisees must address culture and diversity issues (including individual differences, group differences, systems, cultural norms, and many other issues). That is, supervisors must ensure that supervisees conceptualize cases within the context of culture and diversity, a focus that must continue as diagnosis, recommendations, and feedback are discussed. Supervisors should be explicit about ensuring that culture and diversity have been addressed throughout each of these decision-making "touch points" in the assessment process. One way to ensure this diversity awareness is to encourage or require supervisees to articulate exactly how they have considered and addressed culture and diversity issues at each of these points in the assessment process.

Supervisory Relationship

Again, psychological assessment supervisors should adhere to the guidelines presented by APA, but some aspects of assessment supervision have the potential to make maintaining a positive, supportive, collaborative relationship more difficult than in supervision of psychotherapy. This topic has been addressed in the Introduction of this book, so we will not belabor the point here. The overall idea is that the necessarily hybrid nature of psychological assessment supervision, always teetering between directive and non-directive, didactic and self-guided, can make the supervisor's role in the relationship less clear moment-to-moment. This is not at odds with APA's guidance to maintain a collaborative relationship with supervisees, but it can certainly make it *seem* less collaborative, especially in moments when the supervisor is teaching new tests or providing developmental, formative feedback about specific mistakes or missteps on the part of the supervisee, which can be much more salient than those in psychotherapy supervision.

Professionalism

Psychological assessment supervisors are again encouraged to adhere to the guidelines presented by APA in this domain, modeling professional attitudes and behavior throughout their work and providing specific feedback to supervisees about expectations for professional behavior and their developmental achievement against those expectations. There are no additional aspects of this that are specific to psychological assessment supervision.

Assessment/Evaluation/Feedback

Psychological assessment supervisors should be experts at evaluating supervisees and providing them feedback; ironically, this often is not the case. The below two resources, the National Council of Schools and Programs of Professional Psychology's (NCSPP) developmental achievement levels (DALs) and the SPA's framework, provide mechanisms for evaluating supervisees and providing feedback. It can be tempting for assessment supervisors to focus on either forest or trees (that is, on global and general feedback about the supervisee's competency across the board, or on granular and specific problems with, for example, scoring on a single test), but assessment supervisors need to do both. One suggestion is for assessment supervisors to explicitly forewarn supervisees about what they will be scrutinizing, from the outset. Presenting the framework from which a supervisor is evaluating a supervisee can help maintain the collaborative, supportive relationship between the two.

> **DON'T FORGET**
> ....
> Assessment supervisors need to look *both* at granular, specific aspects of the assessment process (such as administration or scoring errors on particular tests) *and* at broader, more global functioning of supervisees (such as how well diversity is addressed by supervisees, or how well they understand the process of conceptualization).

Professional Competence Problems

Like all of the other guidelines, assessment supervisors should adhere to the guidance provided by APA regarding professional competence problems. The major consideration that is specific to assessment supervision is how to address mistakes, missteps, or other problems when they affect clients in a way that is more difficult to fix. For example, tests administered inappropriately can have a significant negative impact on a client, and it may preclude the client from being able to take that test again in the near future, so a supervisor often cannot just go back in and re-administer the test (because of testing/practice effects, etc.). The guideline that supervisors must be skilled at developing and implementing clear, timely remediation plans extends further in assessment supervision, in that supervisors must be skilled at addressing specific, clinically-related assessment mistakes made by supervisees with competence problems.

Ethical, Legal, and Regulatory Considerations

Like other clinical supervisors, assessment supervisors should model ethical and legal behavior in their practice and supervision, including ethical decision-making throughout the assessment and supervision processes. Further, they should make their expectations clear (again, the models below from NCSPP and SPA can be useful in organizing this) and document performance, progress, and feedback. And like other clinical supervisors, they should maintain the wellbeing of the clients first and foremost (see "Professional Competence Problems" above) and serve as gatekeepers to the field of psychology. Specific to psychological assessment supervision, supervisors are encouraged to understand and address areas of competence within the assessment process from a developmental perspective, knowing that training in psychological assessment is often incomplete, at best, as well as the fact that many professionals will not engage in psychological assessment in their professional practice (though it is important to note that it is within their scope of practice, so simply saying that they won't do it in the future is not good enough— they must still be competent to do it). Further, supervisors should be specifically aware of the legal mandates related to ensuring test security, as well as ethical and legal guidance about whether raw test data (record forms, etc.) are or are not part of the medical record, where and for how long they should be stored, and other such issues related to actual test measures administered.

> **CAUTION**
>
> Supervisors and supervisees must be aware of whether raw test data are considered part of the medical record.

NCSPP'S COMPETENCY DEVELOPMENTAL ACHIEVEMENT LEVELS

While not always explicit, it is extremely helpful for supervisors to recognize the endpoint goal of training in order to support supervisees in traveling to that destination. However, for an activity as complex as psychological assessment, it is not a single goal but a set of interrelated goals that must be achieved before supervisees can be deemed competent for independent practice (let alone excellence) in psychological assessment. Furthermore, although knowledge of distal goals is helpful, also necessary are guideposts along the way of a supervisee's training trajectory. These guideposts both direct the supervisory emphasis during any given training segment and also provide the means to ascertain whether a supervisee is failing to keep apace, suggesting the need for remediation in order that the distal goals might ultimately be fulfilled.

Over the last 25 years, national organizations devoted to the training of professional psychologists, such as the NCSPP, have identified the multicomponent, distal goals of training and supervision at different phases of doctoral training (Rodolfa et al., 2005), based largely on works that emerged from important conferences (Kaslow et al., 2004; Krishnamurthy et al., 2004; Peterson et al., 1992). According to Rodolfa and colleagues, competency "is generally understood to mean that a professional is qualified, capable, and able to understand and do certain things in an appropriate and effective manner" (p. 348). The work of Krishnamurthy et al. (2004) considered specifically how students' acquisition of the assessment competencies might be evaluated. They put forth the seminal notion that evaluation must be developmental. That is, trainers (instructors and supervisors) need to have different expectations for students at different levels of training (also see Fouad et al., 2009). This proposition served as a framework for ensuing work on assessment competencies.

Of note, one of the important achievements of the 2005 Competencies Conference was differentiating between those domains required of all professional psychologists and those specific to particular specialty areas (Rodolfa et al., 2005). This distinction is of particular importance for psychological assessment because of the increasingly specialized nature of assessment practice. For example, the areas of neuropsychology, organizational psychology, and school psychology involve assessment methodologies beyond what would be expected of the generalist psychological assessor. This distinction is useful to the assessment supervisor who at times is required to determine the appropriateness of particular types of referrals for students who have generalist backgrounds. For example, supervisors can think through what kinds of questions about a client's memory are more appropriately within the scope of a supervisee who has had neuropsychological training beyond general training in assessment.

With this groundwork laid, NCSPP held the 2007 Clinical Training Conference: Developing Our Competencies in Clinical Training (NCSPP, 2007). In this conference and the resulting publication, *Developmental Achievement Levels* were identified for three key points during the course of training: *the outset of practicum* (generally after some basic training, but only early exposure to application and practice), *the outset of internship*, and *the point of degree completion* (when fully independent practice is expected). For every competency specified (of which assessment is one), at each milestone in training, the *Knowledge, Skills,* and *Attitudes* that should be evident are described. The assessment competency includes four domains of development: (a) interviewing and relationships; (b) case formulation; (c) psychological testing; and (d) ethics and professionalism (Krishnamurthy & Yalof, 2010; NCSPP, 2007). Krishnamurthy and Yalof discuss these competency areas in more detail, but a pared down version for reference is presented below.

Rapid Reference 1.2

NCSPP's Developmental Achievement Levels for Assessment Framework (Adapted from Krishnamurthy & Yalof, 2010)

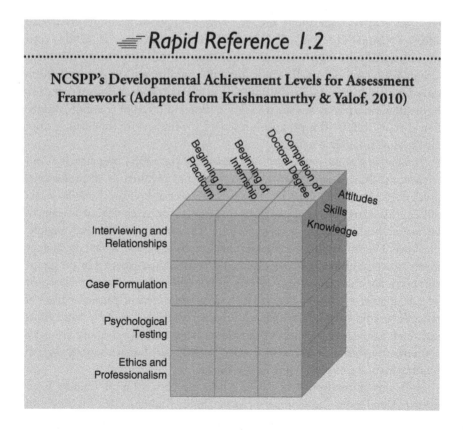

Assessment Supervision Vignettes: Developmental Levels

In order to illustrate how these developmental benchmarks can be used in assessment supervision, we present several vignettes, with discussion. It should be noted that while the DALs tend to be most useful when a supervisee is saliently *not* demonstrating one of the specific competencies, which will be the focus of these vignettes, they can also be used as a way of evaluating the current level of assessment functioning of a supervisee at the outset of the supervisory relationship. Further, the DALs emphasize a developmental approach to supervision; this should not be forgotten. That is, for example, a problem with an ethical aspect of an assessment may trigger a supervisor to determine that a supervisee is "unethical"; however, the DALs would argue that the supervisee has simply not yet reached the appropriate developmental level in the ethics and professionalism domain. This developmental attitude can help supervisors be less punitive and more supportive in the development of their supervisees. A supervisor may choose to use an approach rooted in developmental theory, such as Vygotsky's zone or proximal development (see, for example, James, Milne, Marie-Blackburn, & Armstrong, 2007), to determine and provide appropriate supports to help supervisees achieve the level of development just beyond where they currently are.

REMEMBER

Supervisees' problems and difficulties can be understood from a developmental perspective, with the goal of the supervisor to figure out exactly what supports the supervisee needs to achieve the next level of development.

Vignette 1: First Practicum

A second-year student has completed an intelligence assessment at his placement in a residential treatment setting. This practicum student, only 2 months into the rotation, had been instructed to come to his supervisor for review of the scoring before he shared the findings. A team meeting was held, during which the supervisor was not present. The supervisee reported his findings from the intelligence testing, which had some bearing on treatment planning. Afterward, a team member mentioned to the supervisor the testing findings, which is when the supervisor realized that the supervisee had not complied with her instructions. When she approached the supervisee, he said that he thought the directive not to provide feedback pertained only to the client, not the treatment team.

When determining the level of developmental functioning (competency) this student *should* be demonstrating, competency domains within the beginning of practicum mark are most appropriate. Within the Assessment competency, the student's misstep seems to fall most clearly within the Ethics and Professionalism domain. From a Knowledge vantage, the student appeared to have a "familiarity with external resources, including [one's] supervisor, and how to access them" (Krishnamurthy & Yalof, 2010, p. 94); as such, this is not a developmental problem in knowledge, within the ethics and professionalism domain of the assessment competency. Similarly, the student did not seem to demonstrate an attitude of not valuing ethical standards throughout the assessment process; as such, it does not seem to be a problem with Attitudes. The supervisee's difficulty fell more in the area of Skills, in that he failed to demonstrate an "ability to use supervision constructively to further training and assessment goals" (p. 95). In other words, he neglected to obtain supervision before acting, before sharing assessment findings with the treatment team.

Clearly, even from this brief example, this supervisee demonstrates some developmental lag in his mastery of the assessment DALs for a beginning practicum student. At the same time, he is a beginning practicum student. As such, it is completely understandable that he has not fully mastered every aspect of each of the domains, even within the column focused on a beginning practicum student. Also, and importantly, this particular problem is one that is unlikely to be addressed in an assessment course. As Ritzler (1998) noted, graduate programs often make short shrift of the topic of disseminating assessment findings because of academic course time strictures. Although, with the emergence of Therapeutic Assessment, much more attention is being paid to exploring findings with clients, less attention has been given to professional third parties, such as a treatment

≡ Rapid Reference 1.3

Practicum-Level Skills in Ethics and Professionalism in Assessment (Krishnamurthy & Yalof, 2010, p. 95)

	Beginning practicum
Skills	1. Ability to support decisions about actions
	2. Ability to differentiate self needs from client needs when considering ethical dilemmas
	3. Ability to use supervision constructively to further training and assessment goals

team. Like many other errors committed by students at this level, it is often field experience that provides the opportunity to correct misconceptions and missteps. What makes the DALs helpful in this context is their ability to underscore the specific area in need of developmental attention. The DALs provide insight that this student needs to learn when to seek supervision and when he can function without it. The capacity to make this differentiation will aid the practitioner throughout his or her career. Concretely, this practicum student would benefit from understanding how other staff are likely to regard the communication of test results and what actions such communications could precipitate. The supervisor and supervisee might think about the potential consequences of an assessor's providing incorrect, incomplete, or misleading findings, as well as the potential outcomes of needing to recant.

The supervisor might also help the student to recognize whether any internal or external pressure existed to lead the student to behave the way he did, without getting appropriate supervision. For example, perhaps the student finds it difficult to decline offering testing feedback to staff when they knew that testing had taken place. Perhaps the student feels some sense of pride in being able to share assessment findings, which spurred his action. Such exploratory work in supervision has the potential to be transformational for the supervisee, just as therapeutic assessment (Finn,

DON'T FORGET

The DALs apply to supervisors too! In this case, the Supervision DALs could be applied to the supervisor of the case. For example, the supervisor may question whether she was sufficiently clear with the supervisee about the dissemination of findings. Relevant DALs for Supervision (Malloy, Dobbins, Ducheny, & Winfrey, 2010) at the level of independent practice include:

- *Knowledge.* Of agency policies and structures that affect the work, of the importance of training and mentoring of supervisees, of an evaluation system (such as the DALs), of legal and ethical requirements in supervision, and of one's own limitations as a supervisor

- *Skills.* Ability to balance multiple roles in supervision (like teaching, evaluating, and supporting), ability to provide effective feedback to supervisees, ability to assess and address supervisees' needs, ability to model effective self-reflection, ability to help supervisees recognize ethical dilemmas and think in an ethical manner

- *Attitudes.* Commitment to the wellbeing of the supervisee's clients, valuing supervision as a developmental opportunity, commitment to own supervisees' ethical practice and behavior

2007) can be for a client. The developmental and exploratory nature of supervision using the DALs has the potential to feel less punitive and critical to the supervisee, and it likely provides assurance of fewer problems in the future than were the assessment supervisor merely to say, "You should not have given that feedback without my having supervised it. Now go in to the next meeting, and share the correct findings." (It should be noted that a recent survey of assessment supervisors suggested that very few supervisors tend to use assessment supervision in this exploratory way [Iwanicki & Peterson, 2017].)

As discussed previously, the DALs are not merely helpful in examining the lapses of supervisees. When problems arise, it is crucial for supervisors to engage in a critical analysis of their own behaviors to ascertain their contributions to what works and what does not. The supervisor in this vignette must consider that she might have been insufficiently clear with her supervisee about the dissemination of test findings. At a minimum, the supervisor is assumed to be functioning developmentally in the range of supervision competency of an individual completing a doctoral degree. In addition to understanding a model (in this case a developmental one) of supervision, assessing the supervisee's strengths and weaknesses, and offering formative feedback, the supervisor would need to continue to observe the practicum student to ensure that progress has been made in his development within the ethical and professional issues realm of the assessment competency.

Vignette 2: Beginning of Internship

A psychology intern sent a draft of a psychological assessment to her supervisor. The supervisor carefully reviewed both the report draft and the data, and he recognized that the Rorschach indicated that the client had self-doubt, though all the other data revealed adequate self-esteem. In considering the report, the supervisor could not figure out how the Rorschach data point had been incorporated into the overall conceptualization of the individual, which characterized the client as having healthy self-esteem. In the supervisory meeting, he pursued this matter with the student, who responded that she had noticed the discrepant finding but thought it was an aberration and ultimately disregarded it.

Several Assessment Competency DAL areas apply in this case. First, the supervisor needs to recognize that the

> **DON'T FORGET**
> ....
> Supervisees come into the assessment supervision process with widely varied exposure and practice to advanced assessment work (such as integrating data and reconciling potentially conflicting data). Try to think developmentally about what supports each supervisee needs to help each of them achieve competency in these skills through your work with them.

full and sophisticated integration of data (a Skill DAL) is not developmentally expected until the point of graduation/independent practice. This is an important recognition, so that the supervisor does not behave in an overly critical manner with the intern (who should not be expected to exhibit competency beyond what is typical of her level of education and training). This is a developmental goal for this student, to better integrate data from multiple sources in her overall formulation and conceptualization of cases.

However, there are two specific DAL expectations for the beginning intern that do not seem to be exhibited by this student. The first is the Case Conceptualization Attitude DAL specifying that the supervisee should possess a "willingness to think critically and with an open mind about alternative hypotheses" (Krishnamurthy & Yalof, 2010, p. 93). Notably, this expectation is built upon the successful developmental achievement of the Attitude DAL at the entering practicum level of maintaining a curiosity to enhance the assessment product. The supervisor might note that the student arrived at a premature foreclosure of interpretive hypotheses by disregarding some of the data. Understanding that the Rorschach is a performance-based measure and is less susceptible to impression management than many other (self-report) measures, it may be possible that it is picking up on something that other measures did not. This client may work hard to present him- or herself as having healthy self-esteem, but underlying that may be some significant self-doubt. The intern might have explored how the performance on the Rorschach aligned with that on other performance-based instruments, as compared to self-report measures. Such comparisons, for example, might have yielded insights as to whether a specific, context-based weakness was present, versus a more generalized deficit, for example. By dismissing the incongruous finding, the student demonstrated an incurious attitude and a lack of reflectivity.

≡ Rapid Reference 1.4

Internship-Level Attitudes in Case Formulation in Assessment (Krishnamurthy & Yalof, 2010, p. 93)

	Beginning internship
Attitudes	1. Willingness to think critically and with an open mind about alternative hypotheses

The second Assessment DAL for the intern level that is important is the Skill of consulting with one's supervisor when needed. Although the intern's manner of addressing the pool of assessment data was somewhat developmentally appropriate, her neglect to communicate with her supervisor about her struggle in integrating the data has significance for her development, which is also addressed under the Assessment competency. This student needs to understand her limitations and reach out to her supervisor when she needs to.

Given the discrepancy between the developmental expectations based on the student's level of training and her actual achievement, targeted remediation by the supervisor would be warranted. Kaslow et al. (2007) provide a format for designing a remediation plan, which could be used hand-in-hand with the DALs in Assessment.

- The initial requirement for a good remediation plan is describing for the intern in clear, precise terms the nature of the deficit in relation to the identified benchmark (Kaslow et al., 2007). Such a formulation might read: *Ignores data that do not fit neatly in case conceptualization.*
- The next step is the provision of the program expectation: *Either integrate all data or, if unable, seek assistance from supervisor.* At the internship level, supervisors should not expect students to have fully mastered data integration. In a recent study, Mihura, Roy, and Gracefo (2017) found that only 57% of doctoral programs expected students to write integrated reports during the practicum years. The consequence of this pattern is that much of the training in integration needs to occur at the internship level. At the same time, a minimal appropriate expectation is that the supervisee shares with the supervisor data incongruities that he or she detects.
- Appropriate training methods should be identified. The supervisor could select readings that address the topic of data integration or share examples of disparities he had found in his own assessment work and indicate how he resolved them.
- The remediation plan would then specify the performance indicator, such as: *Completed reports will show a capacity to integrate disparate findings 80% of the time, and the student will seek supervision for integrative challenges 100% of the time.*
- Finally, an assessment method and timeline would be specified, like: *Given that the intern completes one psychological report a month, the supervisor will review on a monthly basis each report for instances in which the student was able to resolve seeming contradictions in the psychological test data. The supervisor will also actively engage the student in conversations about data disparities that are initially challenging for the student to resolve and require that the student disclose the disparities to the supervisor. The supervisor will*

also indicate that occasions might arise when the intern is unable to detect a disparity. The supervisor will also specify that although an occasional difficulty of this sort is not unusual for an intern [here the supervisor is elaborating beyond the DALs, a sometimes necessary step], *the supervisor will evaluate whether such difficulties diminish over the course of the training period.*

Once again, the effective assessment supervisor should reflect upon what can be learned about his or her own assessment supervision from the emergence of this problem. This step would be consistent with the Supervision DAL, "Knowledge of limitations of one's own supervisory competence" (Malloy et al., 2010, p. 166). In this case, the supervisor might ascertain whether the student's weakness was idiosyncratic or one shared by other interns. If data integration were to be found to be a common problem area, the supervisor might decide to build a didactic element into the beginning of the training year to strengthen interns' capabilities in this important skill. Alternatively, the supervisor might specifically look at his own openness and approachability in these matters.

Vignette 3: Ending Doctoral Training

In the tenth month of his 12-month training year, an intern was presented with an assessment referral of an individual who had emigrated from a country in Africa and had lived in the United States for 15 years. The intern noticed that the client's English was very good, despite his struggling with certain consonants. The client vaguely stated that he had come to the United States to pursue work and school opportunities. He went on to describe himself as highly assimilated into American culture. The intern proceeded with the testing as if the client were born in the United States, selecting and using tests and norms that are U.S.-specific. When the client gave evidence on the PAI of manifesting a high level of

≡ Rapid Reference 1.5

Components of an Effective Remediation Plan (Kaslow et al., 2007)

1. Describe the nature of the deficit in clear, precise terms, related to the expected benchmark.
2. Provide the expectation.
3. Identify appropriate training methods.
4. Specify the performance indicator.
5. Specify the assessment method and timeline.

stress, the intern did not consider whether it had an acculturative component. Also, the client was a racial minority in the United States, although he was in the majority in his native country. This aspect remained unexplored. In short, the client's identity status was explored neither with the client nor with the supervisor until it came to the supervisor's attention. The supervisor was taken off guard because the supervisee had recently begun a rotation with the supervisor and this was the first assessment the supervisor had seen. The supervisor felt she had made too many assumptions about the multicultural competence of the supervisee.

One DAL in the Assessment Case Formulation domain is especially relevant to this situation. It specifies that at the point of completing the doctoral degree, the individual should demonstrate "Knowledge of broad range of individual and system characteristics (for example, diversity, psychopathology, development, social context) and how they impact case formulation and diagnosis" (Krishnamurthy & Yalof, 2010, p. 92). While the DALs offer general guidance, it is often important to utilize other resources to enhance and enrich the specificity and depth of the "spirit" of each DAL. In this case, the DAL is enriched by the American Psychological Association (APA)'s *Multicultural Guidelines: An Ecological Approach to Context, Identity, and Intersectionality* (APA, 2017). Particularly relevant is Guideline 8, which states, "Psychologists seek awareness and understanding of how developmental stages and life transitions intersect with the larger biosociocultural context, how identity evolves as a function of such intersections, and how these different socialization and maturation experiences influence worldview and identity" (p. 76). This case involves the intersection of acculturation and race, an intersection that is likely to influence multiple stages of the assessment process. Yet, this intern seemed to give only passing attention to the client's race, his status as an immigrant, and the cultural differences between his native and current environments.

⟱ Rapid Reference 1.6

Doctoral Completion-Level Knowledge in Case Formulation in Assessment (Krishnamurthy & Yalof, 2010, pp. 92–93)

	Complete doctoral degree
Knowledge	1. Knowledge of broad range of individual and system characteristics (e.g., diversity, psychopathology, development, and social context) and how they impact case formulation and diagnosis

Hass (2016) noted that assessing acculturation is a complex matter, particularly because when individuals describe their self-identification patterns, they tend to give socially desirable responses (Tsai, Chentsova-Dutton, & Wong, 2002). Hence, the client's self-description of himself as being "highly assimilated" required some scrutiny and likely further probing, with special care not to invalidate his experience. In order to penetrate the surface of any self-presentation efforts, the student would have had to delve into the client's status with respect to values, goals, customs, and assumptions about the world and others, to name a few, as these elements pertained to both the native and current culture. Discrepancies identified between the two cultures would also reveal the potential for acculturative stress (Williams & Berry, 1991). The interview should also have covered the client's immigration story to ascertain what experiences in the transition process were salient, with particular focus on the everyday experiences of transition from racial majority to minority status. Whether or not the decision to emigrate was voluntary should have been explored as well (Akhtar, 2011). The decision of whether English-language tests were appropriate for him should have been a deliberative one with careful consideration of the purpose of the evaluation. If the aim were to determine the client's highest level of cognitive functioning, thinking explicitly about whether administration of the subtests should be in his primary versus secondary language would be essential. Then, in examining the finding from the PAI that the client was experiencing a high level of stress, the assessor might have been able to determine whether it may be useful to include a narrow-band acculturative stress scale, such as the Societal, Attitudinal, Familial, and Environmental (SAFE) Acculturative Stress Scale (Fuertes & Westbrook, 1996). Ultimately, the client's background should not be ignored (Roysircar & Krishnamurthy, 2018).

As the aforementioned discussion suggests, this assessment case with which the intern was presented was complex. Even though the intern did not approach it optimally, he had not completed his internship year, and thus should not quite yet be expected to have reached all of his competency DALs for the independent practitioner. Even upon completing a doctoral program, most new graduates, particularly those who had not encountered similar cases previously, would require supervision or consultation on such a complex case. In this circumstance, it would be appropriate for the supervisor to do the following: (a) help the supervisee identify how the assessment was deficient; (b) connect these insufficiencies to the guidelines relevant to multicultural assessment; (c) provide didactic/reading experiences to enhance the intern's multicultural competence; (d) monitor future assessments specifically and intensively for this aspect; and (e) provide the student with continuing formative and, ultimately, summative feedback in this area.

Although this example has clear implications for the supervisor's ongoing work with this particular intern, it also has significance for the supervisor's assessment supervision practices in general. This supervisor granted too much autonomy (i.e., decision-making capacity) to an intern who was assigned a challenging case, making assumptions about the intern's developmental level of competency. The supervisor's hands-off approach at the beginning of the case might be seen as not entirely fulfilling the Supervision DAL of demonstrating "[an] ability to assess learning needs of trainees," a capacity that should be fully in place by the point where the supervisor is providing supervision. This example should signify for the supervisor that this is an area in which the supervisor must maintain vigilance that he or she is evaluating supervisees' needs and that nothing else in the supervisor's workload is impeding this process. As Yalof (2018) noted, the supervisor might expand upon the information informally obtained about the success of his or her supervision in promoting diversity sensitivity through use of a supervisory tool like the Supervision Outcome Scale (Tsong & Goodyear, 2014).

SPA'S FRAMEWORK

SPA originally developed its framework for strong assessment practice, using the assessment report as a proxy for the entire process, in order to align with APA's idea of assessment as a proficiency. A proficiency (Alexander, 1997) is a developmental step above competence, showing a mastery of some domain. The framework has evolved into a tool that is driving advanced trainings, CE workshops and presentations, and for the purposes of this chapter, a tool in the supervision of assessment. The framework, and the associated Report Review Form (Rubric), share a common goal, which is entirely aligned with the purpose of supervision: to strengthen and enhance training toward one's eventual clinical work within the field of psychological assessment. Although developed for more traditional clinical assessment, the components within the framework are applicable (and necessary) across most different types of assessments and settings. The SPA Framework aims to clarify a certain standard or expectation for assessment providers, and as such can be an operationalization of expectations in supervision.

The SPA Report Review Form (Rubric)

When developing a process to recognize proficiency in assessment, SPA developed a tool to systematically and granularly review comprehensive psychological assessment reports (SPA, 2015). The SPA Rubric (which is what we will call it throughout the rest of this chapter) considers five main components as essential for any strong,

≋ Rapid Reference 1.7

SPA's Framework

The SPA Rubric includes the following overarching areas that can inform supervision practices:
1. Validity
2. Comprehensiveness
3. Integration
4. Client-Centeredness
5. Overall Writing

comprehensive psychological assessment report: validity, comprehensiveness, integration, person-centeredness, and overall writing style. The SPA Rubric refers to a written report, however the components included directly lend themselves to the multitude of skills trainees need to gain, maintain, and strengthen throughout their training and toward post license proficiency status. Supervision is key in the development of the skills associated with each of the areas identified in the SPA Rubric.

Different instructors and supervisors have played around with how to use the SPA Rubric in supervision (Pade, Stolberg, Baum, Clemence, & Wright, 2018). Some have adapted the rubric itself into developmental benchmarks, taking each individual component in the form and delineating a three-point system of mastery of that item. Others have used it more broadly as an evaluative tool, especially at later stages of training and with consultation with licensed colleagues. One promising way to use the form, which has evidenced some positive results, is having supervisees rate their own performance using the form before submitting any work to their supervisor for evaluation and feedback. That is, the SPA Rubric serves as an ideal self-assessment tool. When supervisees use the form to rate their own reports, they are forced to be deliberate in thinking about the five major areas delineated in the rubric. Supervisees can also use the SPA Rubric to evaluate one another's work in a case conference format, serving the dual purpose of improving the quality of actual reports and building skills in evaluating others' work.

It should be noted that different areas of the SPA Rubric may be more appropriate and applicable at different stages in the supervisory process, and it can be "taken apart" and used in chunks. For example, doing an evaluation at the beginning of the supervisory relationship about the validity of testing is always useful. Ensuring that a supervisee can administer, score, and interpret tests in alignment with empirical evidence or widely-accepted clinical practice—or providing necessary education, training, and support if the supervisee cannot—is typically a good first step in supervision. Evaluating the overall writing style, on the other hand, is often a good final step in evaluating each individual testing report. Supervisors should be deliberate and purposeful throughout supervision with using the SPA framework and associated rubric at moments when they can be most useful.

Validity

It is, we hope, obvious that test and assessment results that are valid (accurate) are the foundation of any good and ethical assessment. Many of the other chapters in this book discuss supervision strategies to ensure that administration, coding, scoring, and interpretation of tests is aligned with empirical literature and widely accepted clinical practice. As such, we will not focus on this as much here. Further, Pade (Summer 2018a) discussed communicating test results in a valid manner. Using supervision to ensure that test findings are valid, though, is one of the trickiest areas to address, as it constitutes perhaps the biggest difference between assessment supervision and general clinical supervision of therapy. That is, the focus on precision and accuracy, to a degree that can easily negatively affect the supervisory relationship, is necessary. Supervisees can easily feel patronized when supervisors "double score" their tests to ensure accuracy. Using the SPA Rubric can provide a frame for supervision, though, with ensuring validity as the first, most basic step. Supervision practices that assure validity in test administration, scoring, and interpretation, as well as ensuring that assertions, conclusions (including diagnostic impressions), and recommendations are consistent with the data collected, align well with the validity section of the SPA Rubric.

> **REMEMBER**
> ....
> Valid test findings are absolutely necessary for ethical assessment practice. Without valid testing, no other aspect of assessment matters!

Comprehensiveness

There are two overarching themes in the Comprehensiveness section of the SPA Rubric: (a) ensuring that the referral questions are clearly delineated and answered and including adequate contextual information (history, behavioral observations, etc.). Identifying a referral question is generally assumed to be quite straightforward and simple to accomplish; however, more is being written now about the clinical skill of helping clients hone and fine-tune their own referral questions (Finn, 2007). For example, a client may come in with a question like: "*Do I have ADHD?*" This is generally entirely answerable in a clinical assessment. However, this is likely not the most useful question to be answered by an evaluation. If the answer is "Yes," then that is extremely helpful to the client. However, if the answer is "No," then the client is left not understanding his or her own experience of poor attention. Supervisees can be encouraged to help clients tailor their assessment questions to what will be most useful for them in the end. In this case, a more useful question may be: "*What is underlying my problem paying attention in school?*" This way, an assessment can both answer the question of whether or not the client has ADHD and also, if the answer is "no," illuminate the actual lived experience of the client having poor attention in his or her everyday life (such as highlighting the role of anxiety, depression, or some other reason for the client's weak attention). This skill is not one that is typically taught in assessment training, so supervisors may need to balance teaching this concept with encouraging supervisees to find their own way to accomplish it.

A similarly seemingly straightforward task in assessment (and thus assessment supervision) is ensuring that all of the referral questions are addressed in the final product (the report, feedback, etc.). Much like clarifying the referral questions, supervisors often assume that this will be easily accomplished and that supervisees are keenly aware of this requirement in the assessment process. However, depending on the level (and personality) of the supervisees, it can be easy for them to miss the forest for the trees. That is, many get so caught up in the specific results of tests and subtests that they struggle to "put it all together" to answer the questions that were posed at the beginning of the assessment process. Supervisors can fall prey to this problem as well, especially when supervisees exhibit problems with the mechanics of testing and require a great deal of hand-holding to ensure valid testing. A special task of supervisors in assessment is to somehow hold onto the big picture while attending to the minor details of the process. The SPA Rubric can serve as a clear reminder, throughout the supervision process, for the supervisor to bring the supervisee back to the ultimate point of the assessment, even when attending to minor scoring issues of single subtests.

> **DON'T FORGET**
> ···
> You have to explicitly answer every question posed by the assessment! Even if the answer is not clear and requires further or different kinds of testing, make this clear in the report and in feedback!

The amount of relevant background, history, context, and behavioral information that is appropriate for any given assessment will vary and very much depend on the individual supervisor and placement. Training clinics, for example, tend to favor extremely comprehensive sections within reports of background information, presumably to ensure that trainees have considered every possible contextual and background factor within the ultimate case conceptualization. Neuropsychological evaluations, on the other hand, tend to favor more targeted, "relevant" background information included in the report. In supervision, supervisors should make absolutely clear what level of background, contextual, and behavioral observation information they want considered in the ultimate case formulation. To ensure comprehensiveness (as the SPA Rubric demands), even information that does not make it into the final report or case conceptualization should at least be *considered* deliberately. Supervisors need to decide how explicit they want to make this process. Some supervisors value a case presentation from the supervisee after the clinical interviewing process, complete with potentially irrelevant background and contextual information, in order to ensure that supervisees are considering all that information and do not have a "blind spot" for any of it. Other supervisors put more trust in and onus on supervisees to whittle down the information to what they think is relevant, with the potential risk of missing some information a supervisee does not think is relevant but a supervisor would. Using the SPA Rubric, either way (or somewhere in between), forces supervisors and supervisees to at least be deliberate in their handling of background, contextual, and behavioral observation data.

Integration

Perhaps one of the most complex and difficult aspects of the assessment process is taking all the information (data) collected and integrating it into a coherent, narrative "whole" of the person. This is perhaps the most "psychologisty" aspect of the assessment process, tying together information, resolving any potentially or apparently discrepant or conflicting data, and presenting a coherent formulation of what is going on with the client, tying his or her functioning into psychological theory. The British Psychological Society's Division of Clinical Psychology (2010) summarized clinical formulation as "the summation and integration of the knowledge that is acquired by [the] assessment process.... . The formulation will draw on psychological theory and research to provide a framework for describing a client's problems or needs, how it developed and is being maintained" (pp. 5–6). Helping supervisees navigate the process of integrating data is perhaps the most important and difficult task in assessment supervision. While it starts in the SPA Rubric as including three different assessment methods, an easy task, it quickly becomes more difficult as the rubric asks that interpretations are presented in a cross-method, integrated manner and any discrepant or conflicting data are adequately addressed.

Aligned with Wright's (2010) process for integrating data in a methodical, stepwise manner, supervision can again be thought of in developmental terms. The major steps in the integration process using that model are (a) Listing data that emerge from measures; (b) Identifying preliminary themes; (c) Reorganizing the data by themes; (d) Finalizing themes; and (e) Putting the themes together in a conceptual framework rooted in theory. For either supervisees early in their training or simply at the beginning of a new supervisory relationship, it can be helpful to have supervisees present the data (step 1) and the supervisor and supervisee identify preliminary themes (step 2) together. Once the supervisor is comfortable that the supervisee can adequately identify preliminary themes, he or she may ask the supervisee to present the data with preliminary themes identified (step 2), at which point the supervisor may help the supervisee revise those themes. Even further in training or comfort, a supervisor may ask the supervisee just to present the reorganized data by themes (step 3), so that the supervisor and supervisee can together look at the data across methods within themes to ensure that they are coherent. It is strongly recommended that supervision not skip past this part of the process, as deciding which data belong within which psychological construct or theme is too important to the process not to pause and get supervision. For example, if the supervisory dyad is looking at all the data that emerged from the measures (including observations, clinical interview, tests, records reviews, etc.) related to interpersonal functioning, it is important to pause at this point and make sure all the data are appropriately categorized and are emerging as a clear description of what is going on interpersonally/socially for the client. The supervision process can help determine whether the theme has enough cross-method data to sustain itself, whether it is telling more than one clear story and should be separated into multiple themes (such as social skills and interpersonal perception), or whether there are conflicting data that need to be explained. A question that all supervisors should ask explicitly during the process is: "*Were there any test or other findings that seem to conflict with the rest of the data?*" Assessors (and certainly those in training) are often too quick to ignore outlier or discrepant data, as was illustrated above in Vignette 2 of the NCSPP DALs section.

≡ Rapid Reference 1.8

Wright's (2010) Process for Integrating Data

1. List data that emerge from measures, by measure, regardless of potential relevance.
2. Identify preliminary themes, categorizing each piece of data within a psychological construct/theme.
3. Reorganize the data by themes, using a table with themes down the side and measures/methods across the top.
4. Finalize themes, ensuring that each theme is telling a clear story and is substantiated across methods/measures.
5. Put the themes together in a conceptual framework rooted in theory.

Again, following Wright's (2010) model, the other major touchpoint in the data integration process that needs explicit supervision is the final step, the formulation, tying together the themes that emerge and situating them within culture, context, and psychological theory. When few themes emerge from the data, this can be relatively straightforward. When more emerge, though, tying them together in a way that is psychologically coherent (that is, makes sense given our understanding of psychological theories, constructs, and functioning) can be quite difficult, and supervisors need to help supervisees navigate this process. As always, supervisors should take a developmental approach to this, helping guide their supervisees more directively in earlier stages, and asking supervisees to develop their own conceptualizations/formulations and present them in supervision in later stages.

Person-Centeredness

This section of the SPA Rubric focuses on two major, overarching areas: (a) that the writing within the report is person-focused rather than test-focused and (b) that recommendations are clear, specific, reasonable, and make intuitive, coherent sense given the conclusions of the assessment process. Ensuring that language in a report (and thus in feedback) is geared toward describing the client him- or herself, rather than focusing on tests, subtests, and other data, is a skill that must often be taught or re-taught in supervision. That is, much of our training in testing is geared toward understanding tests and test scores, so as students we become comfortable writing about those (even though, ironically, before assessment training we would likely be much more comfortable writing about people!). Writing about tests and test scores often needs to be unlearned by supervisees, who at times need to be reminded that they are talking about a person; writing about a person's abilities (rather than his or her test scores) makes the report more personally meaningful to the client (Pade, Winter 2018b). Supervisors can ask and re-ask the question: "*Is there a way this can be communicated that is more about the person, and less about the scores?*" Like many other items within the SPA Rubric, this section forces supervisors and supervisees to at least think deliberately about the issue of person-centered communication (in writing and feedback).

The issue of recommendations is the focus of another chapter in this book, so we will not discuss it thoroughly here. However, again, using the SPA Rubric as a sort of checklist forces supervisees (and their supervisors) to consider whether their recommendations (a) Are linked clearly and directly to the conclusions, referral questions, history, culture, and context of the individual being assessed and (b) Are clear, specific, and reasonable. Supervisors may want to engage supervisees in a discussion about what kinds of recommendations are reasonable, given any individual limitations or constraints of the client. For example, the evidence base to recommend a specific type of therapy to a client might be strong, but if the client will not have access to that type of therapy (for any reason, such as proximity issues, availability issues, cost issues), it is not reasonable to make that recommendation. Supervisees often need encouragement to investigate the real-world viability of recommendations.

> **REMEMBER**
>
> Supervisors should engage supervisees in a specific discussion about whether recommendations included in the assessment are clear, specific, reasonable, and directly tied to the outcomes of the assessment itself.

Overall Writing Skills

The written report is often the one piece of documentation that best illustrates the work of the assessment psychologist (and the supervisee). It is meant to describe the various aspects of the assessment process and provide enough details to be clear and meaningful, but also somehow concise and reader-friendly. Because supervising the writing of reports is the focus of another chapter in this volume, we will not discuss it at length here. However, the SPA Rubric singles out several basic components of report writing that are of note: that the report is clear and mostly jargon-free; that it is well-written and organized; and that test scores and examples are used appropriately throughout the report. The first two are likely the focus of many supervisors (we spend way too much time copyediting reports!). When considering the last component, what constitutes the "appropriate" use of test scores and examples will vary widely between supervisors, types of assessments, and settings. Supervisors are encouraged to be specific about how they expect test scores and examples to be used, which can often be accomplished by providing a few sample test reports to supervisees. The more specific supervisors are at the outset about what they expect to see in a report, the less time they will spend revising the writing.

> **REMEMBER**
>
> The more specific supervisors are at the outset about what they expect to see in an assessment report, the less time they will have to spend revising the writing!

Diversity Issues

The SPA framework and associated rubric do not have a separate section devoted to cultural or diversity issues in the assessment process; however, diversity is infused throughout the SPA Rubric, which can serve again as a supervisory tool. While there is one item in the rubric that specifically addresses diversity in the interpretation of test results (under the umbrella of Validity), diversity permeates many of the other criteria in the SPA Rubric. The rubric approaches diversity from the stance that individualization of our work is critical in assessment and report writing to accurately represent the individual in appropriate life contexts. For example, the concept of comprehensiveness and inclusion of relevant background and observational information addresses attention to an individual's specific upbringing and demographic factors that are relevant to the assessment. Validity assumes that cultural factors are considered when utilizing norms and interpreting test results, including recognizing limitations and potential problems with such data. Integration inherently brings together information about the person assessed, including personal context and situation and unique characteristics, in a meaningful way. Client-centeredness further helps ensure that the individual, rather than scores and measures, is the focus of the report. This helps personalize the descriptions to make them meaningful and useful for that specific individual, which includes attention to culture and diversity.

Those who apply the SPA Rubric to their own assessment work will find themselves needing to apply their knowledge of cultural and individual differences and diversity in two primary ways. First, they must use appropriate tests and test norms, whenever possible. That is, supervisees must understand and utilize knowledge that different cultural groups may be inadequately assessed by certain measures or may have different cut-off thresholds on specific tests, subtests, or indices on tests. Many tests (such as the MMPI-2) have specific norms for different cultural groups. In the absence of such norms, supervisees must understand the limitations of comparing an individual's test scores to "general" population norms for any given test, and supervisors can help them adapt their interpretation of those test scores accordingly. Second, in addition to culturally-relevant interpretation of individual test scores, those using the SPA Rubric will find themselves having to situate all interpretations and findings from data sources within a cultural context. While the former task deals with individual test scores from different measures, this latter task relates to integrating the test data into a conceptualization of the individual being assessed that is sensitive to culture and diversity. Using the SPA Rubric as a tool in supervision will ensure that, at the very least, these two areas of diversity are being explicitly considered by supervisees and their supervisors.

CONCLUSION

Supervision in general can easily become unfocused and unwieldy; although this is perhaps less true with assessment supervision than general clinical supervision, it can still occur. Assessment supervisors can easily either make false assumptions about their supervisees' competencies or overly focus on certain aspects of the assessment process (such as test scoring and interpretation), at the expense of other aspects. Using any or all of the above three sets of guidelines/frameworks can help ensure that supervisors are attending to every aspect of the assessment process. They provide guidance for supervisors themselves (especially the APA Supervision Guidelines), for supervisees in the process (especially the SPA Framework), and for how to evaluate and provide appropriate feedback and guidance to supervisees (especially the NCSPP's DALs). Together, these three sets of guidelines can strengthen not only the supervision of assessment, but also the actual assessment services being provided to the public.

🐾 TEST YOURSELF 🐾

1. **A remediation plan should include all of the following EXCEPT:**
   (a) A precise description of the problem
   (b) A standard period for the completion of remediation
   (c) Operational statement of the program expectation
   (d) Specification of an indicator of adequate performance
   (e) A remediation plan should include all of the above.

2. **Generally, the skill of integrating psychological test data is mastered:**
   (a) Prior to embarking upon a practicum
   (b) During the practicum years
   (c) During the internship years
   (d) Following completion of the doctoral program

3. **The NCSPP DALs assist the supervisor in**
   (a) Establishing goals for particular phases of training
   (b) Maintaining a supportive posture throughout phases of training
   (c) Creating an appropriate a remediation plan when a supervisee fails to demonstrate a competency
   (d) All of the above

4. **Assessment supervision is rarely a topic of professional or graduate training. True or False?**

5. **When supervisees exhibit difficulties, supervisors should focus both on how to remediate the problems as well as their own supervisory capabilities that might have created the context for the emergence of difficulties. True or False?**

Answers: 1. e; 2. d; 3. d; 4. True; 5. True.

REFERENCES

Akhtar, S. (2011). *Immigration and acculturation: Mourning, adaptation, and the next generation.* New York, NY: Jason Aronson.

Alexander, P. A. (1997). Mapping the multidimensional nature of domain learning: The interplay of cognitive, motivational, and strategic forces. In M. L. Maehr & P. R. Pintrich (Eds.), *Advances in motivation and achievement* (Vol. 10, pp. 213–250). Greenwich, CT: JAI Press.

American Psychological Association. (2015). Guidelines for clinical supervision in health service psychology. *The American Psychologist, 70*(1), 33–46.

American Psychological Association (APA). (2017). Multicultural guidelines: An ecological approach to context, identity, and intersectionality. Retrieved from: http://www.apa.org/about/policy/multicultural-guidelines.pdf.

Division of Clinical Psychology. (2010). *Clinical psychology: The core purpose and philosophy of the profession.* Leicester, United Kingdom: British Psychological Society.

Finn, S. E. (2007). *Our clients' shoes: Theories and techniques of therapeutic assessment.* New York, NY: Taylor & Francis.

Fouad, N. A., Grus, C. L., Hatcher, R. L., Kaslow, N. J., Hutchings, P. S., Madson, M. B., … Crossman, R. E. (2009). Competency benchmarks: A model for understanding and measuring competence in professional psychology across training levels. *Training and Education in Professional Psychology, 3*(4S), S5–S26.

Fuertes, J. N., & Westbrook, F. D. (1996). Using the Social, Attitudinal, Familial, and Environmental (S.A.F.E.) Acculturative Stress Scale to assess adjustment needs of Hispanic college students. *Measurement and Evaluation in Counseling and Development, 29,* 67–76.

Hass, G. A. (2016). The integration of gender and immigration in the personality assessment of women. In V. Brabender & J. A. Mihura (Eds.), *Handbook of gender and sexuality in psychological assessment* (pp. 439–466). New York, NY: Routledge.

Iwanicki, S., & Peterson, C. (2017). An exploratory study examining current assessment supervisory practices in professional psychology. *Journal of Personality Assessment, 99* (2), 166–174.

James, I. A., Milne, D., Marie-Blackburn, I., & Armstrong, P. (2007). Conducting successful supervision: Novel elements towards an integrative approach. *Behavioural and Cognitive Psychotherapy, 35*(2), 191–200.

Kaslow, N. J., Borden, K. A., Collins, F. L., Forrest, L., Illfelder-Kaye, J., Nelson, P. D., … Willmuth, M. E. (2004). Competencies conference:

Future directions in education and credentialing in professional psychology. *Journal of Clinical Psychology*, 60(7), 699–712.

Kaslow, N. J., Rubin, N. J., Forrest, L., Elman, N. S., Van Horne, B. A., Jacobs, S. C., ... Grus, C. L. (2007). Recognizing, assessing, and intervening with problems of professional competence. *Professional Psychology: Research and Practice*, 38(5), 479–492.

Krishnamurthy, R., VandeCreek, L., Kaslow, N. J., Tazeau, Y. N., Miville, M. L., Kerns, R., ... Benton, S. A. (2004). Achieving competency in psychological assessment: Directions for education and training. *Journal of Clinical Psychology*, 60(7), 725–739.

Krishnamurthy, R., & Yalof, J. A. (2010). The assessment competency. In M. B. Kenkel & R. L. Peterson (Eds.), *Competency-based education for professional psychology* (pp. 87–104). Washington, DC: American Psychological Association. https://doi.org/10.1037/12068-005

Malloy, K. A., Dobbins, J. E., Ducheny, K., & Winfrey, L. L. (2010). The management and supervision competency: Current and future directions. In M. B. Kenkel & R. L. Peterson (Eds.), *Competency-based education for professional psychology* (pp. 161–178). Washington, DC: American Psychological Association.

Mihura, J. L., Roy, M., & Graceffo, R. A. (2017). Psychological assessment training in clinical psychology doctoral programs. *Journal of Personality Assessment*, 99(2), 153–164.

National Council of Schools and Programs of Professional Psychology (NCSPP). (2007). Competency developmental achievement levels. Retrieved from: http://ncspp.net/wp-content/uploads/2017/08/DALof-NCSPP-9-21-07.pdf

Pade, H. (Summer 2018a). The MAC report: Components of proficient report writing: Part II. *SPA Exchange*, 30(2), 5–8.

Pade, H. (Winter 2018b). The MAC report: Components of proficient report writing: Part I. *SPA Exchange*, 30(1), 6–8.

Pade, H., Stolberg, R., Baum, L., Clemence, A. J., & Wright, A. J. (2018). Utility of the proficiency report review form in assessment coursework and clinical training. Roundtable discussion conducted at the annual meeting of the Society for Personality Assessment, Washington, D.C.

Peterson, R. L., McHolland, J. D., Bent, R. J., Davis-Russell, E. E., Edwall, G. E., Polite, K. E., ... Stricker, G. E. (1992). *The core curriculum in professional psychology*. Washington, DC: American Psychological Association.

Ritzler, B. (1998). Teaching dissemination of assessment results. In L. Handler & M. J. Hilsenroth (Eds.), *Teaching and learning personality assessment* (pp. 413–427). Mahwah, NJ: Lawrence Erlbaum.

Rodolfa, E., Bent, R., Eisman, E., Nelson, P., Rehm, L., & Ritchie, P. (2005). A cube model for competency development: Implications for psychology educators and regulators. *Professional Psychology: Research and Practice*, 36(4), 347–354.

Roysircar, G., & Krishnamurthy, R. (2018). Nationality and personality assessment. In S. R. Smith & R. Krishnamurthy (Eds.), *Diversity-sensitive personality assessment* (pp. 151–178). New York, NY: Routledge.

Society for Personality Assessment SPA. (2015). Personality Assessment Proficiency: Report Review Form. Retrieved from: http://storage.jason-mohr.com/http://www.personality.org/General/pdf/Proficiency%20Report%20Review%20Form%202015.pdf

Tsai, J. L., Chentsove-Dutton, Y., & Wong, Y. (2002). Why and how researchers should study ethnic identity, acculturation, and cultural orientation. In G. C. N. Hall & S. Okazaki (Eds.), *Asian American psychology: The science of lives in context* (pp. 41–65). Washington, DC: American Psychological Association.

Tsong, Y., & Goodyear, R. K. (2014). Assessing supervision's clinical and multicultural impacts: The Supervision Outcome Scale's psychometric properties. *Training and Education in Professional Psychology*, 8(3), 189–195.

Williams, C. L., & Berry, J. W. (1991). Primary prevention of acculturative stress among refugees: Application of psychological theory and practice. *American Psychologist*, 46, 632–641.

Wright, A. J. (2010). *Conducting psychological assessment: A guide for practitioners*. Hoboken, NJ: Wiley.

Yalof, J. (2018). Supervision and training of personality assessment with multicultural and diverse clients. In S. Smith & R. Krishnamurthy (Eds.), *Diversity-sensitive personality assessment* (pp. 349–362). New York, NY: Routledge.

Two

SUPERVISING COGNITIVE ASSESSMENT

Robert Walrath
John O. Willis
Ron Dumont

ognitive assessment is a mainstay of practice for school psychologists (Bramlett, Murphy, Johnson, Wallingsford, & Hall, 2002), neuropsychologists, and many clinical psychologists, educational diagnosticians, specialists in assessment of intellectual functioning, and other professionals, typically conducted as part of psychoeducational evaluations and evaluations of neuropsychological, psychological, and academic functioning. At the beginning of one's career, classroom instruction is, of course, very important, but supervised practice is essential for developing and maintaining advanced skills across one's professional life.

Given the important decisions that are often made from assessment results, competency in the administration, scoring, interpretation, integration of, and ultimately decision-making from assessment tools is of utmost importance. Moral, ethical, and legal obligations hold psychologists accountable for the work they do (American Psychological Association [APA], 2016; National Association of School Psychologists [NASP], 1997, 2010). Unfortunately, even though most evaluators may feel they are competent in the accurate administration and scoring of cognitive measures, the reality is that errors are all too common. Effective supervision of assessments conducted by practicum and internship students and

Essentials of Psychological Assessment Supervision, First Edition.
Edited by A. Jordan Wright.
© 2020 John Wiley & Sons, Inc. Published 2020 by John Wiley & Sons, Inc.

by practicing evaluators is essential for improving and maintaining competence in cognitive assessment and serves as the necessary foundation for the higher level skills of conceptualizing, diagnosing, and making appropriate recommendations.

One aspect of maintaining accountability in this area of psychological work is supervision. Once a person has graduated from a training program, it can be difficult to obtain supervision. Most states do not mandate that psychologists and school psychologists maintain mentorship arrangements for direct supervision. The NASP (2016) advocates and provides some guidelines for early career mentoring of school psychologists. The APA (2015) provides guidelines for clinical supervision, and the NASP (2018) has a new position paper on supervision.

Cognitive assessment supervision shares many of the demands, needs, and parameters of the other aspects of supervision discussed in this volume. We attempt as much as possible to focus on the special issues of supervision of cognitive assessment. Supervision of assessment occurs at many levels, including practice for beginning students and internships for advanced graduate students; supervision of staff in schools, clinics, hospitals, and agencies; and supervision or peer consultation for experienced professionals. The differences among these situations are more a matter of degree than fundamental components, so we are considering them together.

> **DON'T FORGET**
> ....
> Moral, ethical, and legal obligations hold psychologists personally accountable for the work they do (APA, 2016; NASP, 2010).

MODELS OF SUPERVISION

As master's and doctoral level training of clinical and school psychologists has moved toward more competency-based approaches (Falender & Shafranske, 2004; Fenning et al., 2015; Kaslow, 2004), trainers and supervisors have moved to more evidence-based supervision models (Connors, Arora, Curtis, & Stephan, 2015). Vannucci, Whiteside, Saigal, Nichols, and Hileman (2017), building on the work of Dumont and Willis (2003), describe clinical competencies that are unique to psychological assessment and suggest a developmental supervision model to "customize supervision," stating that "linking skills assessment, goal setting, and evaluation are important for successful student outcomes" (p. 114). Finkelstein and Tuckman (1997) have long advocated for a similar framework, guiding supervisees through eight distinct phases of skill attainment and thinking.

In their discussion of "thinking errors" in the context of the trainee's heuristics and cognitive biases, Wilcox and Schroeder (2015) address an often neglected aspect of supervision: clinical reasoning and diagnostic decision-making in assessment. Using the assessment process (referral, data gathering, data analysis, and decision making), Wilcox and Schroeder present a compelling case for the need to intentionally teach school psychology students to use both deductive and inductive reasoning, to determine when and how reasoning is likely to be subject to error, and to prevent those errors through didactic instruction, supported practice, and teaching self-regulation strategies (p. 657).

Tawfik, Landoll, Blackwell, Taylor, and Hall (2016) developed the Multi-level Assessment Supervision and Training (MAST) approach, which adds peer supervisors to the more traditional supervision done by licensed clinicians in clinic-based settings, with the goal of increasing supervision through observation of trainees' test administration and better evaluation of assessment competencies. Marks and Kasky-Hernandez (2016) advocate for student-to-student supervisory relationships, not just to improve skills, but also to provide better training in supervision in general.

Costello, Belcaid, and Arthur-Stanley (2018), citing Gatti, Watson, and Siegel (2011), advocate for "the reflective supervision model [which] promotes reflective practice in the context of collaborative growth-promoting between professionals" to allow "professionals to step back to examine complex situations and make thoughtful, informed decisions about next steps" (p. 4). Although the focus of this chapter is on promoting accuracy and effectiveness in cognitive assessments, reflective supervision peer groups with trained leaders may help evaluators maintain best practices in the face of job stress and administrative pressure.

Finally, Yalof and Abraham (2009) developed an integrated model combining Finkelstein and Tuckman's (1997) developmental stages, Allen's (2007) multicultural assessment supervision, Krishnamurthy, VandeCreek, and Kaslow's (2004) competency-based training in assessment, and Johnson's (2007) transformational supervision. While these models are useful constructs and helpful for both supervisors and trainees in creating a framework for supervision, we believe that there are concrete activities or components necessary for effective supervision that we will operationalize below.

CONSIDERATIONS SPECIFIC TO COGNITIVE ASSESSMENT SUPERVISION

Inexperienced, and even experienced, test administrators often do not fully grasp the importance of adhering to standardized administration of psychological tests (e.g., Lee, Reynolds, & Willson, 2003) or the chances for making errors when administering and scoring these tests. Alfonso and Pratt (1997), Kaufman,

Raiford, and Coalson (2016), Loe, Kadlubek, and Marks (2007), Oak, Viezel, Dumont, and Willis (2018), Raiford (2017), Rodger (2011), Styck and Walsh (2016), and many others have noted that examiners will make errors on Wechsler scales test record forms due to administration errors, mathematical mistakes, ambiguity of scoring rules, and general carelessness, including very simple clerical errors. Rollins and Raiford (2017a,b) report distressing numbers of errors by qualified examiners submitting record forms for review as part of test standardization!

CAUTION

High rates of administration and scoring errors are common among students and practitioners on the several tests that have been studied. Constant vigilance is the price of accuracy!

These errors may result in substantial, meaningful differences between the scores on the record form and the scores that the person tested truly earned or should have earned. If a score is incorrect, any interpretation based on that score and any recommendations based on that interpretation are likely to be wrong and possibly harmful. Kaufman et al. (2016), in summarizing the literature regarding errors made on cognitive assessment instruments by examiners (both graduate students and experienced practitioners), noted that "the errors are numerous and have serious consequences" (p. 38). Almost a quarter of a century ago, Kaufman (1994, p. 331) said:

> Virtually no studies have investigated the competence in administration and scoring of instruments such as the SB-IV, DAS, WJ-R COG, and KAIT. It is likely that errors in administration and scoring of these instruments occur with the same or similar frequency as the Wechsler scales given the minimal instruction provided on these newer instruments in most graduate training programs. (p. 331)

Rodger (2011) was able to confirm Kaufman's prediction. Three primary measures of intellectual assessment, the Wechsler scales, the Woodcock-Johnson III Tests of Cognitive Abilities (WJ III COG; Woodcock, McGrew, Schrank, & Mather, 2001/2007), and the Differential Ability Scales, Second Edition (DAS-II; Elliott, 2007) were examined. Errors were tabulated and analyzed from 295 Wechsler protocols, 257 DAS-II protocols, and 258 WJ III COG protocols record forms completed by master's and doctoral-level students and practicing school psychologists. The numbers of errors, regardless of the test administered, were essentially the same. Also, Spenceley, Flanagan, Vonderohe, and Clawson (2016) reviewed 48 Woodcock-Johnson IV (WJ IV COG; Schrank, McGrew, & Mather, 2014) record forms completed by 12 first-year graduate students. Each student administered the test four times with feedback after each administration. Nonetheless, every record form included at least one error. There was significant improvement from the first to the last administration, but no significant improvement after the second administration. Similarly, Ramos, Alfonso, and Schermerhorn (2009) reported that 36 graduate students made 500 errors on 108 administrations of the WJ III COG. Common errors included the use of incorrect ceilings, failure to record errors, and failure to encircle the correct row for the total number correct.

There are several important components to supervising assessment, whether one is supervising students, interns, or staff members or sharing peer supervision with colleagues. These components can be broken down into aspects of the evaluation process and methods of supervision. Aspects of the evaluation process include planning fruitful and appropriate assessments; flawlessly administering and scoring tests; collecting other important data, interpreting findings thoughtfully and responsibly; communicating accurately, both verbally and in written form, the results in ways appropriate for the consumer (e.g., child, parent, school personnel, other psychologists); and offering helpful recommendations. Methods of supervision include observation of or participation in activities (e.g., actual test sessions, feedback meetings with client or client parents), and reviews of test record forms and subsequent reports.

> **DON'T FORGET**
> ....
> • Flawlessly accurate administration and scoring are essential skills that prove difficult to attain, but attention must also be given to interpretation, promoting reasoning, helping supervisees avoid errors in thinking, and the development of recommendations.
> • Important goals to achieve as a result of assessment supervision include: planning appropriate assessments; flawlessly administering and scoring tests; collecting important data, interpreting findings thoughtfully and responsibly; communicating the results in ways appropriate for the consumer; and offering helpful recommendations.

Written Feedback on Test Record Forms and Evaluation Reports

When reviewing test record forms and evaluation reports from students, interns, staff members, and colleagues, we use a system of writing numbers in the margins of the test record form and typing a numbered list of comments, calling attention to all observed or suspected errors on the record form. The numbered list allows comments to be as long as necessary and to include as much explanation as may be needed. The supervisor can also retain a paper or electronic copy of the list of comments, which facilitates tracking progress (or lack thereof). Because record forms can be, and often are, reviewed in cases that end up in debate, such as due process hearings, and because clients, parents, and sometimes attorneys have a legal right to review the record forms themselves, the use of the numbers associated with a separate key may reduce the fear a supervisee or his or her boss may have with marking up the actual test record form—particularly when the marks are highlighting errors.

When supervisees submit paper copies of their evaluation reports, we correct minor errors directly on the report, using standard proofreader marks, but we include more extensive comments in another numbered list. However, we usually work with electronic copies of reports and use the Microsoft Word™ review function with track changes, new comment, and so forth. Comments can include an explanation of the reason for a correction in text (e.g., explanation of a rule for grammar, style, spelling, or punctuation) or a discussion of an important principle of assessment or reporting. When we find ourselves writing the same comment many times, we add the comment to the automatic text list in the word processor so that the comment can be inserted with just a few keystrokes. We find that students and staff begin to correct their writing errors more quickly when they are given the reasons for our corrections. The opportunity to provide detailed discussions allows us to explain in depth important principles of assessment, assign remedial readings, and individualize our feedback as much as necessary. We retain copies of these comment sheets so we can track the progress of each supervisee.

One cautionary note regarding the use of the track changes feature is the tendency for a supervisee to simply use the "accept all changes" feature of the document. When the changes/edits are small and unimportant, this is not a problem. When the edits are more substantial, placing them in a comment box requires the supervisee to take a more active role in making the changes to the document itself.

Supervising Fruitful and Appropriate Assessments

Supervision is necessary at all steps of the assessment process. Supervision must be reduced, maintained, or increased on the basis of the supervisee's performance.

Planning the Assessment

The evaluator should be responsible for selecting the specific tests and other instruments and procedures to be used, as well as for planning how (e.g., when, where, number of sessions) the assessment will actually be carried out. The supervisor must ensure that the evaluator is choosing instruments and procedures that are not only the most reliable and otherwise psychometrically trustworthy, but also the most valid and useful for the intended purpose.

The supervisor should consult with the supervisee between receipt of the referral and the beginning of the assessment to assist in the planning process. The frequency of such meetings and amount of assistance offered will depend on both the skill and experience of the supervisee. This is a process that is frequently neglected, potentially resulting in a flawed evaluation that is difficult to repair after the fact. Before an assessment strategy can be developed, relevant information must be gathered and reviewed. Attention should be given to file reviews, portfolio assessments, observations, interviews, self-report inventories, questionnaires and rating scales, informal methods of assessment, and other means of evaluation in addition to normed tests.

Other aspects of this pre-assessment review that a supervisor should be stressing include the following. The goal is for the supervisee to become an independently thorough detective, dedicated to finding and integrating all relevant information.

- Have all reports (including the client's self-report and all previous evaluations and case reports) and referral questions from other sources such as teachers, therapists, parents, employers, job supervisors, rehabilitation counselors, and the client been reviewed, and, if no reports are available, has the supervisee actively solicited reports and referral questions and concerns?
- Have all the concurrent findings of other evaluators been reviewed and the data integrated, with commonalties being given due weight and disparities acknowledged and discussed?
- Before a final decision is made as to how to proceed with an assessment, have multiple sources of convergent data been sought, provided, or found, and have these data then been taken into account?
- Have contradictory data been sought and given due emphasis? For example, do prior cognitive scores seem reasonable given the client's adaptive, academic, and vocational functioning or observed behaviors?
- Are prior scores on tests of working memory consistent with performance on a job such as air traffic controller or wait staff in a restaurant? If, for instance, most data support a tentative diagnosis of intellectual disability or of obsessive-compulsive disorder (OCD), is there any contradictory information that also must be considered? Are there prior assessment data that can be used for comparison? Do they support the tentative formulation or do they require further consideration?

This step in planning the assessment is an essential opportunity for the supervisor to help the supervisee to learn to guard against confirmation bias.

Selecting an Assessment Battery

Review of the collected information, as well as answers to the guiding questions below, is necessary to choose an appropriate assessment battery. For example, it is not unusual for a child, referred for an evaluation, to have already been assessed before, sometimes recently.

- Will the new assessment repeat tests already administered, or will different tests be chosen? Issues related to practice effects, the difficulty of measuring change with instruments that are not identical, and the Flynn Effect should be discussed with the supervisee.
- Is the choice of tests sufficient to sample behaviors for the specific purpose of the assessment (e.g., psychoeducational or vocational testing, application for accommodations on an examination [e.g., SAT], or eligibility for the death penalty), and is the choice of tests appropriate to the test-taker in terms of sensory and motor abilities, language, and culture?
- Are the chosen tests as free from bias as possible, considering the standardization sample and the test-taker? Are the tests chosen able to distinguish between skills rather than lumping them together? For example, can visual-motor skills be distinguished from visual-spatial skills? Can measures of working memory assess potential differences between verbal and visual domains? Can the measure of working memory distinguish between simple memory span and working memory with mental manipulation?

> **REMEMBER**
>
> Planning the assessment is an opportunity for the supervisor to help the supervisee do a thorough and helpful evaluation, rather than a routine evaluation that does little for the client.

These pre-assessment meetings may be a good opportunity for the supervisor to acquaint the supervisee with new tests and procedures; to assign reading of test manuals, test reviews, and textbooks; and, if necessary, to teach or review statistical principles of reliability, validity, and factor analysis.

To the extent that the planning meetings before the assessment are deliberately scaled back over time (due to expected supervisee development), neglected, or ineffective, the supervisor will need to point out any resulting lapses in planning that are evident in the supervisee's evaluation report, using the written feedback system discussed above. If lapses are frequent or serious, the supervisor will need to resume meeting with the supervisee between the referral and the beginning of the assessment.

Flawlessly Administering and Scoring Tests

One preliminary issue here is the supervisor's need to instill within supervisees motivation, attitudes, and beliefs about the technical aspects of test administration. Some clinicians do not seem to think that highly accurate administration and scoring and statistically sound interpretation are really very important. They know that the testing needs to be reasonably accurate, but they may not see any need to be "obsessive" about the process. They may see testing as just one small part of a larger, higher process of helping the client that should not be overemphasized. One task, then, is helping supervisees learn and believe that testing needs to be done precisely or not at all.

The following set of questions may help supervisors when assessing supervisees' administration and scoring of the tests:

- Were all basal and ceiling rules obeyed, and were they the correct ones, since the rules vary from test to test and even from subtest to subtest within a test?
- Were the test instructions and items read verbatim, with appropriate demonstrations and samples given as instructed in the test manual, and without any coaching, helping, or teaching given, except as instructed? Was any unauthorized feedback given?
- Did the examiner follow all standardized instructions, avoiding any ad-libbing? Were the instructions delivered in a smooth, conversational tone?
- Were all time limits, timed presentations, and timed delays adhered to? Did the evaluator refrain from answering questions from test-takers in greater detail than the test manual allows?
- For a client with severe or low-incidence disabilities, did the examiner *adopt* appropriate tests rather than *adapt* inappropriate ones (Willis & Dumont, 2002)? Was the client tested in the client's specific native language (e.g., Puerto Rican vs. Castilian Spanish or American Sign Language vs. Signed English), with tests normed in that language?

We use three approaches to encourage error-free administration and scoring: observation, reviews of test record forms, and corrective action. These are described below. There is no excuse for making errors in administering and scoring tests, and the consequences of such errors can be very serious. Our experience sadly confirms the distressing frequency of errors reported by Erdodi, Richard, and Hopwood (2009), Kaufman et al. (2016), Kuentzel, Hetterscheidt, and Barnett (2011), Raiford (2017), and others.

Observation

We believe that supervisors should occasionally observe evaluation sessions directly or review videotapes of evaluations. This should take place with greater frequency in the beginning stages of training to ensure the supervisor can correct deficiencies before they become "bad habits." Once the supervisor can be sure of the trainee's obsessive attention to detail, the frequency can be reduced. Videotaping may be less intrusive than direct observation and allows the supervisor to study administration techniques as closely as necessary by using the pause and rewind functions, even using a stopwatch to check timing of subtests and rate of reading digits aloud (e.g., one or two digits per second) on digit recall tests.

Reviews of Test Record Forms

We urge supervisors to review all test record forms. There seems to be, in our experience as well as that of others (e.g., Belk, LoBello, Ray, & Zachar, 2002; Oak et al., 2018; Raiford, 2017; Rodger, 2011), no limit to the errors that can be made, even by experienced professionals. Supervisors must train examiners to check everything, including basals, ceilings, correct assignment of bonus points, and scoring of all items. The written feedback system is effective for correcting scoring errors. When training or supervising evaluators, it is essential to provide feedback on one case before the supervisee begins the next. Supervisors must respond quickly, and supervisees must wait for the feedback before testing again. Otherwise, errors may be practiced several times before they can be corrected. With sufficient practice in making a particular error, the supervisee may form an unbreakable erroneous habit.

> **DON'T FORGET**
> ....
> Whenever possible, supervisees should be required to see their clients again to correct errors in test administration that the supervisor is able to discern from the test record form. Supervisees should not be given the impression that errors do not matter.

Despite the fact that many tests now have computer scoring programs available to evaluators, we highly recommend that the supervisee be required to, whenever possible, score the test by hand using the scoring manuals provided. Some tests (e.g., WJ IV) require the use of computer scoring, but if a test can be scored by hand, it is often a useful practice so the supervisee can gain (and demonstrate) familiarity with and understanding of the test scoring procedures. Once an evaluator is able to demonstrate complete accuracy in hand scoring a test, the use of a computer program can be introduced.

Corrective Action

Supervisees should be required to correct their errors. Some errors, such as assigning the wrong point value to a response or an addition error may be corrected simply on a resubmitted

record form. Others, such as failing to establish a basal or ceiling, may require the supervisee to see the client again and then resubmit a corrected record form. This form of corrective action, although highly desirable, may be feasible only for students taking assessment courses and not those providing formal reports to parents or schools, but it should be used whenever possible with practicum students, interns, and supervised staff members. Noting or even criticizing an error without requiring corrective action sends a message that the error did not really matter all that much. Some errors, though, are subtle and complicated (Overholser & Fine, 1990). Cruise (2018) provides a helpful discussion of the delicate challenge of giving feedback effectively.

Interpretation of Evaluation Results

Guiding supervisees to administer and score tests with perfect accuracy is simple, albeit very difficult and apparently seldom successful. Interpreting (accurate) test

---

≡ Rapid Reference 2.1

Tips for Corrective Action in Assessment Supervision

- Use a combination of participation, observation, written review of record forms and reports, and corrective action when supervising evaluations. Each of these interactions provides opportunities to give feedback and, when necessary, to assign or recommend additional reading.
- Supervisors can make brief corrections on supervisees' test record forms and reports and make longer comments by keying numbered lists of comments to numbers written on the record forms and reports.

results, history, and other information is a more complicated process and very difficult to teach through supervision, although we have found that supervision is probably a better venue than classroom instruction for teaching interpretation and formulation of recommendations. Individual supervision allows for a more thorough discussion of the multiple steps required for integrating the specific results of a single examinee's testing into specific, individualized recommendations. Group supervision with a norm of open feedback among supervisees can be an excellent venue for teaching interpretation, especially if the supervisees have heterogeneous backgrounds.

The supervisor should be alert to indications that the supervisee lacks the requisite knowledge to make sensible interpretations for a particular examinee. In those cases, the supervisee needs to be directed to resources to develop knowledge of the disability, medical conditions, culture, relevant teaching or therapy methods, or other information essential to understanding the examinee and interpreting the data. (A certified school psychologist who was a supervisee of one of the authors commendably took it upon herself to volunteer in a special education program to gain needed personal experience with classroom teaching of children with disabilities.)

There is a risk of concentrating so hard on errors in administration and scoring (which must be eliminated if interpretation and recommendations are to have any validity at all) that insufficient attention is given to integrating test results with all of the other historical, observational, and interview information about the examinee. The supervisor must help supervisees step back, consider the "big picture," draw on knowledge of personality and social issues, and use logical reasoning (e.g., Wilcox & Schroeder, 2015) to put the cognitive test results in a meaningful context. Cognitive assessment is one part of a complete psychological evaluation, and personality issues and styles interact with cognitive functioning. This necessary integration can be taught in class, but it is really learned with actual practice guided by a competent supervisor (Barnett, Erickson Cornish, Goodyear, & Lichtenberg, 2007). Discussions in group supervision can be especially effective in broadening perspective.

DON'T FORGET
....
Test interpretation is not based on scores alone. Behavioral observations, interviews, and the client's history are also essential components and must be integrated into a cohesive picture of the client's functioning.

≡ Rapid Reference 2.2

Questions to Pose in Evaluating a Supervisee's Report

1. Does the supervisee report genuinely germane observations from test sessions, while at the same time being clear that behaviors in a test session may be unique to that test session and may never be seen in any other context?

2. Does the supervisee pay attention to the reported observations? For example, if a supervisee cites the client's boredom or fatigue, it would not make sense to declare, "Test results are assumed to be valid."

3. Does the supervisee integrate the behavioral observations, interviews, and background information into a comprehensive understanding of the client's cognitive functioning?

4. Does the supervisee distinguish clearly among different tests, clusters, factors, subtests, and scores with similar titles? For example, "processing speed" may not be the same skills on different tests.

5. For the purpose of clarity and ease of understanding, does the supervisee explain with words and figures all the statistics used in the reports?

6. Does the supervisee explain differences between different statistics (e.g., standard scores vs. scaled scores, percentile rank vs. percentage) for different tests that are included in the report?

7. Are qualitative descriptors (e.g., "Below Average") for the statistics used in the reports clearly explained?

8. Does the supervisee explain the differences between names for the same scores (e.g., standard score, age-equivalent, classification labels) on various tests that are used in the report or, alternatively, explain how and why scores on various tests were converted to a single metric?

9. If a disability is identified, does that identification demonstrate a reasoned, clinical judgment, rather than simply an exercise in arithmetic?

10. Does the supervisee explain the mechanism of the disability? For example, according to the IDEA (Individuals with Disabilities Education Act) Final Regulations, 2006, Section 300.8(c)(10), a specific learning disability is a disorder in one or more of the basic psychological processes involved in understanding or in using language, spoken or written, that may manifest itself in the imperfect ability to listen, speak, think, read, write, spell, or to do mathematical calculations.

11. Does the supervisee make an attempt to describe the student's specific disorder(s)? For example, the IDEA Final Regulations, 2006, Section 300.8(c)(4)(i) define emotional disturbance in part as "a condition exhibiting one or more of the following characteristics over a long period of time and to a marked degree that adversely affects a child's educational performance . . ."

12. Does the supervisee make an attempt to describe the student's specific condition and to specify the characteristics?

13. Does the supervisee answer the specific questions generated and included in the "reason for referral" section?

14. Does the supervisee distinguish clearly between findings and implications?

15. Do the interpretation and recommendations demonstrate an understanding of the suspected problems identified in the referral questions?

16. Does the report offer specific, detailed recommendations and give a rationale for each?

17. Does the supervisee appraise the entire pattern of the client's abilities, not merely weaknesses?

18. Does the supervisee base conclusions and recommendations on multiple sources of convergent data (not just test scores), consider contradictory information, and avoid interpretation beyond the limits of the tests/measures?

CONSIDERATIONS RELATED TO SUPERVISING DIGITAL ASSESSMENT

Although we consider some tests much easier to administer, score, and interpret than others, the literature cited above (e.g., Oak et al., 2018; Ramos et al., 2009; Rodger, 2011; Spenceley et al., 2016) makes it clear that high rates of error are seen in students and practicing professionals on every test that has been studied. Some tests take longer than others to teach, but students make errors on all of them and continue to make errors in professional practice.

Recent technological advances have led to the increasing trend of "online" or digital assessment across all areas of psychology. Notably, with Pearson's Q-Global and Q-interactive systems, cognitive assessments can now be administered, scored, and interpreted almost entirely online. Clark, Gulin, Heller, and Vrana (2017) note that there is limited research, beyond Pearson's own studies on the equivalence of paper-and-pencil compared to digital administration of the Wechsler scales (Daniel, Wahlstrom, & Zhang, 2014), on the implications of this change. Dumont, Viezel, Kohlhagen, and Tabib (2014) and Kaufman et al. (2016) provide detailed reviews of the mechanics of administration of the WISC-V using Q-interactive, but with virtually no comments on its implications for training and practice. Wahlstrom, Daniel, Weiss, and Prifit-

> ## CAUTION
>
> Adhering to standardized administration of psychological tests is of utmost importance. If the assessment is not administered correctly, there is no way to tell the impact (large or small) of any errors made by the examiner. Invalid test scores prevent valid interpretation.

era (2016) also reviewed the Q-interactive platform development and use and provided some suggestions for training, in that "trainers have expressed excitement that they will be able to spend less instructional time on the mechanics of assessment…" (p. 370).

Clark et al. (2017) provide the most helpful review of the training and supervision implications for the Q-interactive system we have found to date. They suggest that training should not be wholly dedicated to digital format and that trainees still need significant experience with paper-and-pencil test administration. They found "that Q-interactive's autoscoring and interpretation system almost completely eradicates computation errors … however, failing to record a response was the most frequent administrative error" (pp. 151–152).

As with any new technology, there are pros and cons. The following comes from the experience of one of the authors teaching the WISC-V through Q-interactive over several semesters. One very helpful addition to the program is a set of training modules that students can complete independently on all aspects of the administration and scoring on the WISC-V, covering both paper-and-pencil and digital versions. Students can print a certification showing completion to ensure they have successfully completed each module. Instructors or supervisors can then spend less time on teaching these activities and more on other aspects of the test, such as interpretation. Another helpful feature is the ability to print "item level responses," which is essentially the entire record of the test administration. Supervisors can see everything entered into the program, either digitally or by writing stylus, to review administration and scoring with the supervisees.

One drawback to the WISC-V Q-interactive is the lack of opportunity for trainees to observe examinee behaviors and interactions with the test materials, which has traditionally provided rich information for a process approach interpretation. This is especially true on the digital administration of both Coding and Symbol Search. One last caveat: *Assess,* the Q-interactive program that is installed on the iPad to deliver the administration, records the entire interaction if given access to the iPad microphone. Supervisors and students should be aware of state laws and school district policies regarding recording students and the potential need for additional releases or consents.

Finally, when supervising administration of digital assessments, supervisors should observe the actual digital administration. The supervisor can, as the supervisee administers the digital test, make a verbatim paper-and-pencil recording of the test session on a separate record form and, after the sessions, compare that to the digital outcome. This will allow for a direct comparison of the computer-scored results with the paper-and-pencil recording. Any differences in scores or response recordings should be discussed.

CAUTION

Users of online or digital assessment still need significant experience with paper-and-pencil test administration.

Overall, the supervisor should not rely solely on digital training with any test instrument. "Hands on" administration and scoring opportunities should always be provided for the most effective supervision.

SUPERVISOR COMPETENCE

The Roman poet Juvenal asked "Quis custodiet ipsos custodes?" ("Who will guard the guards themselves?") Who will train and supervise the supervisors? We recommend, in addition to studying the literature on supervision, that supervisors solicit anonymous feedback from supervisees (or foster a relationship with a single or very small group of supervisees that encourages candid feedback). A peer supervision group of supervisors would be very helpful, and a supervisor might invite a peer to occasionally sit in on supervision sessions. As noted above, Marks and Kasky-Hernandez (2016) recommend student-to-student supervisory relationships, which could improve students' skills and also prepare them some day to be more effective supervisors. Guiney (2018) provides a thoughtful and practical discussion of issues involved in collaboration between university faculty and the supervisors working directly with supervisees. Guiney offers general principles and specific recommendations to make the collaborative supervision process as productive and rewarding as possible. Supervisors can also vary their approaches and explicitly observe the results of different approaches.

DIVERSITY ISSUES

As illustrated by, for just one example, *Larry P. v. Riles* (1979; see also Powers, Hagans, & Restori, 2004), racial and other diversity issues are very important in assessment, and it is easy for supervisees to lose track of this concern as they strive to master the seemingly objective mechanics of assessment. Ideally, graduate classes and seminars, practicum and internship sites, and work settings would offer assessors broad diversity of gender identities; racial, ethnic, and cultural groups; ages; socio-economic statuses; languages; religions; political beliefs; and other personal characteristics among their clients, peers, supervisors, and teachers. However, that is often not the case (two of the authors have taught assessment in a small, Catholic university in New Hampshire, so diversity in our doctoral classes usually consisted of one white, male middle-class guidance counselor in a group of white, female, middle-class teachers). Commentary, feedback, and insights shared by diverse peers can be even more effective than lectures and readings, but that goal is difficult for a campus or work site supervisor to achieve unilaterally.

As in other areas of psychological training, supervisors must strive to keep issues of diversity clearly in mind throughout instruction and supervision of assessment, keep raising diversity issues during individual and group supervision sessions and when responding to evaluation reports, and encourage supervisees to reflect on diversity issues as they plan assessments, conduct assessments, write reports, and meet with clients and staff about their assessments. Supervisors need to maintain and increase their own cultural competence as it relates to assessment.

The topic of diversity issues in assessment could easily fill an entire chapter or book. Three valuable resources are discussed below.

Explicitly for supervisors, Allen (2007) describes multicultural assessment supervision as involving cultural differences between supervisor and supervisee, supervisee and client, or the client and the samples of persons tested during development and standardization of the tests. Allen presents a multicultural assessment competency model covering most aspects of assessment and supervision of assessment.

For examiners (and, therefore, supervisors), Sattler (2018, pp. 64–66, 137–182, and elsewhere; 2014, pp. 125–159) discusses in depth many of the practical and legal issues involved in assessing children of diverse backgrounds. Ortiz, Piazza, Ochoa, and Dynda (2018) discuss diversity issues in detail with emphasis on potential bias and threats to validity. They note that bias against linguistically and culturally diverse individuals "is not related to any technical or psychometric flaws within the tests themselves, but primarily to the assumption of comparability" (pp. 549–550) between culturally and linguistically diverse individuals and mainstream, native speakers of English. Sattler and Ortiz, Piazza, Ochoa, and Dynda emphasize that these are complex issues that do not have simple or complete solutions. For example, verbal cognitive tests depend on the dominant U.S. vocabulary and language comprehension and expression. Timed performance tasks on cognitive tests assume that the examinee is comfortable with attempting to excel by working as quickly as possible, a specific cultural value. Rules for administering tests assume typical, dominant-culture expectations for adult–child or adult-to-adult interactions in a professional setting. One goal of supervision should be to foster and encourage continuing personal reflection by supervisees to attempt to discover and offset as much as possible their own biases and assumptions, both during assessments and in post-evaluation meetings with clients, with clients and parents, or with other audiences.

SUPERVISORY RELATIONSHIP

This admonition should not need to be written, especially in the age of the #MeToo and Time's Up movements, but it still does. The relationship between a supervisor and supervisee often becomes very close, with mutual admiration and sometimes affection, and it may outlast the period of supervision. Mutual respect and some degree of warmth are important for a successful supervision experience, but there are several risks.

Personal Relationships

First, of course, is the absolute rule that supervisors must avoid any personal or, especially, romantic involvement with their supervisees. More subtle are concerns that personal feelings may interfere with the supervision process in various ways. For example, a supervisor may withhold needed criticism and correction from a favored supervisee, may attempt to overcompensate by being too harsh with a favored supervisee, or may be unduly and unhelpfully critical of a less favored one. In group supervision, perceived favoritism toward one student is toxic to the group process. A supervisee may divert effort from developing professional skills to attempting to please the supervisor. And there may, of course, be even more serious personal, professional, and legal consequences. If a supervisor, even with help from a wiser colleague or the supervisor's own supervisor, cannot prevent the development of an inappropriately personal relationship, it may be necessary to find another supervisor for the supervisee.

Availability

Supervisees often face problems that must be addressed very quickly. An effective supervisor will ensure as much availability as possible for genuine emergencies. Email and text messages are notorious for concerns about the security of confidential information, so telephone calls are normally more secure. Crespi and Dube (2005) discuss the low participation rate in supervision by school psychologists as problematic due to the increasing complexity of students' problems in school, making availability of the supervisor much more important.

Supervisor Characteristics

Supervision, whether of students, new staff, or experienced staff, requires a delicate balance between setting and maintaining high standards and being supportive of supervisees who may be struggling (Guiney, 2018). This general concern may be especially problematic in supervision of cognitive assessment because of the need for constant, firm correction of the myriad errors made by supervisees in administration and scoring of tests, even toward the end of the period of supervision. Supervisees need to feel accepted and respected by their supervisors while being continually and inflexibly corrected. Supervisors must consider the experiences and perceptions of supervisees who come from different cultures and pay attention to diversity in how they relate to supervisees and in how they model respect for diversity for their supervisees (Barnett et al., 2007), while insisting on absolute precision in administration and scoring.

Remember, all effective supervision is based on the relationship between supervisor and trainee. While there is much research on satisfaction and effectiveness in psychotherapy supervision (Watkins, 2011), and less in assessment supervision (Iwanicki and Peterson, 2017), cognitive assessment supervision may be unique is some ways due to the focus on the psychometrics of assessment instruments (Vannucci et al., 2016) and the potential need for more didactic supervision and mastering of multiple competencies, as we have described elsewhere. Guiney (2018) aptly describes the process of supervising school psychology interns and collaborating with university and site supervisors as "coparenting," which may be the best way to sum up the supervisor–supervisee relationship as well, but it is coparenting while teaching flawless driver safety skills.

PROFESSIONALISM

Professionalism is very important in the supervisory process, but "sometimes, you will be forced to choose between being unprofessional or being unethical. Go with unprofessional every time" (R. R. Moore, personal communication, February 10, 1976). For example, in reviewing previous assessments of a client, supervisees may discover significant errors in a previous evaluation. Correcting an error made by another professional that may have had an important impact on the client may be interpreted as unprofessional, especially since the previous evaluator was probably a licensed psychologist or certified school psychologist. However, if the error would otherwise continue to harm the client, it would be unethical to let it stand unchallenged.

Unfortunately, in one study, Ladany (2002) found more than 50% of trainees surveyed reported that they perceived their supervisors to have engaged in at least one unethical practice during the course of the supervision, a finding that raises great concerns for the profession (Barnett et al., 2007, p. 270). Professionalism in assessment is a behavior that must be modeled, not just taught. Oakland (1986) provides a comprehensive overview of professionalism in school psychology that serves as a model for practice.

ETHICAL, LEGAL, AND REGULATORY CONSIDERATIONS

Assessors, like all psychologists, face many legal, ethical, and technical issues. Some concerns specific to cognitive assessment include choosing appropriate test batteries in light of new research on existing tests, completely mastering new tests and new editions of old tests that are being published (and deciding whether they are acceptable), understanding and applying the developing research on Flynn Effects (e.g., Flynn, 2010; Kaufman & Weiss, 2010), determining when old tests that have not been revised must be retired, assessing the possible effects of retesting, the positive and negative outcomes associated with adding more and more tests and test scores to an evaluation, and such factors as test/examinee bias, confirmatory bias, and illusory correlations. Training and peer supervision short of an entire course on a new test or edition may be very difficult for a practicing psychologist to obtain. Supervisors need to take opportunities to reinforce these issues. A serious concern is the type and amount of supervision in assessment that psychologists have been given over the course of their careers. For example, Silva, Newman, Guiney, Valley-Gray, and Varrett (2016) surveyed 700 early-career school psychologists and found that only 38% reported having access to professional supervision, and nearly 30% reported feeling pressure to practice outside their competence because of the lack of mentoring or supervision. The most frequently reported obstacles were time, availability, and proximity to a supervisor. Less frequent were access to technology, supervisor interest, and cost. Similarly, Chafouleas, Clonan, and Vanauken (2002) found that many school psychologists in their nationwide sample did not have sufficient professional supervision to meet their needs or professional standards. These issues may be particularly serious for psychologists performing cognitive assessments because of the important, but detailed technical issues involved with assessment instruments.

> **REMEMBER**
>
> Remind (or teach) supervisees about issues like the datedness of tests, the effects of retesting, the positive and negative outcomes associated with adding more and more tests and test scores to an evaluation, and test/examinee bias, confirmatory bias, and illusory correlations.

There are several factors, regardless of the academic training level of the person providing psychological assessment, for which each psychologist is responsible. The following guidelines set out the minimum responsibilities for psychologists who perform psychological assessments (adapted from the APA, 2016):

a. providing assessment services efficiently and effectively.
b. offering assessments in only those areas for which they have established their competence.
c. obtaining training and adequate supervision when extending their areas of assessment competence to new areas; this training may include formal course work, research, individual study, applied training, and/or supervision.
d. maintaining current knowledge of scientific and professional developments that are directly related to the assessments they render.
e. monitoring, reviewing, or evaluating the effectiveness of the assessments to ensure that user needs are met.
f. actively participating in procedures established by the profession of psychology for the purpose of review and evaluation of psychological practice.
g. not providing services when the ability to do so is impaired by alcohol, drugs, physical or psychological disturbance, or other dysfunction.

Psychologists providing supervision of assessments under the provisions of the Individuals with Disabilities Education Act (IDEA, 2004) must adhere to the following standards (adapted from IDEA Final Regulations, 2006, Section 300.304):

a. Tests are selected and administered so as to be nondiscriminatory toward the child. For those children suspected of having impaired skills, assessment tools are also selected and administered so as to ensure that the results accurately reflect whatever factors the test purports to measure, rather than reflecting the child's impaired sensory, manual, or speaking skills (unless those skills are the factors that the test purports to measure).
b. The child is assessed in his or her native language or other mode of communication, unless it is clearly not feasible to do so. For a child with limited English proficiency, the tests and procedures that are chosen are administered in such a way so as to ensure that they measure the extent to which the child has a disability and needs special education, rather than measuring the child's English language skills.
c. A variety of assessment tools and strategies are used to gather relevant functional and developmental information.

d. Standardized tests must have been validated for the specific purpose(s) for which they are used, and they must be administered by trained and knowledgeable personnel in accordance with the instructions provided by the producer of the tests. Clear explanations of any variation from standardized conditions (e.g., the qualifications of the person administering the test, or the method of test administration) must be included in the evaluation report.

e. The child is assessed in all areas related to a suspected disability, including, if appropriate, health, vision, hearing, social and emotional status, general intelligence, academic performance, communicative status, and motor abilities. The evaluation must be sufficiently comprehensive to identify all of the child's special education and related services needs, whether or not commonly linked to the disability category in which the child has been classified.

f. Evaluators must use technically sound instruments that may assess the relative contribution of cognitive and behavioral factors, in addition to physical or developmental factors, and that provide relevant information that directly assists persons in determining the educational needs of the child.

In our teaching and supervision, we have always insisted that students download and save copies of federal and their state special education regulations to the hard drive of a portable device so that they can quickly search those documents for needed information, even in a meeting. See IDEA Final Regulations (2006) to download the federal regulations for IDEA (2004). Links to special education regulations for each state and the District of Columbia can be found at McBride (n.d.). Supervisors and supervisees can find many sources of legal and regulatory information, for example, details about IDEA for assessment providers in McBride, Dumont, and Willis (2011), frequent articles on legal issues in school psychology by Perry Zirkel (e.g., Zirkel, 2018) in the NASP journal *Communiqué*, and recent special education law news posted at McBride, Dumont, and Willis (n.d.). An important role for supervisors is to teach and model efforts to remain up to date on legal and regulatory issues. Supervisees need to be able to tactfully, but verifiably, refute erroneous legal claims from the people with whom they work.

CONCLUSION

As we have noted in this chapter, cognitive assessment is an important professional function in which most, if not all, psychologists are in some way involved.

While some psychologists routinely administer cognitive assessments, others trust and utilize the results of the assessments done by other professionals. Regardless of the involvement one has with cognitive assessments, it is essential that the assessments and the results be accurate. Given the various important life-impacting decisions that might be made as a result of these assessments (e.g., special education eligibility, medical determination of other health impairment [OHI], death penalty determination), we cannot stress enough the need for competence in the administration, scoring, and interpretation of assessment tools. However, many studies have demonstrated that inaccurate administration and scoring are common, which in turn impairs the validity of interpretation. One important procedure for developing and maintaining the necessary competence is the use of collaborative supervision by all professionals involved with cognitive assessment. While obviously important for student trainees, professionals at all levels of expertise should seek out and utilize professional supervision of their practice, when appropriate.

🐟 TEST YOURSELF 🐟

1. **Research shows that experienced professionals make fewer errors on standardized assessments than do students being trained to administer assessments. True or False?**

2. **Which of the following does not address accountability for assessment professionals?**
   (a) American Psychological Association (APA) (*Ethical Principles of Psychologists and Code of Conduct*, 2016)
   (b) National Association of School Psychologists (NASP) (Standards for the credentialing of school psychologists, 2010)
   (c) American Educational Research Association (AERA) (*Standards for Educational and Psychological Testing*, 2014)
   (d) National Association of School Psychologists (NASP) (*Principles for Professional Ethics*, 2010)

3. **Which is *not* one of the main approaches to supervising assessment?**
   (a) Observation of actual test sessions
   (b) Teaching test administration with the supervisee before testing
   (c) Reviews of test record forms
   (d) Requiring corrective action

4. **Which of the following is not considered an important aspect related to competent assessment?**

    (a) Years of experience

    (b) Knowledge regarding specific topics

    (c) Ability to effectively apply knowledge

    (d) Judgment necessary to use both knowledge and skill effectively

5. **Which of the following is not typically useful in the development of competence?**

    (a) Formal education

    (b) Specialized training

    (c) Supervised experience

    (d) Ongoing professional development

6. **Because competency-based and evidence-based models have not been developed, supervisors must rely on models based on experience and intuition. True or False?**

7. **Supervision models discussed in this chapter include all but which of the following?**

    (a) Reflective Supervision

    (b) Multilevel Assessment Supervision and Training

    (c) Didactic Supervision

    (d) Multicultural Assessment Supervision

8. **Intensity of supervision in different aspects of assessment:**

    (a) Can only be reduced on the basis of supervisee performance.

    (b) Can only be increased on the basis of supervisee performance.

    (c) Can be reduced or increased on the basis of supervisee performance.

    (d) Can be reduced or increased only as scheduled at the beginning of supervision.

9. **Administration and scoring errors are common:**

    (a) Only on the Wechsler scales.

    (b) On several tests that have been studied.

    (c) Only at the beginning of training.

    (d) Unless examiners know they are submitting record forms for review.

10. **Although test administration and scoring are taught in university classes, supervisors need to check the testing done even by supervisees who have taken those courses. True or False?**

11. **Group supervision may be especially helpful in teaching:**

    (a) Test administration

    (b) Test scoring

    (c) Test statistics

    (d) Test interpretation

12. **With tests that offer both hand and online scoring and interpretation,**
    (a) Supervisees should first learn to hand score tests that allow hand scoring.
    (b) Supervisees should practice hand scoring the test after they have mastered online scoring.
    (c) Supervisees should always hand score tests that allow hand scoring.
    (d) Supervisees should never hand score tests that allow online scoring.

13. **The major cognitive test batteries are normed on carefully selected, random, stratified national samples that closely match U.S. Census data for gender, ethnicity, geographic region, parental education, family income, and other important variables.**
    (a) Therefore, cultural diversity is not an issue if supervisees are using one of the major tests.
    (b) Nonetheless, cultural competence is essential in selecting, administering, and interpreting the tests.
    (c) Therefore, examiners and examinees should be matched on the basis of demographic variables.
    (d) Nonetheless, scoring rules should be modified for some groups.

14. **Even though supervisees are working professionals or graduate students training to be working professionals, sensitivity to diversity issues is important for supervisees' personal comfort and learning as well as for modeling cultural awareness. True or False?**

15. **Once certified and employed, school psychologists report being satisfied with the quality and amount of professional supervision they receive. True or False?**

16. **This chapter cites readily available sources of information about special education law appropriate for psychologists. True or False?**

Answers: 1. False; 2. b; 3. b; 4. a; 5. a; 6. False; 7. c; 8. c; 9. b; 10. True; 11. d; 12. a; 13. b; 14. True; 15. False; 16. True.

REFERENCES

Alfonso, V. C., & Pratt, S. I. (1997). Issues and suggestions for training professionals in assessing intelligence. In D. P. Flanagan, J. L. Genshaft, & P. L. Harrison (Eds.), *Contemporary intellectual assessment: Theories, tests and issues* (pp. 326–344). New York, NY: Guilford Press.

Allen, J. (2007). A multicultural assessment supervision model to guide research and practice. *Professional Psychology: Research and Practice*, 38(3), 248–258. https://doi.org/10.1037/0735-7028.38.3.248

American Educational Research Association (AERA). (2014). *Standards for educational and psychological testing*. Washington, DC: Author.

American Psychological Association (APA). (2015). Guidelines for clinical supervision in health service psychology. *American Psychologist*, 70(1), 33–46.

American Psychological Association (APA). (2016). *Ethical principles of psychologists and code of conduct*. Washington, DC: Author. Retrieved from http://www.apa.org/ethics/code/index.aspx

Barnett, J. E., Erickson Cornish, J. A., Goodyear, R. K., & Lichtenberg, J. W. (2007). Commentaries on the ethical and effective practice of clinical supervision. *Professional Psychology: Research and Practice*, 38(3), 268–275. https://doi.org/10.1037/0735-7028.38.3.268

Belk, M. S., LoBello, S. G., Ray, G. E., & Zachar, P. (2002). WISC-III administration, clerical, and scoring errors made by student examiners. *Journal of Psychoeducational Assessment*, 20(3), 290–300. https://doi.org/10.1177/073428290202000305

Bramlett, R. K., Murphy, J. J., Johnson, J., Wallingsford, L., & Hall, J. D. (2002). Contemporary practices in school psychology: A national survey of roles and referral problems. *Psychology in the Schools*, 39(3), 327–335. https://doi.org/10.1002/pits.10022

Chafouleas, S. M., Clonan, S. M., & Vanauken, T. L. (2002). A national survey of current supervision and evaluation practices of school psychologists. *Psychology in the Schools*, 39(3), 317–325. http://dx.doi.org/10.1002/pits.10021

Clark, S. W., Gulin, S. L., Heller, S. B., & Vrana, S. R. (2017). Graduate training implications of the Q-interactive platform for administering the Wechsler intelligence scales. *Training and Education in Professional Psychology*, 11(3), 148–155. https://doi.org/10.1037/tep0000155

Connors, E. H., Arora, P., Curtis, L., & Stephan, S. H. (2015). Evidence-based assessment in school mental health. *Cognitive and Behavioral Practice*, 2260–2273. https://doi.org/10.1016/j.cbpra.2014.03.008

Costello, L. H., Belcaid, E., & Arthur-Stanley, A. (2018). Reflective supervision: A clinical supervision model for fostering professional growth. *Communiqué*, 46(7), 4–6. Retrieved from https://www.nasponline.org/resources-and-publications/periodicals/communiqu%C3%A9-volume-46-number-7-(may-2018)/reflective-supervision-a-clinical-supervision-model-for-fostering-professional-growth

Crespi, T. D., & Dube, J. B. (2005). Clinical supervision in school psychology: Challenges, considerations, and ethical and legal issues for clinical supervisors. *The Clinical Supervisor*, 24(1–2), 115–135. https://doi.org/10.1300/J001v24n01_06

Cruise, T. K. (2018). Supervision: Feedback and evaluation. *Communiqué*, 47(1), 4–6. Retrieved from http://www.nasponline.org/publications/periodicals/communique/issues/volume-47-issue-1/supervision-feedback-and-evaluation

Daniel, M. H., Wahlstrom, D., & Zhang, O. (2014). *Equivalence of Q-interactive and paper administrations of cognitive tasks: WISC–V* (Q-interactive Tech. Rep. No. 8). Retrieved from http://www.helloq.com/research.html.

Dubin, S. S. (1972). Obsolescence or lifelong education: A choice for the professional. *American Psychologist, 27*, 486–498.

Dumont, R., Viezel, K. D., Kohlhagen, J., & Tabib, S. (2014). A review of Q-interactive assessment technology. *Communiqué, 43*(1), 8–12. Retrieved from http://www.nasponline.org/publications/periodicals/communique/issues/volume-43-issue-1/technology-a-review-of-q-interactive-assessment-technology

Dumont, R., & Willis, J. O. (2003). Issues regarding the supervision of assessment. *The Clinical Supervisor, 22*(1), 159–176. https://doi.org/10.1300/J001v22n01

Elliott, C. D. (2007). *Differential ability scales (2)*. San Antonio, TX: The Psychological Corporation.

Erdodi, L. A., Richard, D. S., & Hopwood, C. (2009). The importance of relying on the manual: Scoring error variance in the WISC-IV vocabulary subtest. *Journal of Psychoeducational Assessment, 27*(5), 374–385. https://doi.org/10.1177/0734282909332913

Falender, C. A., & Shafranske, E. P. (2004). *Clinical supervision: A competency-based approach*. Washington, DC: The American Psychological Association.

Fenning, P., Diaz, Y., Valley-Gray, S., Cash, R., Spearman, C., Hazel, C. E., … Harris, A. (2015). Perceptions of competencies among school psychology trainers and practitioners: What matters? *Psychology in the Schools, 52*(10), 1032–1041. https://doi.org/10.1002/pits.21877

Finkelstein, H., & Tuckman, A. (1997). Supervision of psychological assessment: A developmental model. *Professional Psychology: Research and Practice, 28*, 92–95. https://doi.org/10.1037/0735-7028.28.1.92

Flynn, J. R. (2010). Problems with IQ gains: The huge vocabulary gap. *Journal of Psychoeducational Assessment, 28*(5), 412–433. https://doi.org/10.1177/0734282910373342

Gatti, S. N., Watson, C. L., & Siegel, C. F. (2011). Step back and consider: Learning from reflective practice in infant mental health. *Young Exceptional Children, 14*(2), 32–45. https://doi.org/10.1177/1096250611402290

Guiney, M. C. (2018). Addressing problems of professional competence: Collaborating with university training programs to support struggling supervisees. *Communiqué*, 46(6), 4, 6–7. Retrieved from https:// www.nasponline.org/resources-and-publications/periodicals/ communiqu%C3%A9-volume-46-number-6-(march/april-2018)/ addressing-problems-of-professional-competence-collaborating-with-university-training-programs-to-support-struggling-supervisees

IDEA Final Regulations, Assistance to States for the Education of Children With Disabilities and Preschool Grants for Children With Disabilities, 34 CFR Parts 300 and 301, 71 Fed. Reg. 46,540 – 46,845 (2006). Retrieved from https://sites.ed.gov/idea/statuteregulations

Individuals with Disabilities Education Act of 2004 (IDEA 2004), Pub. L. No. 108-446, 118 Stat. 2647 (2004).

Iwanicki, S., & Peterson, C. (2017). An exploratory study examining current assessment supervisory practices in professional psychology. *Journal of Personality Assessment*, 99(2), 165–174. https://doi.org/10.1080/00223891.2 016.1228068

Johnson, W. B. (2007). Transformational supervision: When supervisors mentor. *Professional Psychology: Research and Practice*, 38(3), 259–267. https://doi.org/10.1037/0735-7028.38.3.259

Kaslow, N. J. (2004). Competencies in professional psychology. *American Psychologist*, 59, 774–781. https://doi.org/10.1037/0003-066x.59.8.774

Kaufman, A. S. (1994). *Intelligent testing with the WISC-III*. Hoboken, NJ: Wiley.

Kaufman, A. S., Raiford, S. E., & Coalson, D. L. (2016). *Intelligent testing with the WISC-V*. Hoboken, NJ: Wiley.

Kaufman, A. S., & Weiss, L. G. (2010). Guest editors' introduction to the special issue of JPA on the Flynn effect. *Journal of Psychoeducational Assessment*, 28(5), 379–381. https://doi.org/10.1177/0734282910373344

Krishnamurthy, R., VandeCreek, L., & Kaslow, N. J. (2004). Achieving competency in psychological assessment: Directions for education and training. *Journal of Clinical Psychology*, 60(7), 725–739. https://doi.org/10.1002/jclp.20010

Kuentzel, J. G., Hetterscheidt, L. A., & Barnett, D. (2011). Testing intelligently includes double-checking Wechsler IQ scores. *Journal of Psychoeducational Assessment*, 29(1), 39–46. https://doi.org/10.1177/0734282910362048

Ladany, N. (2002). Psychotherapy supervision: How dressed is the emperor? *Psychotherapy Bulletin*, 37(4), 14–18.

Larry P.v. Riles. US District Court for the Northern District of California - 495
F. Supp. 926 (N.D. Cal. 1979). Retrieved from https://law.justia.com/cases/
federal/district-courts/FSupp/495/926/2007878

Lee, D., Reynolds, C. R., & Willson, V. L. (2003). Standardized test
administration: Why bother? *Journal of Forensic Neuropsychology*, 3, 55–81.
https://doi.org/10.1300/J151v03n03_04

Loe, S. A., Kadlubek, R. M., & Marks, W. J. (2007). Administration and
scoring errors on the WISC-IV among graduate student examiners.
Journal of Psychoeducational Assessment, 25, 237–247. https://doi.
org/10.1177/0734282906296505

Marks, I., C., & Kasky-Hernandez, L. (2016). Student to student supervision
in graduate training programs. *Communiqué*, (1), 45. Retrieved from http://
www.nasponline.org/publications/periodicals/communique/issues/volume-
45-issue-1/student-to-student-supervision-in-graduate-training-programs

McBride, G. M. (n.d.). State regulations, Part B agencies, state forms, and state
RTI links. [Page on the My School Psychology website.] Retrieved from
http://www.myschoolpsychology.com/federal-regulations/state-regulations-
part-b-agencies-and-state-rti-links

McBride, G. M., Dumont, R., & Willis, J. O. (2011). *Essentials of IDEA for
assessment professionals*. Hoboken, NJ: Wiley.

McBride, G. M., Dumont, R., & Willis, J. O. (n.d.). *My school psychology*
[Website]. Retrieved from www.myschoolpsychology.com.

National Association of School Psychologists (NASP) (1997). *Standards for the
provision of school psychological services*. Washington, DC: Author.

National Association of School Psychologists (NASP) (2010). *Principles for
professional ethics*. Bethesda, MD: Author. Retrieved from http://www.
nasponline.org/standards-and-certification/professional-ethics

National Association of School Psychologists (NASP) (2016). *Guidance for
post-graduate mentorship and professional support*. Bethesda, MD: Author.
Retrieved from http://www.nasponline.org/publications/periodicals/
communique/issues/volume-45-issue-4/guidance-for-post-graduate-
mentorship-and-professional-support

National Association of School Psychologists (NASP) (2018). Supervision
in school psychology (position statement). *Communiqué*, 46(8), 12–13.
Retrieved from http://www.nasponline.org/publications/periodicals/
communique/issues/volume-46-issue-8/supervision-in-school-psychology

Oak, E., Viezel, K. D., Dumont, R., & Willis, J. O. (2018). Wechsler
administration and scoring errors made by graduate students and school

psychologists. *Journal of Psychoeducational Assessment.* Article first published online July 11, 2018. https://doi.org/10.1177/0734282918786355

Oakland, T. D. (1986). Professionalism within school psychology. *Professional School Psychology,* 1(1), 9–27. https://doi.org/10.1037/h0090496

Ortiz, S. O., Piazza, N., Ochoa, S. H., & Dynda, A. M. (2018). Testing with culturally and linguistically diverse populations: New directions in fairness and validity. In D. P. Flanagan & E. M. McDonough (Eds.), *Contemporary intellectual assessment: Theories, tests, and issues (4)* (pp. 684–712). New York, NY: Guilford Press.

Overholser, J. C., & Fine, M. A. (1990). Defining boundaries of professional competence: Managing subtle cases of clinical incompetence. *Professional Psychology: Research and Practice,* 21, 462–469.

Powers, K., Hagans, K., & Restori, A. (2004). Twenty-five years after Larry P.: The California response to overrepresentation of African Americans in special education. *The California School Psychologist.,* 9, 145–158. https://doi.org/10.1007/BF03340915

Raiford, S. E. (2017). *Essentials of WISC-V integrated assessment.* Hoboken, NJ: Wiley.

Ramos, E., Alfonso, V. C., & Schermerhorn, S. M. (2009). Graduate student administration and scoring errors on the Woodcock-Johnson III tests of cognitive abilities. *Psychology in the Schools,* 46(7), 650–657. https://doi.org/10.1002/pits.20405

Rodger, E. R. (2011). Errors on cognitive assessments administered by graduate students and practicing school psychologists. (Doctoral dissertation). Retrieved from ProQuest (UMI No. 3515304.)

Rollins, K. M., & Raiford, S. E. (2017a). Intelligent WISC-V integrated administration. In S. E. Raiford (Ed.), *Essentials of WISC-V integrated assessment* (pp. 35–89). Hoboken, NJ: Wiley.

Rollins, K. M., & Raiford, S. E. (2017b). WISC-V integrated scoring. In S. E. Raiford (Ed.), *Essentials of WISC-V integrated assessment* (pp. 90–122). Hoboken, NJ: Wiley.

Sattler, J. M. (2014). *Foundations of behavioral, social, and clinical assessment of children (6).* La Mesa, CA: Jerome M. Sattler, Publisher Inc.

Sattler, J. M. (2018). *Assessment of children: Cognitive foundations and applications (6).* La Mesa, CA: Jerome M. Sattler, Publisher Inc.

Schrank, F. A., McGrew, K. S., & Mather, N. (2014). *Woodcock-Johnson IV tests of cognitive abilities.* Rolling Meadows, IL: Riverside Publishing.

Silva, A. E., Newman, D. S., Guiney, M. C., Valley-Gray, S., & Varrett, C. A. (2016). Supervision and mentoring for early school psychologists:

Availability, access, structure, and implications. *Psychology in the Schools*, 53(5), 502–516. https://doi.org/10.1002/pits.21921

Spenceley, L., Flanagan, S., Vonderohe, S., & Clawson, A. (2016, February). Trainee errors in scoring and administration of the WJ-IV. Poster session presented at the annual meeting of the National Association of School Psychologists, New Orleans, Louisiana.

Styck, K. M., & Walsh, S. M. (2016). Evaluating the prevalence and impact of examiner errors on the Wechsler scales of intelligence: A meta-analysis. *Psychological Assessment*, 28, 3–17. https://doi.org/10.1037/pas0000157

Tawfik, S. H., Landoll, R. R., Blackwell, L. S., Taylor, C. J., & Hall, D. L. (2016). Supervision of clinical assessment: The multilevel assessment supervision and training (MAST) approach. *The Clinical Supervisor*, 35(1), 63–79. https://doi.org/10.1080/07325223.2016.1149751

Vannucci, M. J., Whiteside, D. M., Saigal, S., Nichols, L., & Hileman, S. (2017). Predicting supervision outcomes: What is different about psychological assessment supervision? *Australian Psychologist*, 52, 114–120. https://doi.org/10.1111/ap.12258

Wahlstrom, D., Daniel, M., Weiss, L. G., & Prifitera, A. (2016). Digital assessment with Q-interactive. In L. G. Weiss, D. H. Saklofske, J. A. Holdnack, & A. Prifitera (Eds.), *WISC-V assessment and interpretation* (pp. 347–372). San Diego, CA: Academic Press.

Watkins, C. J. (2011). Psychotherapy supervision since 1909: Some friendly observations about its first century. *Journal of Contemporary Psychotherapy*, 41(2), 57–67. https://doi.org/10.1007/s10879-010-9152-2

Wilcox, G., & Schroeder, M. (2015). What comes before report writing? Attending to clinical reasoning and thinking errors in school psychology. *Journal of Psychoeducational Assessment*, 33(7), 652–661. https://doi.org/10.1177/0734282914562212

Willis, J. O., & Dumont, R. (2002). *Guide to identification of learning disabilities (3)*. Peterborough, NH: Authors. Available from authors: willissaif@gmail.com

Woodcock, R. W., McGrew, K. S., Schrank, F. A., & Mather, N. (2001/2007). *Woodcock-Johnson III normative update*. Rolling Meadows, IL: Riverside Publishing.

Yalof, J., & Abraham, P. (2009). An integrative approach to assessment supervision. *Bulletin of the Menninger Clinic*, 73(3), 188.

Zirkel, P. A. (2018). The legal meaning of special education eligibility: The latest case law. *Communiqué*, 46(7), 14–16. Retrieved from https://www.nasponline.org/resources-and-publications/periodicals/communiqu%C3%A9-volume-46-number-7-(may-2018)/the-legal-meaning-of-special-education-eligibility-the-latest-case-law

Three

SUPERVISING PERSONALITY ASSESSMENT

Robert F. Bornstein

Supervision is the Rodney Dangerfield of psychological competencies: It has received modest attention—and little respect—from clinicians and policymakers who discuss the knowledge, skills, and values that are essential in clinical practice. Although the American Psychological Association (APA) includes supervision as a core competency in health care psychology (APA, 2006), and a sizeable proportion of psychologists perform supervision at some point during their careers, from a pedagogical perspective clinical supervision is like classroom teaching: most do it with little formal training (Scott, Ingram, Vitanza, & Smith, 2000), being left on their own to navigate unfamiliar territory. We devote much effort to enhancing beginning psychologists' knowledge and skills, but we devote comparatively little attention to helping them impart this knowledge and enhance the skills of others.

The majority of writing on supervision in psychology focuses on psychotherapy; the literature on supervision of psychological assessment is sparse, and that on supervision of personality assessment is even more sparse (DeCato, 2002; Iwanicki & Peterson, 2017). Thus, although there are established principles for evidence based assessment (Bornstein, 2017), and guidelines for evidence based supervision (Holt et al., 2011), given the state of the discipline, there is no such thing as "evidence based assessment supervision" (see Kaslow & Egan, 2017).

This chapter discusses the conceptual and empirical underpinnings of personality assessment supervision, including practical challenges in helping

Essentials of Psychological Assessment Supervision, First Edition.
Edited by A. Jordan Wright.
© 2020 John Wiley & Sons, Inc. Published 2020 by John Wiley & Sons, Inc.

early career psychologists develop competence in this important domain of clinical practice. I begin by defining the two core constructs of *personality* and *personality assessment*, and discuss the evolving context for personality assessment supervision in contemporary psychology. Conceptualizing personality assessment supervision as a multidimensional task that involves multiple stakeholders (e.g., supervisee, client, referent) and complex roles (e.g., teacher, mentor, gatekeeper), I discuss considerations specific to personality assessment supervision, the seven areas of competence that are necessary to thrive as a personality assessment supervisor, and how these considerations can be used to facilitate supervisee growth as personality assessment supervision moves from the theoretical to the practical— from principle to practice.

DEFINING THE DOMAIN: PERSONALITY AND PERSONALITY ASSESSMENT

A discussion of opportunities and challenges in personality assessment supervision requires an understanding of the core constructs that comprise this domain. Supervisors and supervisees should be familiar with the key elements of *personality* and *personality assessment*.

≡ Rapid Reference 3.1

Key Sources Regarding Psychological Assessment and Assessment Supervision

All assessors and assessment supervisors should be familiar with the *Standards for Educational and Psychological Testing* and the *International Guidelines for Test Use*; APA's *Guidelines for Clinical Supervision in Health Service Psychology* will also be helpful to those who supervise personality assessment (and psychological assessment more generally). Citations for all three are below:

- American Educational Research Association, American Psychological Association, and National Council on Measurement in Education. (2014). *Standards for educational and psychological testing.* Washington, DC: Author.
- American Psychological Association. (2015). Guidelines for clinical supervision in health service psychology. *American Psychologist, 70,* 33–46.
- International Test Commission. (2001). International Guidelines for Test Use. *International Journal of Testing, 1,* 93–114.

What Is Personality?

Although they differ in the details, classic and contemporary definitions of personality have much in common. Allport (1961) defined personality from a trait perspective as "the dynamic organization within an individual of those psychophysical systems that determine his characteristic behavior and thought" (p. 28); several decades later, Pervin (1996) offered a more nuanced definition of personality as "the complex organization of cognitions, affects, and behaviors that gives direction and pattern (coherence) to the person's life. Like the body, personality consists of both structures and processes and reflects both nature (genes) and nurture (experience). In addition, personality includes the effects of the past, including memories of the past, as well as constructions of the present and future" (p. 414).

Many psychologists today ascribe to some variant of the definition offered by the *APA Dictionary of Psychology* (APA, 2007), wherein personality is defined as: "The configuration of characteristics and behavior that comprises an individual's unique adjustment to life, including major traits, interests, drives, values, self-concept, abilities, and emotional patterns" (p. 689). Consistent with this definition, Millon (2011), Mischel and Shoda (2008), and others have argued that personality traits and behavioral predispositions can be understood in terms of characteristic ways of thinking (e.g., the introvert's belief that social engagement is fraught with danger), core motives (e.g., a desire to minimize shame and embarrassment), characteristic emotional responses (e.g., high levels of anxiety around unfamiliar people), and behavior patterns (e.g., a tendency to engage in solitary activities rather than those that involve a great deal of interpersonal contact).

Utilizing a similar framework, the *Diagnostic and Statistical Manual of Mental Disorders* (DSM) has traditionally identified four domains of personality functioning—cognition, affectivity, interpersonal relatedness, and impulse control—that comprise the core components of personality pathology (see American Psychiatric Association [APsA], 1994, 2000). Adopting a more parsimonious approach, the current version of the manual, DSM-5 (APsA, 2013), emphasizes two domains of functioning: self (which includes identity and self-direction), and relatedness (comprised of empathy and intimacy). This two-pronged definition is consistent with theoretical and empirical writings from psychoanalysis (Luyten & Blatt, 2013), cognitive theory (Beck, Freeman, & Davis, 2004), and trait and circumplex models (Hopwood, Zimmermann, Pincus, & Krueger, 2015), all of which conceptualize personality development and dynamics with reference to these two complementary and synergistic developmental lines.

What Is Personality Assessment?

Just as the competent supervisor should have a clear understanding of the underlying dynamics and core components of personality, so should the supervisor appreciate the distinguishing features of personality assessment. Psychologists often use the terms *testing* and *assessment* interchangeably, but in fact they mean very different things. As Meyer et al. (2001) noted:

> Testing is a relatively straightforward process wherein a particular test is administered to obtain a specific score. Subsequently, a descriptive meaning can be applied to the score based on normative, nomothetic findings. In contrast, psychological assessment is concerned with the clinician who takes a variety of test scores, generally obtained from multiple test methods, and considers the data in the context of history, referral information, and observed behavior to understand the person being evaluated, to answer the referral questions, and then to communicate findings to the patient, his or her significant others, and referral sources. (p. 143)

DON'T FORGET

Testing versus Assessment
Even psychologists sometimes confuse these two terms, so remember:
- Testing involves the administration, scoring, and interpretation of individual psychological tests.
- Assessment involves integrating these test data with other information (for example, historical records) to develop a more complete understanding of the patient's psychological functioning.

There are many forms of psychological assessment (e.g., cognitive assessment, neuropsychological assessment, assessment of intelligence, aptitude, and achievement). What distinguishes personality assessment from these other domains? Wright (2011) contrasted personality assessment with other forms of assessment based on the types of measures used and the way assessment data are treated, noting that:

> Whereas cognitive assessment is almost exclusively performed using performance-based instruments, personality and emotional assessments generally include self-report, symptom-focused measures, self-report inventory measures, and some performance-based measures. Additionally, whereas many of the individual domains of cognitive functioning can be assessed using a single test (or even a subtest), assessment of personality and

emotional functioning necessitates the use of multiple measures in order to rule out or confirm hypotheses about individual functioning. (p. 76)

As Wright's (2011) description suggests, in contrast to other forms of psychological assessment, personality assessment is characterized by use of an *integrated test battery*, with this battery comprised of measures that employ *different formats* and tap *contrasting response processes*, allowing the examiner to draw inferences regarding key domains of the respondent's psychological functioning, including underlying psychological dynamics (e.g., motives, affective responses) that may not be amenable to assessment by self-report (see also Bram & Peebles-Klieger, 2014). Use of an integrated, multi-method battery enhances case formulation, facilitates risk management, and enables the examiner to address a broad range of clinical issues (e.g., reality testing, impulse control, potential to benefit from therapy).

THE CONTEXT FOR PERSONALITY ASSESSMENT SUPERVISION: AN EVOLVING LANDSCAPE

Krishnamurthy and Yalof (2009) and Krishnamurthy et al. (2004) discussed core features of the assessment competency as developed by APA and others (e.g., the National Council of Schools and Programs of Professional Psychology). Like other competencies in psychology, personality assessment and assessment supervision have evolved over time in response to changes in professional practice and evolving social norms. Two trends in particular provide important context for personality assessment supervision today.

First, there has been a gradual decline in emphasis on personality assessment in doctoral training programs in recent years, which mirrors the overall decline in attention to psychological assessment relative to other clinical competencies (e.g., psychotherapy). There has also been a shift toward briefer, mono-method assessment in lieu of the traditional multi-method test battery. Consistent with the results of earlier analyses (e.g., Clemence & Handler, 2001), Mihura, Roy, and Graceffo's (2017) survey of assessment measures, methods, and topics in clinical training programs confirmed that there has been a decrease in performance-based testing and multi-method assessment and found differences in these trends as a function of program characteristics (e.g., multi-method assessment is more common in scientist-practitioner and scholar-practitioner programs than in clinical science programs, which tend to emphasize mono-method assessment). Similar results were obtained by Iwanicki and Peterson (2017), who surveyed supervisors regarding the topics most commonly addressed in assessment supervision.

Second, as Edwards, Burkard, Adams, and Newcomb (2017) and others (e.g., Suzuki & Ponterotto, 2008) noted, in recent years there has been an increase in multicultural assessment training, including training and supervision in multicultural personality assessment, impelled in part by demographic shifts within the United States and elsewhere that have resulted in increased diversity among both providers and recipients of psychological services. This pedagogical evolution has been facilitated by the development of psychological tests and scoring rubrics that are sensitive to cultural and subcultural differences (e.g., Costantino et al., 2014), and by accumulating evidence regarding the advantages (as well as the challenges) of multicultural assessment (Dadlani, Overtree, & Perry-Jenkins, 2012). Survey data confirm that increased attention to cultural issues in assessment are positively perceived by trainees and training directors (Rings, Genuchi, Hall, Angelo, & Cornish, 2009), and also point to the need for stronger theoretical and conceptual frameworks to guide work in this area (Edwards et al., 2017).

⚊ Rapid Reference 3.2

Information Regarding Diversity Issues in Personality and Personality Assessment

Here are some sources that will be helpful to the beginning personality assessor, and to the assessment supervisor as well.

- American Psychological Association. (2017). *Multicultural guidelines: An ecological approach to context, identity, and intersectionality.* http://www.apa.org/about/policy/multicultural-guidelines.aspx
- Caldwell-Harris, C. L., & Aycicegi, A. (2006). When personality and culture clash: The psychological distress of allocentrics in an individualist culture and idiocentrics in a collectivist culture. *Transcultural Psychiatry, 43,* 331–361.
- Church, A. T. (Ed) (2017). *The Praeger handbook of personality across cultures.* Santa Barbara, CA: Praeger.
- Cuéllar, I., & Paniagua, F. A. (Eds.) (2000). *Handbook of multicultural mental health.* San Diego, CA: Academic Press.
- Dadlani, M. B., Overtree, C., & Perry-Jenkins, M. (2012). Culture at the center: A reformulation of diagnostic assessment. *Professional Psychology: Research and Practice, 43,* 175–182.
- Hays, P. A. (2016). *Addressing cultural complexities in practice: Assessment, diagnosis, and therapy* (3rd ed.). Washington, DC: American Psychological Association.
- Ryder, A. G., Sunohara, M., & Kirmayer, L. J. (2015). Culture and personality disorder: From a fragmented literature to a contextually grounded alternative. *Current Opinion in Psychiatry, 28,* 40–45.

CONSIDERATIONS SPECIFIC TO PERSONALITY ASSESSMENT SUPERVISION

With these contemporary trends and evolving emphases in mind, there are several considerations specific to personality assessment supervision—considerations that are more salient here than in other domains of assessment supervision. Among the most important of these are:

- *A stark contrast between categorical and dimensional models of personality.* A great deal of attention has been devoted to this issue in recent years, and debates regarding the advantages and limitations of these contrasting conceptual frameworks have occasionally become emotionally charged, with advocates of the trait perspective arguing that dimensional models have greater heuristic value than categorical models, and proponents of the categorical approach arguing that dimensional models—though psychometrically sound—lack clinical utility.

  Although some promising integrative perspectives have emerged (e.g., Hopwood et al., 2015), this debate is likely to continue as proposed revisions for DSM-5.1 and ICD-11 are discussed (see Herpertz et al., 2017). Theoretical controversies notwithstanding, personality assessment supervision should always be informed by multiple theoretical perspectives, embracing diverse conceptual frameworks.

- *A focus on multi-method assessment and test score discontinuity.* Personality assessment is unique in its emphasis on the value of interpreting test score discontinuities—meaningful divergences in test results that sometimes emerge when similar constructs are assessed using different methods (e.g., self-report versus performance-based; see Bornstein, 2009; Mihura, 2012). A complete understanding of these test score discontinuities requires a process-focused approach, wherein test results are contextualized with respect to the psychological processes engaged by different instruments (Bornstein, 2011).

- *A shift from doctoral training to internship.* Because graduate programs devote less time to personality assessment than they once did, responsibility for teaching some basic personality assessment skills has shifted to internship supervisors. Clinical science programs in particular have de-emphasized personality assessment relative to scientist–practitioner and practitioner–scholar programs. This situation differs markedly from that involving psychotherapy (where trainees typically enter internship with stronger backgrounds and more fully developed skills) and is complicated by the fact that competence in personality assessment is inherently multi-disciplinary, requiring an understanding of research in cognitive, social, developmental, and neuropsychology.

- *Strongly held beliefs regarding different measures and methods.* Clients and members of the public often have strongly held (and often erroneous) beliefs regarding personality assessment, and about specific tests as well; social media is exacerbating this problem. Similarly, some psychologists—supervisors as well as supervisees—have test preferences that are rooted in their background, training, and theoretical orientation, rather than on evidence regarding the construct validity and clinical utility of scores derived from different measures (e.g., compare criticisms of the Rorschach Inkblot Method [RIM] by Wood, Nezworski, Lilienfeld, & Garb, 2003, with meta-analytic evidence bearing on RIM score validity by Hiller, Rosenthal, Bornstein, Berry, & Brunell-Neulieb., 1999, and Mihura, Meyer, Dumitrascu, & Bombel, 2013). Like many strongly held beliefs, these attitudes are resistant to change and can result in selection of tests based on personal preferences rather than each test's ability to address aspects of a referral question.

⫸ *Rapid Reference 3.3*

Process-Focused Classification of Personality Tests

Interpreting and integrating the results obtained from different personality tests requires an understanding of the psychological processes engaged by each test. Self-report tests, tests that require respondents to interpret ambiguous stimuli (like inkblots), and tests that require respondents to generate their own images or narratives involve different mental activities.

- *Self-report tests* (sometimes described as "objective tests") typically take the form of questionnaires wherein people are asked to acknowledge whether or not each of a series of statements is true of them or rate the degree to which these statements describe them accurately. When people complete items on self-report tests, they engage in an autobiographical memory search to see whether they can recall instances of having exhibited the behavior described in that item (e.g., "I often have trouble controlling my temper"). To the extent that such memories come to mind easily, the person is likely to rate him- or herself high on that item.
- *Stimulus attribution tests* (also called "projective tests") require people to interpret ambiguous stimuli, and here the fundamental task is to attribute meaning to a stimulus that can be interpreted in multiple ways. This process occurs in much the same way as the attributions that each of us make dozens of times each day as we navigate the ambiguities of the social world: just as an inkblot can be interpreted in multiple ways, so can our friend's failure to greet us as we pass on the street. Both are attribution processes; both reflect how we perceive and interpret events in our world.
- *Constructive tests* are distinguished from stimulus-attribution tests because constructive tests require respondents to create—literally to "construct"—novel products (e.g., drawings, written descriptions) with minimal guidance from the examiner. The Draw-a-Person test is an example of a constructive test; so are tests that ask the person to provide open-ended descriptions of parents or other significant figures.

COMPETENCE IN PERSONALITY ASSESSMENT SUPERVISION: DOMAIN, TASKS, AND TENSIONS

Falender et al. (2004) outlined the key elements of an *Integrated Supervision Competencies Framework*, describing the knowledge, skills, and values necessary for competence in assessment supervision; they also discussed some of the broader social issues and interpersonal dynamics that create important context for the supervision process (e.g., attention to diversity, ethical and legal considerations, creation of a supportive climate to facilitate supervisee growth). Surveys of internship training directors' views regarding the importance of various supervision competencies confirm that the elements articulated by Falender et al. (2004) are in fact valued by those working on the "front lines" of personality assessment supervision (see Rings et al., 2009, Table 2).

> **DON'T FORGET**
> ....
> Clinical Competence
> Personality assessment supervision aims to enhance the supervisee's knowledge (i.e., the accumulation of information regarding personality tests and test scores) and skills (i.e., test administration, scoring, and interpretation), but the ultimate goal is to enhance supervisees' clinical competence in real-world clinical settings.

The writings of Falender et al. (2004), Rings et al. (2009), and others (e.g., Krishnamurthy et al., 2004; Rudd, Cukrowicz, & Bryan, 2008) helped form the basis for APA's (2015) *Supervision Competency Guidelines*, which discuss seven domains of supervision competency. In the following sections these seven domains are discussed with respect to supervision of personality assessment.

Supervisor Competence

As Bornstein (2010) noted, personality testing is essentially a behavioral task, while personality assessment is analytic and integrative; he went on to suggest that whereas "testing requires precision, objectivity, and the kind of scientific detachment that facilitates accurate data-gathering...assessment involves integration, synthesis, and clarification of ambiguous—even conflicting—evidence obtained during the testing process" (p. 147). Adopting a more metaphoric stance, Berant, Saroff, Reicher-Atir, and Zim (2005) likened personality assessment supervision to the apprenticeship of a novice painter to a more experienced artist, wherein the mentor helps the apprentice to hone basic skills (e.g., drawing, use of perspective), as well as to develop his or her own approach to integrating complex information so that, fully synthesized, it emerges as a cohesive whole.

The competent personality assessment supervisor must be able to enhance the supervisee's performance in both testing and assessment, which involve different knowledge bases and skill sets.

A second challenge in personality assessment supervision involves breadth of knowledge and experience: because personality assessment data are often used in case conceptualization and treatment planning, competence in personality assessment supervision requires a working knowledge of assessment, treatment, and how the former informs the latter. In this respect, personality assessment supervision may actually be more complex than supervision of psychotherapy. As is true of psychotherapy supervision, however, effective personality assessment supervision requires the capacity for mentalization and self-reflection (and the ability to foster these processes in supervisees), as well as *meta-competence*—knowing what one is competent to do effectively and in which areas additional consultation may be needed.

Diversity Issues

Although each person's cultural background and unique experience affect all aspects of psychological functioning, personality assessment may be more strongly embedded than other assessment domains (e.g., cognitive assessment) in an individual's life history and culture (see Mio, Barker, & Rodriguez, 2015). As a result, the competent supervisor must be knowledgeable regarding current work on the self-concept (Wilson, 2009), construction of life narratives (McAdams & McLean, 2013), and the impact of imagined "future selves" on present-day experience and behavior (Urminsky, 2017). As Brabender and Mihura (2016) noted, individual difference variables beyond gender, race, and ethnicity have received relatively modest attention by writers, but these variables (e.g., age, sexuality, religiosity) are also salient in personality assessment, and should be in personality assessment supervision as well (see Gutierrez et al., 2012).

Thus, training in multicultural assessment must not only include attention to the impact of individual difference variables on personality development and dynamics, but it should incorporate the identities of client, supervisee, and supervisor, with attention to intersectionality (Dadlani et al., 2012; Edwards et al., 2017), as well as an appreciation of the fact that even individuals not physically present (e.g., the client) may still be psychologically present during the supervision process. In addition, understanding of the complex nature of test bias (beyond group differences in test scores) is crucial for effective personality assessment supervision: the competent supervisor should have a working knowledge of different ways test bias may be manifest (e.g., content bias versus outcome bias; see Reynolds & Suzuki, 2013), as well as the ways that test content, test instructions and labels, and the obvious and subtle dynamics of the testing situation impact clients' psychological responses during testing and thereby influence assessment results (Bornstein, 2009; Masling, 2002).

Supervisory Relationship

Thomas (2007) argued that just as informed consent on the part of the client is important in clarifying roles, expectations, and boundaries and in setting the stage for

≡ *Rapid Reference 3.4*

Understanding Test Bias

Psychologists typically associate bias in psychological testing with group differences in test scores (for example, when members of Group A consistently obtain higher intelligence scores than do members of Group B). But test bias is more complicated than that, and comes in several different forms. Among the most important of these are *content bias, outcome bias,* and *stereotype threat:*

- *Content bias* occurs when information in a personality test item means different things in different cultural groups. For example, one item on the Minnesota Multiphasic Personality Inventory (MMPI) asks respondents whether they have ever communicated with dead ancestors; a positive response to this question has traditionally been interpreted as evidence of psychosis. However, such experiences are normative in some cultures, and, unless these cultural norms are taken into account, the assessor may risk misinterpreting this response.
- *Outcome bias* occurs when the same test score means different things in different groups. If, for example, a score of 10 on a narcissism scale is associated with significant impairment in men, but that same score is associated with only mild dysfunction in women, then that test shows outcome bias: it "over-predicts" impairment in women and may cause some women to be incorrectly diagnosed. (This particular example could potentially be corrected by having separate norms for women and men.)
- *Stereotype threat* occurs when members of a group believe that a test may uncover some flaw or deficit, and as a result they become anxious ("threatened") as they take the test, and their performance suffers. If, for example, members of a particular group are convinced that the Rorschach will make them look bad, they may become anxious when completing the measure, and this excess anxiety will impair their performance in certain domains (e.g., Rorschach indices of stress tolerance).

effective intervention, the same is true of assessment supervision. Because supervisee self-disclosure tends to occur more frequently in personality assessment supervision than in other types of assessment supervision (e.g., neuropsychological), informed consent on the part of the supervisee is helpful in clarifying responsibilities, expectations, and relationship boundaries. As a number of writers have pointed out, in order for consent to be most helpful, it should be fully informed and voluntary (i.e., agreed to freely, with no hint of coercion; see Knapp & VandeCreek, 1997). As Thomas (2007) noted, however, given the contingencies of doctoral and internship training (e.g., requirements for graduation and licensure), truly voluntary consent to supervision may be more aspirational than fully achievable.

APA (2015) noted that "management of supervisee's emotional reactivity and interpersonal behavior" (p. 36) is an important task for all clinical supervisors; given that disclosure of personal information is particularly salient in personality assessment supervision, this task becomes even more important. The dynamics of personality assessment supervision differ to some degree as a function of theoretical orientation (e.g., personal disclosure and discussion of the supervisee–client and supervisee–supervisor relationship may occur more frequently in psychodynamically oriented supervision than in other types of supervision). As Levendosky and Hopwood (2017) pointed out, however, these inter- and intrapersonal dynamics must be addressed regardless of theoretical orientation (see Levendosky & Hopwood, 2017, Table 1, for a summary of considerations in this domain).

Professionalism

Two issues regarding professionalism are particularly germane to personality assessment supervision. First, to a greater extent than in other assessment domains, supervisors and supervisees often have strong preferences for particular test modalities (e.g., self-report, performance-based). In those instances where the assessment supervisor frequently utilizes a particular assessment tool or method (or conducts research regarding the validity and clinical utility of a particular tool or method), they may be invested in the continued use of that measure in clinical settings. Supervisors vary in the degree to which they are consciously aware of potential biases and their impact on the supervision process. As in other areas of professional practice, consultation with colleagues can be helpful in this regard.

Second, as is true of laypersons and professionals in other areas, it is not uncommon for beginning psychologists to experience psychological distress and dysfunction, which may range from mild depression and anxiety to more significant psychopathology (e.g., see Mongrain & Blackburn, 2015). Personality pathology is common in psychology trainees and in professional psychologists as well (see Berant et al., 2005; McWilliams, 2011). Even subsyndromal personality dysfunction can impair supervisee performance (e.g., the supervisee with border-line features may become dysregulated when emotionally aroused; the obsessive supervisee may become overwhelmed with detail and have difficulty integrating psychological test data). Supervisors should pay close attention to personality and emotional variables of supervisees and how they may influence their interactions with clients, interpretations of tests, case conceptualizations, and other aspects of the personality assessment process.

Assessment, Evaluation, and Feedback

Humans are flawed processors of information (Kahneman, 2003). Even the most conscientious and experienced psychologists make errors (Flores, Cobos, & Hagmayer, 2018), and the same is true of other health care professionals (Hutchinson & Romero, 2016). Similarly, there is no such thing as flawless test administration or errorless scoring, even when self-report measures are used (see Dumont & Willis, 2003). Given the complexity of personality testing and the contrasting skills required for test administration and test score integration, the personality assessment supervisor's expectations regarding supervisee performance must be tempered and realistic.

Providing constructive feedback regarding supervisee performance is an important part of personality assessment supervision, helping the beginning psychologist refine the knowledge, skills, and attitudes necessary to achieve competence in this domain. By providing feedback that is not only helpful and constructive, but also empathic and couched in language that the supervisee can assimilate, the supervisor is modeling effective assessment feedback as it occurs in clinical contexts—teaching by example. APA (2015) recommends "bi-directional feedback between the super-visor and supervisee" (p. 35); an important component of this feedback involves the supervisee's responses to the supervisor's "teaching style."

Multi-method assessment of competence (including live observation of the supervisee and review of audio- or videotaped performance) is the gold standard of personality assessment supervision. When observation is coupled with evaluation of test and assessment results, and with supervisees' self-evaluations, discontinuities may emerge (e.g., the supervisee's self-assessment may not dovetail with the supervisor's evaluation of the supervisee's performance). In this respect, multi-method assessment of supervisee competence parallels the dynamics of personality assessment itself. Just as the client's self-assessment does not always mirror evidence from other assessment modalities, supervisee self-assessment—although inherently imperfect—can illuminate areas of unrecognized difficulty and help build meta-competence skills.

Professional Competence Problems

Supervisees sometimes perceive personality assessment as less challenging (and less valuable) than therapy, so they may be less invested in the process and less responsive to corrective feedback. As the Society for Personality Assessment (SPA, 2006) noted, however, the opposite may be true: because they become part of the client's medical record, personality assessment results actually have a more pervasive and long-lasting impact on the client than do psychotherapy notes, which remain confidential in most situations. Beyond formalizing expectations, goals, and relationship boundaries, a supervision contract along the lines of that described by Thomas (2007) can be helpful in prompting dialogue regarding the value of personality assessment, as well as the challenges inherent in test administration, creation of an assessment report, and provision of feedback to the client and others.

Although Finn's (2007) Therapeutic Assessment (TA) model was initially designed to facilitate work with clients, it has been extended to personality assessment supervision as well (see Handler, 2008), and it provides an optimal framework for addressing competence problems in supervisees. Finn's TA model divides feedback provided by assessor to client (and that provided by supervisor to supervisee) into three levels. "Level 1" information is congruent with the individual's self-concept, and, as a result, this type of feedback is readily accepted and assimilated into the person's life narrative. "Level 2" information is mildly discrepant from the individual's self-view but can—if delivered empathically—modify in a beneficial way that person's understanding of him- or herself. "Level 3" findings are those that are highly discrepant from the person's habitual way of thinking. This kind of feedback is typically very anxiety-provoking, requires considerable cognitive and affective accommodation, and mobilizes the person's characteristic coping strategies and defense mechanisms.

Vannucci, Whiteside, Saigal, Nichols, and Hileman (2017) found that the ability to manage anxiety predicts supervisee success in assessment training: students who perform poorly in this domain report greater focus on basic skills and show greater inaccuracy in self-assessment. Beyond providing feedback constructively, empathically, and with attention to the supervisee's capacity to assimilate the feedback and use it productively, the competent personality assessment supervisor can help the supervisee address professional competence problems by modeling self-reflection and critical thinking, as well as by discussing the use of debiasing strategies (e.g., avoidance of premature closure, "consider the opposite" thinking; see Croskerry, 2016; Croskerry, Singhal, & Mamede, 2013) as needed.

≡ Rapid Reference 3.5

Debiasing Strategies

A number of strategies can be useful in helping personality assessors (and personality assessment supervisors) diminish the impact of stereotypes, expectancy effects, and other biases that affect our perceptions of other people, as well as interpretation of assessment results. Useful discussions of these "debiasing strategies" are provided by Bornstein (2017), Croskerry et al. (2013), and Graber (2009). Among the more useful debiasing strategies are the following:

• Utilize evidence-based guidelines, rubrics, and scoring methods to enhance comprehensiveness and rigor in assessment-related decision-making.
• Become familiar with use of actuarial approaches to maximize the accuracy and clinical utility of personality test data.
• Receive ongoing training in theories of reasoning, sources of bias and distortion in human decision-making (e.g., heuristics, stereotypes, affect biases), and effective debiasing techniques.
• Self-monitor for fatigue, distraction, or cognitive overload during testing, assessment, and provision of feedback.
• Focus on personal accountability when making assessment-related decisions; avoid engaging in behaviors that lead to diffusion of responsibility.

Ethical, Legal, and Regulatory Considerations

Yalof and Brabender (2001) provided an excellent overview of ethical issues in personality assessment training; Matthews and Matthews (2006) provide a helpful discussion of competence in personality assessment from the perspective of a state licensing board. Because personality assessment naturally overlaps with assessment of psychopathology and risk (both with respect to referral questions and the information yielded by various tests), ethical and legal issues must be addressed openly and directly, including the limits of supervision confidentiality. This can be complex because personality assessment is conducted in multiple settings (hospitals, clinics, schools, forensic settings), each with their own norms and regulations. Moreover, as Rudd et al. (2008) noted, risk of self-harm and harm to others is salient in personality assessment, and therefore in personality assessment supervision.

Beyond risk management, ethical issues may arise when trainees complete self-report personality tests (e.g., the MMPI) to experience these measures themselves or administer performance-based tests (e.g., the RIM) to each other, or to friends, as a way of gaining experience before administering these tests to clients. Use of practice participants raises significant ethical and risk management questions (e.g., how to proceed if evidence of significant psychopathology or likelihood of self-harm emerges). Copyright issues (e.g., use of pirated test materials) sometimes raise important ethical questions as well: because personality test materials are expensive, copyright violations are distressingly common among trainees and are often tolerated by well-meaning supervisors who are sensitive to students' fiscal constraints.

FROM PRINCIPLE TO PRACTICE: THE EFFECTIVE SUPERVISOR

Beyond the traditional goals of facilitating case conceptualization and treatment planning, an important (if often unintended) consequence of personality assessment is that it changes the way the client understands him- or herself. In the process, the client may revise his or her life narrative to accommodate this changed understanding. Personality assessment not only prompts self-reflection in the client, but in the assessor as well, and personality assessment supervision should explore this self-reflection process to help the beginning psychologist enhance clinical skills and meta-skills. With this in mind, it is fair to say that effective personality assessment supervision not only impacts the life of the client, and that of the assessor, but it impacts the supervisor as well.

In moving from principle to practice, three issues emerge. These issues provide helpful context for the personality assessment supervisor in today's evolving health care milieu.

The Supervision Dialectic

Clinical psychology has long been characterized by a tension between the nomothetic and idiographic traditions, and the same is true of personality assessment. Although it is built on a scientific foundation of construct validity and clinical utility, when applied to the individual client, personality assessment remains an art. Berant et al. (2005) put it well when they wrote, "Much like artistic training, supervision of personality assessment is a complex process that calls for creative integration of different working processes, some more technical and formal and others broader and more complex" (p. 205).

Rather than being minimized or ignored, the inherent tension between the nomothetic and idiographic traditions that characterizes personality assessment is an opportunity for beginning psychologists to understand that although many competencies in applied psychology are rooted in science, they require real-world experience coupled with integration of feedback to be used effectively *in vivo*. Just as one cannot become a competent driver by reading driving manuals, one cannot become a competent assessor by reading textbooks and journal articles.

The Future of Personality Assessment Supervision

It is impossible to predict with confidence where personality assessment is headed, but current trends allow us to make some reasonable inferences regarding changes that may occur in this domain during the next decade and beyond. It is clear that telehealth (e.g., online testing, client–assessor interaction via video link) will play an increasing role in psychological assessment, including personality assessment, during the coming years. Aside from the professional challenges of telehealth, remote testing and long-distance assessment raise concerns regarding confidentiality, as well as some unique risk management issues.

Another emerging supervision domain involves personality assessment in primary care settings. Advances in this area are driven in part by a desire to tailor medical interventions to patient characteristics, culture, and preferences, and also by accumulating evidence that personality characteristics help shape the relationship between patients and health care professionals and affect treatment process and outcome (e.g., see Magidson et al., 2012). Personality assessment and assessment supervision in primary care settings present unique challenges (e.g., providing feedback to colleagues who may not be fluent in the language of personality dynamics), in addition to affording unique opportunities (e.g., an opportunity to educate physicians, nurses, and other allied health professionals regarding the value of personality assessment in treatment and management of medical conditions).

Good Intentions Sometimes Lead to Unintended Consequences

Several years ago a new RIM scoring and interpretation system was developed, which seemed to have some significant advantages over existing RIM scoring and interpretation systems. After considering the costs and benefits of shifting to the new system, the clinical psychology doctoral program at my university decided to make the shift. We trained our incoming cohort of students in the new RIM system, and—feeling very good about ourselves—sent them out to their externship placements.

Imagine our surprise when we began to receive calls from externship directors asking us to slow things down a bit and continue training students in the older scoring and interpretation system—even as many of these colleagues acknowledged that the new system might be better. The problem, we were told, was that few of their on-site personality assessment supervisors were trained in the new system; it would take at least another couple of years for that transition to occur. Needless to say, our students—who now had to become familiar with a second RIM scoring rubric—were not altogether pleased with this turn of events.

In clinical work, as in many areas of life, good intentions sometimes lead to unintended consequences. Aside from the ability to enhance the requisite knowledge, skills, and values in trainees, some flexibility—and the occasional dose of good humor—is central to effective personality assessment supervision.

 TEST YOURSELF

1. **Which core feature/component of personality is reflected in an introverted person's belief that social engagement is fraught with danger?**
   (a) Characteristic ways of thinking
   (b) Basic motives
   (c) Characteristic emotional responses
   (d) Behavior patterns

2. **According to Wright (2011), a distinguishing feature of personality assessment is:**
   (a) Exclusive reliance on structured interviews
   (b) Use of an integrated multi-method test battery
   (c) Reliance on questionnaires to assess psychopathology
   (d) Poor reliability and validity evidence

3. **In recent years there has been a decline in emphasis on personality assessment in doctoral training programs. True or False**

4. **Which of the following is *not* one of the three core constituencies served by personality assessment supervision?**
   (a) The supervisee
   (b) The client
   (c) The profession of psychology
   (d) The medical community

5. **Although the focus of personality assessment supervision has traditionally been on _____, in recent years there has been an increasing emphasis on _____.**
   (a) Growth, deficit
   (b) Normal functioning, abnormal functioning
   (c) Knowledge acquisition, outcome/performance-based evaluation
   (d) Questionnaires, performance-based tests

6. **Trainees typically enter internship training with stronger skills in psychotherapy than in psychological assessment. True or False**

7. **Which of the following is *not* one of the three core elements of clinical competence as specified by the American Psychological Association (APA) and others?**

   (a) Knowledge

   (b) Skills

   (c) Attitudes/values

   (d) Teaching ability

8. **When a test score predicts an outcome more effectively in members of Group A than in members of Group B, this may be an example of:**

   (a) Content bias

   (b) Outcome bias

   (c) Self-report confounds

   (d) Instructional deficiency

9. **Thomas (2007) suggests that informed consent on the part of supervisees is helpful, but also notes that given the contingencies of doctoral training truly voluntary informed consent might not be possible. True or False**

10. **An optimal framework for addressing competence problems in supervisees is:**

    (a) Finn's (2007) Therapeutic Assessment model

    (b) Mischel and Shoda's (2008) interactionist model

    (c) The role-reversal pedagogy model

    (d) An ethical violation centered model

Answers: 1. a; 2. b; 3. True; 4. d; 5. c; 6. True; 7. d; 8. b; 9. True; 10. a.

REFERENCES

Allport, G. W. (1961). *Pattern and growth in personality.* New York, NY: Holt, Rinehart, & Winston.

American Psychiatric Association. (1994). *Diagnostic and statistical manual of mental disorders* (4). Washington, DC: Author.

American Psychiatric Association. (2000). *Diagnostic and statistical manual of mental disorders* (4, text revision). Washington, DC: Author.

American Psychiatric Association. (2013). *Diagnostic and statistical manual of mental disorders* (5). Washington, DC: Author.

American Psychological Association (APA). (2006). Evidence-based practice in psychology. *American Psychologist*, 61, 271–285.

American Psychological Association (APA). (2007). *APA dictionary of psychology*. Washington, DC: APA Books.

American Psychological Association (APA). (2015). Guidelines for clinical supervision in health services psychology. *American Psychologist*, 70, 33–46.

Beck, A. T., Freeman, A., & Davis, D. D. (2004). *Cognitive therapy of personality disorders (2)*. New York, NY: Guilford.

Berant, E., Saroff, I., Reicher-Atir, I., & Zim, S. (2005). Supervising personality assessment: The integration of intersubjective and psychodynamic elements in the supervisory process. *Journal of Personality Assessment*, 84, 205–212.

Bornstein, R. F. (2009). Heisenberg, Kandinsky, and the Heteromethod convergence problem: Lessons from within and beyond psychology. *Journal of Personality Assessment*, 91, 1–8.

Bornstein, R. F. (2010). Psychoanalytic theory as a unifying framework for 21st century personality assessment. *Psychoanalytic Psychology*, 27, 133–152.

Bornstein, R. F. (2011). Toward a process-focused model of test score validity: Improving psychological assessment in science and practice. *Psychological Assessment*, 23, 532–544.

Bornstein, R. F. (2017). Evidence based psychological assessment. *Journal of Personality Assessment*, 99, 435–445.

Brabender, V. M., & Mihura, J. L. (Eds.) (2016). *Handbook of gender, sex, and psychological assessment*. New York, NY: Routledge/Taylor & Francis.

Bram, A. D., & Peebles-Klieger, M. J. (2014). *Psychological testing that matters: Creating a road map effective treatment*. Washington, DC: APA Books.

Clemence, A. J., & Handler, L. (2001). Psychological assessment on internship: A survey of training directors and their expectations for students. *Journal of Personality Assessment*, 76, 18–47.

Costantino, G., Litman, L., Waxman, R., Dupertuis, D., Pais, E., Rosenzweig, C., … Canales, M. M. F. (2014). Tell-Me-A-Story (TEMAS) assessment for culturally diverse children and adolescents. *Rorschachiana*, 35, 154–175.

Croskerry, P. (2016). Our better angels and black boxes. *Emergency Medicine Journal*, 33, 242–244.

Croskerry, P., Singhal, G., & Mamede, S. (2013). Cognitive debiasing 2: Impediments to and strategies for change. *BMJ Quality and Safety*, 22, ii65–ii72.

Dadlani, M. B., Overtree, C., & Perry-Jenkins, M. (2012). Culture at the center: A reformulation of diagnostic assessment. *Professional Psychology: Research and Practice*, 43, 175–182.

DeCato, C. M. (2002). A quantitative method for studying the testing supervision process. *Psychological Reports*, 90, 137.

Dumont, R., & Willis, J. O. (2003). Issues regarding the supervision of assessment. *The Clinical Supervisor*, 22, 159–176.

Edwards, L. M., Burkard, A. W., Adams, H. A., & Newcomb, S. A. (2017). A mixed-method study of psychologists' use of multicultural assessment. *Professional Psychology: Research and Practice*, 48, 131–138.

Falender, C. A., Cornish, J. A. E., Goodyear, R., Hatcher, R., Kaslow, N. J., Leventhal, G., … Sigmon, S. T. (2004). Defining competencies in psychology supervision: A consensus statement. *Journal of Clinical Psychology*, 60, 771–785.

Finn, S. E. (2007). *In our client's shoes: Theory and techniques of therapeutic assessment*. New York, NY: Routledge/Taylor & Francis.

Flores, A., Cobos, P. L., & Hagmayer, Y. (2018). The diagnosis of mental disorders is influenced by automatic causal reasoning. *Clinical Psychological Science*, 6, 177–188.

Graber, M. L. (2009). Educational strategies to reduce diagnostic error: Can you teach this stuff? *Advances in Health Science Education*, 14, 63–69.

Gutierrez, F., Vall, G., Peri, J. M., Bailles, E., Ferraz, L., Garriz, M., & Caseras, X. (2012). Personality disorder features through the life course. *Journal of Personality Disorders*, 26, 763–774.

Handler, L. (2008). Supervision in therapeutic and collaborative assessment. In A. K. Hess, C. D. Hess, & T. H. Hess (Eds.), *Psychotherapy supervision: Theory, research, and practice* (pp. 200–222). Hoboken, NJ: Wiley.

Herpertz, S. C., Huprich, S. K., Bohus, M., Chanen, A., Goodman, M., Mehlum, L., … Sharp, C. (2017). The challenge of transforming the diagnostic system of personality disorders. *Journal of Personality Disorders*, 31, 577–589.

Hiller, J. B., Rosenthal, R., Bornstein, R. F., Berry, D. T. R., & Brunell-Neulieb, S. (1999). A comparative meta-analysis of Rorschach and MMPI validity. *Psychological Assessment*, 11, 278–296.

Holt, H., Beutler, L. E., Kimpara, S., Macias, S., Haug, N. A., Shiloff, N., … Stein, M. (2015). Evidence-based supervision: Tracking outcome and teaching principles of change in clinical supervision to bring science to integrative practice. *Psychotherapy*, 52(2), 185–189.

Hopwood, C. J., Zimmermann, J., Pincus, A. L., & Krueger, R. F. (2015). Connecting personality structure and dynamics: Towards a more empirically-based and clinically useful diagnostic system. *Journal of Personality Disorders*, 29, 431–448.

Hutchinson, L., & Romero, D. (2016). Precision or imprecision medicine? *Clinical Oncology*, 13, 712–713.

Iwanicki, S., & Peterson, C. (2017). An exploratory study examining current assessment supervisory practices in professional psychology. *Journal of Personality Disorders*, 99, 165–174.

Kahneman, D. (2003). A perspective on judgment and choice: Mapping bounded rationality. *American Psychologist*, 58, 697–720.

Kaslow, N. J., & Egan, G. J. (2017). A competency-focused commentary on the Special Section on Teaching, Training, and Supervision in Personality and Psychological Assessment. *Journal of Personality Assessment*, 99, 189–191.

Knapp, S., & VandeCreek, L. (1997). Ethical and legal aspects of clinical supervision. In C. E. Watkins (Ed.), *Handbook of psychotherapy supervision* (pp. 589–599). Hoboken, NJ: Wiley.

Krishnamurthy, R., VandeCreek, L., Kaslow, N. J., Tazeau, Y. N., Miville, M. L., Kerns, R., ... Benton, S. A. (2004). Achieving competency in psychological assessment: Directions for education and training. *Journal of Clinical Psychology*, 60, 725–739.

Krishnamurthy, R., & Yalof, J. A. (2009). The assessment competency. In M. B. Kenkel & R. L. Peterson (Eds.), *Competency-based education for professional psychology* (pp. 87–104). Washington, DC: American Psychological Association.

Levendosky, A. A., & Hopwood, J. C. (2017). Terminating supervision. *Psychotherapy*, 54, 37–46.

Luyten, P., & Blatt, S. J. (2013). Interpersonal relatedness and self-definition in normal and disrupted personality development. *American Psychologist*, 68, 172–183.

Magidson, J. F., Collado-Rodriguez, A., Madan, A., Perez-Camoirano, N. A., Galloway, S. K. B., J., J., ... Miller, J. D. (2012). Addressing narcissistic personality features in the context of medical care: Integrating diverse perspectives to inform clinical practice. *Personality Disorders: Theory, Research, and Treatment*, 3, 196–208.

Masling, J. M. (2002). Speak, memory, or goodbye Columbus. *Journal of Personality Assessment*, 78, 4–30.

Matthews, J. R., & Matthews, L. H. (2006). Personality assessment training: View from a licensing board. *Journal of Personality Assessment*, 86, 46–50.

McAdams, D. P., & McLean, K. C. (2013). Narrative identity. *Current Directions in Psychological Science*, 22, 233–238.

McWilliams, N. (2011). *Psychoanalytic diagnosis: Understanding personality structure in the clinical process* (rev. ed.). New York, NY: Guilford.

Meyer, G. J., Finn, S. E., Eyde, L. D., Kay, G. G., Moreland, K. L., Dies, R. R., … Reed, G. M. (2001). Psychological testing and assessment: A review of evidence and issues. *American Psychologist*, 56, 128–165.

Mihura, J. L. (2012). The necessity of multiple test methods in conducting assessments: The role of the Rorschach and self-report. *Psychological Injury and Law*, 5, 97–106.

Mihura, J. L., Meyer, G. J., Dumitrascu, N., & Bombel, G. (2013). The validity of individual Rorschach variables: Systematic reviews and meta-analyses of the comprehensive system. *Psychological Bulletin*, 139, 548–605.

Mihura, J. L., Roy, M., & Graceffo, R. A. (2017). Psychological assessment training in clinical psychology doctoral programs. *Journal of Personality Assessment*, 99, 153–164.

Millon, T. (2011). *Disorders of personality (3.)*. Hoboken, NJ: Wiley.

Mio, J., Barker, L., & Rodriguez, M. D. (2015). *Multicultural psychology (4)*. Oxford, UK: Oxford University Press.

Mischel, W., & Shoda, Y. (2008). Toward a unified theory of personality: Integrating dispositions and personality dynamics within the cognitive-affective processing system. In O. P. John, W. Robins, & L. A. Pervin (Eds.), *Handbook of personality* (3, pp. 208–241). New York, NY: Guilford.

Mongrain, M., & Blackburn, S. (2015). Cognitive vulnerability, lifetime risk, and the recurrence of major depression in graduate students. *Cognitive Therapy and Research*, 29, 747–768.

Pervin, L. A. (1996). *The science of personality*. New York, NY: Wiley.

Reynolds, C. R., & Suzuki, L. A. (2013). Bias in psychological assessment: An empirical review and recommendations. In J. R. Graham, J. A. Naglieri, & I. B. Weiner (Eds.), *Handbook of psychology, Volume 10: Assessment psychology* (pp. 82–113). Hoboken, NJ: Wiley.

Rings, J. A., Genuchi, M. C., Hall, M. D., Angelo, M. A., & Cornish, J. A. E. (2009). Is there consensus among predoctoral internship training directors regarding clinical supervision competencies? A descriptive analysis. *Training and Education in Professional Psychology*, 3, 140–147.

Rudd, M. D., Cukrowicz, K. C., & Bryan, C. J. (2008). Core competencies in suicide risk assessment and management: Implications for supervision. *Training and Education in Professional Psychology*, 2, 219–228.

Scott, K. J., Ingram, K. M., Vitanza, S. A., & Smith, N. G. (2000). Training in supervision: A survey of current practices. *The Counseling Psychologist*, 28, 403–422.

SPA Board of Trustees. (2006). Standards for education and training in psychological assessment: Position of the Society for Personality Assessment. *Journal of Personality Assessment*, 87, 355–357.

Suzuki, L., & Ponterotto, J. (2008). *Handbook of multicultural assessment: Clinical, psychological and educational applications*. San Francisco, CA: Jossey-Bass.

Thomas, J. T. (2007). Informed consent through contracting for supervision: Minimizing risks, enhancing benefits. *Professional Psychology: Research and Practice*, 38, 221–231.

Urminsky, O. (2017). The role of psychological connectedness to the future self on decisions over time. *Current Directions in Psychological Science*, 26, 34–39.

Vannucci, M. J., Whiteside, D. M., Saigal, S., Nichols, N., & Hileman, S. (2017). Predicting supervision outcomes: What is different about psychological assessment supervision? *Australian Psychologist*, 52, 114–120.

Wilson, T. D. (2009). Know thyself. *Perspectives on Psychological Science*, 4, 384–389.

Wood, J. M., Nezworski, M. T., Lilienfeld, S. O., & Garb, H. N. (2003). *What's wrong with the Rorschach? Science confronts the controversial inkblot test*. San Francisco, CA: Jossey-Bass.

Wright, A. J. (2011). *Conducting psychological assessment: A guide for practitioners*. Hoboken, NJ: Wiley.

Yalof, J., & Brabender, V. M. (2001). Ethical dilemmas in personality assessment courses: Using the classroom for in vivo training. *Journal of Personality Assessment*, 77, 203–213.

Four

SUPERVISING INTEGRATION IN ASSESSMENT

Steven R. Smith
Ana Romero-Morales

After tests have been scored and historical information gathered, the next phase of a comprehensive assessment is the integration of all assessment material. The integration of test results and clinical data in a complex, person-centered manner allows for rich and useful interpretations that go beyond any one test score. Assessment integration is a difficult process and one that requires a great deal of skill, knowledge, and experience. As noted by Handler and Meyer (1998):

> The focus [of psychological assessment] is not on obtaining a single score, or even a series of test scores. Rather, the focus is on taking a variety of test-derived pieces of information, obtained from multiple methods of assessment, and placing these data in the context of historical information, referral information, and behavioral observations in order to generate a cohesive and comprehensive understanding of the person being evaluated. These activities are far from simple; they require a high degree of skill and sophistication to be implemented properly. (pp. 4–5)

Clearly, this more complex process of assessment requires a great deal of skill and care. For that reason, careful supervision of trainees as they progress from facility with administering a few tests to competence in integrated psychological assessment is vital.

Essentials of Psychological Assessment Supervision, First Edition.
Edited by A. Jordan Wright
© 2020 John Wiley & Sons, Inc. Published 2020 by John Wiley & Sons, Inc.

MODEL OF ASSESSMENT SUPERVISION

Yalof (2018) notes that few models for assessment supervision exist, despite the range of available models for psychotherapy or counseling. According to Krishnamurthy and Yalof (2010), assessment integration represents the highest level of assessment competence and is not expected prior to internship. Supervisors of trainees should remember that assessment is both complex and challenging, and their expectations for student performance should be adjusted accordingly. As in all forms of training, a developmental approach is essential.

Finkelstein and Tuckman (1997) outlined a concise developmental model for assessment supervision that focuses on the needs of supervisees at increasingly autonomous levels. Their work emphasizes the importance of the supervisor-supervisee relationship and how the process of growing competence shifts the supervisee's perspective of the supervisor from assessment magician to trusted consultant. Particularly important for assessment supervision is their suggestion that supervisors not forget to explain their thinking in great detail. Experienced supervisors can be prone to making "internal leaps" that rapidly combine and alter several forms of test data with history and other information. Finkelstein and Tuckman remind supervisors to slow down and explain each step fully until the supervisee has enough experience to engage in the process without those full explanations.

> **DON'T FORGET**
> ....
> Integrating assessment data is complex and represents the most sophisticated competency in assessment, so supervisors need to adjust their expectations accordingly.

CONSIDERATIONS SPECIFIC TO SUPERVISING INTEGRATION IN ASSESSMENT

Before we can discuss assessment integration, it is important to consider what types of information are being integrated. History, interview data, reason for referral, setting, diversity factors, cognitive assessment scores, personality assessment scores, behavioral assessment data, reports of others, and medical information are all forms of data that can be a part of a comprehensive assessment process. All of these data sources can interact with one another, and interpretations will need to be modified accordingly. For example, scores in the average normative range obtained from an adolescent in an inpatient setting will be interpreted differently than similar scores obtained in an outpatient setting. Likewise, personality assessment scores obtained from a client with cognitive difficulties should be interpreted differently from personality assessment scores obtained from a client who tests as cognitively above average.

Data Modification and Meaning

One of us has written about the integration of neuropsychological and personality/emotional data (Smith, 2007). In that chapter, I argued that neuropsychological data and personality assessment data affect each other differently. Personality assessment seems to affect neuropsychological data at the level of *interpretation*. That is, when personality assessment data suggest that a client is depressed, easily frustrated, or lacking in motivation, it might suggest that his or her effort, speed, or motivation for completing neuropsychological tests might be compromised. In those cases, clinicians might interpret those neuropsychological tests as an underestimate of their true abilities.

In contrast to interpretation, neuropsychological processes can affect personality assessment results at the more fundamental level of *meaning* (Smith, 2007). Stated differently, if a client struggles with a neurocognitive weakness or deficit, that weakness

REMEMBER

Interpretations of scores from tests need to be made in the context of scores from other tests and other data collected.

Part of understanding what is being integrated is having a nuanced understanding of what each test *is*. Supervisors should not assume that all supervisees understand these nuances well. For example, we can easily say that the Minnesota Multiphasic Personality Inventory-2 (MMPI-2) is a measure of personality, but the truth is that it is a measure of explicit self-representation that is completed in a particular setting, for a particular reason, at a particular time. In the case of self-report measures, the context of the assessment is also being implicitly measured. As another example, Block Design from the Wechsler Adult Intelligence Scale (WAIS) is a measure of nonverbal processing, but it also has components of processing speed (for the timed items), visuospatial reasoning, fine motor control, visual-motor integration, pattern recognition, frustration tolerance, and even performance anxiety. Supervisors must help supervisees recognize that all tests measure multiple components of performance and that any of those components might be driving an obtained score.

might impact how he or she interacts with personality assessment materials, items, or stimuli. For example, a client with dyslexia might experience frustration when completing a lengthy self-report measure (and that frustration might elevate some scores or impact measures of validity). Similarly, a client with deficits in visuospatial processing might have some challenges decoding the Rorschach task.

≋ *Rapid Reference 4.1*

Interaction Between Neuropsychology, Personality, and Assessment

How neuropsychological functioning affects personality/emotional assessment, and how personality/emotional functioning affects neuropsychological tests (Smith, 2007):

1. Supervisors should help supervisees understand how to *interpret* neuropsychological data within the context of personality and emotional functioning. For example, depression, anxiety, or obsessive perfectionism can alter how a client performs on certain neuropsychological measures that require processing speed, concentration, etc.

2. Supervisors should help supervisees understand the *meaning* of scores obtained on personality and assessment measures within the context of neuropsychological functioning. For example, problems with visuospatial processing or attention can affect how a client can approach certain tests of personality and emotional functioning.

This shift in how we understand the meaning of personality/emotional test scores based on neuropsychological processing must be considered when integrating data.

Importance of Theory

Another important point of supervision is to help supervisees create their theoretical and conceptual model for normative human functioning. Without a complex theory of personhood, test interpretations tend to be piecemeal, score-centered, and lacking in depth and integration (e.g., Sugarman, 1991). Part of what makes supervision of assessment so challenging is that supervisors must not only teach facility with test administration and scoring, as well as interviewing, but also broad theories of personality and neurocognitive functioning (and the interactions between the two). Without a broad theory of cognitive and psychological processes (that encapsulates a sensitivity to diversity factors), integration of assessment data is nearly impossible.

A number of authors have posited complex frameworks for data integration. Blais and Smith (2014; based on the work of Mayer, 1998, 2005) offer a four-part model of functioning that can serve as a transtheoretical model for data organization and integration:

1. *Nature and quality of thinking*: Data from neuropsychological and cognitive test data, including memory processes, attention, language, executive functions, processing speed, etc. This domain also includes data from personality measures that capture thought processes, psychotic experiences, coping style, and capacity for metacognition. Finally, history information related to education, head injuries, and even substance use can be helpful for understanding the nature and quality of a client's thinking.
2. *Emotional processing*: Data from personality tests, history, and interviews can tell us about the presence of mood or anxiety disorders, self-reported mood and anger, and accessibility of a range of feelings. It is particularly important to consider cultural variables and how they might impact the expression of affect and affective distress (which will be discussed in more detail below).
3. *Self system*: Cognitive and affective processes combine and help form a sense of self. In that self system are feelings about ourselves (self-esteem) and the complexity of our thoughts, images, and ideas about ourselves (self-concepts). The self system contains and controls our personal narratives, how we understand the nature of our difficulties, and it has a bidirectional relationship with how we understand the motives and actions of others.
4. *Interpersonal processing*: The combination of cognitive and affective processes and sense of self will then impact our relationships with others. Interpersonal processes not only include actual interpersonal behavior, but our expectations and experiences of others as well.

Of course, these processes are not mutually exclusive, and there is a transactional relationship among and between all four of these systems. Furthermore, Blais and Smith (2014) note that all of these processes can operate on an explicit or implicit (unconscious) basis. Although the model is complex, it can be distilled and easily communicated to supervisees who are struggling to integrate different forms of assessment data.

Integration Process

Supervisors are urged to work through this integration process in a step-by-step fashion so that they have a framework to use with increasingly complex cases. All of these steps presume basic knowledge of each test's psychometrics, as well as a complex theory of personality and cognitive functions. In all cases, supervisors and supervisees are encouraged to remember culture, context, and the reason(s) for referral. That is, the assessment data should be couched within real world conflicts, issues, and functioning.

Step 1. Assessment measures should be scored using standardized systems and the best available normative sample. Supervisees should make note of the adequacy of the norms relative to the demographics of their particular client.

Step 2. Supervisees and supervisors should make themselves aware of the research literature about the strengths and weaknesses of each measure for addressing the reason(s) for referral. Supervisees should be aware of the psychometric limitations of each measure and note any validity concerns, particularly as they relate to diversity factors and acculturation status.

Step 3. Supervisees should begin to interpret each test independently and organize the test data into the four domains described above. We find that organizing data into a grid format (see Table 4.1) helps with this process. By transposing data sources onto one table that can be easily reviewed, supervisees and supervisors can take a "bird's eye view" of the data, including consistencies and inconsistencies. Part of what supervisors will help supervisees do is remember each test's strengths and weaknesses and where in the assessment results to look for all four of the domains.

Step 4. In keeping with the model above, supervisors and supervisees should start with the cognitive assessment data. Basic attention, reasoning, language, and memory processes should be summarized and considered. Furthermore, personality measures can tell us about a client's clarity of thought and thinking processes. All initial interpretations should be held as tentative until the full picture of client functioning is reviewed.

Step 5. Following a review of their cognitive processing, supervisees should engage in a basic review of emotional processes. Presence of anxiety or depression, lability, or defenses should be carefully considered in context of the assessment setting (Baity et al., 2018) and interpersonal dynamics (Estrada, 2018). Initial hypotheses can be made at this point about how emotional functioning might have impacted cognitive test scores (e.g., slowing, effort, or frustration tolerance); the initial cognitive interpretations can then be altered accordingly. Likewise, if the client had significant deficits on cognitive measures, supervisors and supervisees should consider how that might have impacted the client's ability to fully engage in the personality assessment process.

Step 6. Once cognitive and affective data are considered, supervisors and supervisees can consider the client's intrapersonal processing (self system). Cognitive data tell us the resources that clients have and can use to consider themselves and their functioning; emotional processes tell us how complex their feelings about themselves might be.

Step 7. Finally, we can consider the client's interpersonal functions. That is, how do they think about relationships and the motivations of others? Are they likely to be introverted or do they gain energy from their interactions? Interpersonal functioning then influences and shapes how clients feel about themselves, which further adds complexity to the interpretations made in Step 6.

Step 8. At this point in the integration process, supervisees and supervisors should start the process over and modify, review, and add nuance to the interpretive picture they're creating. Because the four domains of functioning addressed here are not orthogonal—they interact and intersect in a myriad of ways—taking a step back and reviewing each domain of data in the context of the other domains will help create a complex picture of client functions.

Table 4.1 Data organization table with example data

Name of assessment	Cognitive/Thinking processes	Emotional functioning	Self system	Interpersonal processing
MMPI-2	Moderate elevation on Scales 8 and 6.	No elevations on 2 or 7.	Some elevation on 3, perhaps suggesting neediness. High L and K suggest some self-protection or lack of insight.	Moderate elevation on 6; likely to be guarded.
WAIS-V	Low average FSIQ, issues with processing speed and WM. Likely to be impulsive and have difficulty performing under pressure.	Frustration tolerance was adequate.	Made a few disparaging remarks: "I'm not good at this."	Behaviorally pleasant, but wary.
History	History of educational problems. Required tutors throughout school. History of ADHD diagnosis with failed medication trials.	Reports of history of depression and anxiety in childhood.	Has difficulty noting strengths. Currently unemployed despite having basic working skills.	Reports getting into fights in recent years. No romantic relationships. Heterosexual. Disconnected from family.

≋ Rapid Reference 4.2

Eight Stages of Supervising Data Integration

1. Assessment measures should be scored according to standardized procedures and norms.
2. Relevant literature should be reviewed in order to adequately assess validity for the particular client.
3. Each test should be interpreted independently and entered into a table that captures cognitive, affective, self, and interpersonal data.
4. Cognitive measures should be addressed first, and initial interpretations should be made regarding overall cognitive functioning, thought processes, memory, language, and efficiency.
5. Affective functions should then be reviewed, including presence of depression or anxiety, comfort with affect, range of affect, frustration tolerance, etc. Once affective data are considered, cognitive interpretations should be reconsidered.
6. In the context of both cognitive and affective findings, self system processes (including complexity of self concept, self esteem, etc.) should be addressed.
7. Finally, interpersonal processes (both real and imagined) should be addressed, and any self system data should then be modified accordingly.
8. As a final step, steps four through seven should be revisited in order to see whether the interpretations might change after all data are known.

Throughout this multistep process, supervisors must guide their supervisees and add complexity to the initial interpretations. Although a supervisee should be able to adequately administer and score each test, make basic interpretations, and visit the relevant literature, the higher-level work of assessment integration might be a challenge for those who are earlier in their assessment training or experience. Evidence-based practice in psychology (EBPP; APA Presidential Task Force on Evidence-Based Practice, 2006) is defined as practice that takes into account information from the best available research, clinician expertise, and the needs, wishes, and demographics of a particular client. Importantly, EBPP is flexible practice *that relies heavily on clinician expertise and experience.*

Of course, supervisees cannot acquire expertise for several years, so in essence, they must borrow the expertise of their supervisors. Supervisors must have expertise and experience with the measures, the type of assessment setting, and the reason(s) for referral, as well as any information about local history or context (Smith & Krishnamurthy, 2018). Supervisors must convey that evidence-based practice is flexible practice and that simple score-centric interpretations should be held lightly.

Dealing with Inconsistencies

In all assessment batteries, inconsistencies between test scores will arise. As noted by Wright (2018), there are several forms of inconsistencies between scores. We suggest that when glaring inconsistencies arise, the first step should be to check the administration or scoring of the measures. Measures that have several steps to obtain a score (e.g., adding item scores, accounting for basals, etc.), complicated instructions, or where there is some degree of clinician judgment about a score (e.g., whether to give one or two points for a vocabulary item) are particularly prone to clinician error. Thus, supervisors should check administration and scoring of measures, even for supervisees who are quite advanced. There have been several instances where we have puzzled over a particular data inconsistency only to learn that the supervisee administered the test incorrectly. Some very puzzling score inconsistencies have been easily reconciled by simply noting a mathematical or clinician error.

Once a supervisor sees that all assessments have been administered and scored correctly and inconsistencies still exist, a plan must be made for how to address them. Wright (2018) notes four types of data inconsistencies. First are *apparent inconsistencies*, where data appear to be in conflict but are easily reconciled based on theory or nuanced understanding of psychopathology. Cognitive test scores often also appear to be in conflict with one another until we remember that each test measures several things. It might be a weakness on one component of a test that makes it appear discrepant (e.g., differences in scores between nonverbal reasoning tests might occur when only one of the tests relies on motor processing, such as Matrix Reasoning versus Block Design). Another form of apparent inconsistency can arise when supervisees rely too heavily on the names of scales given by test authors (and thus do not have a deep understanding of what tests actually measure). Two tests might purport to measure depression, but one test might actually be measuring something closer to anhedonia, while the other measures constructs more in keeping with a DSM-V diagnosis of major depression. Supervisor expertise on the measures is needed to help supervisees understand these apparent conflicts. In cases of apparent inconsistencies, supervisees just need to describe the discrepancy and explain it in a clear way, which may require some psychoeducation for the audience of the report.

The second type of inconsistency noted by Wright relates to *process or method effects*. The literature is clear that different test methodologies rarely correlate, even when they purport to measure the same thing. The magnitude of measurement error and the fact that different methods might be measuring different aspects of the same construct often account for discrepancies in data. This underscores the importance of visiting the literature to note any convergent validity data that might exist on the measures being used. Also, research literature will help shape nuanced interpretations that might be different for the measures in question.

The third source of data inconsistencies are *context effects*. When the context of an assessment shifts or historical events impact the client, this can give rise to data discrepancies. Furthermore, the setting in which an assessment takes place can also give rise to differences between tests (e.g., an adolescent in a juvenile facility might deny any behavioral issues on self-report, inconsistent with their actual history of truancy or crime). Importantly, diversity factors have a large effect on assessment data. Consider the notion of stereotype threat, where individuals from non-majority groups will perform on tests in keeping with prevalent stereotypes about their group (Steele & Aronson, 1995). Finally, even basic rapport (or lack thereof) with the clinician might give rise to differential test performance, yielding inconsistent findings. For all three of these types of data inconsistency, Wright suggests that clinicians carefully and thoroughly explain them in the report.

The final form of data inconsistency is more problematic: *test error or outlier-driven discrepancies* (Wright). In this case, none of the prior forms of inconsistency explanations apply (and all of the tests were administered and scored correctly), but inconsistencies remain. These inconsistencies might be due to unexplainable flukes in test taking (that might be driven by variables like low motivation, drug use, hunger, or poor attention that the clinician might not be aware of). Diversity factors are particularly important here, given that outlier scores might be due to inadequate norms or validity for the client's cultural group. In such cases where score inconsistency exists, supervisors and supervisees must decide which score(s) to exclude from analysis.

≡ Rapid Reference 4.3

Model for Addressing Data Discrepancies/Inconsistencies (Adapted from Wright, 2018)

1. Ensure that all tests and measures were administered and scored correctly.
2. Determine whether the discrepancies are *apparent discrepancies* that simply need explaining to a lay audience.
3. Determine whether the conflicting data are due to *process or method effects*, as different methods measure different aspects of constructs in different ways.
4. Determine whether the conflicting data are due to *context effects*, attributable to the immediate context in which different measures were administered.
5. If not attributable to any of the above reasons, consider the fact that every test has error, and some *test error or outliers* will exist, and try to determine which data can be excluded from analysis.

Interpersonal Considerations

As is true for all forms of clinical work, the clinician's feelings about, and experiences of, the client are important sources of data. In all assessment batteries, there will be inconsistencies and test scores that point in different directions. In those situations, there are often considerable consequences for interpreting one data source over another. Although we have posited some ways of dealing with those inconsistencies, it is worth noting that clinician feelings about a client can potentially steer interpretation in one direction over another.

It is easy for supervisees and supervisors to get lost in the data and behavioral observations of an assessment case, particularly when the data are complex or compelling in some way. However, supervisors must remind supervisees that their experiences of the client are important and should be addressed. All of us have had clients we were "rooting for" during an assessment, where we really wanted someone to perform well or generate a relatively "normal" personality assessment profile. Likewise, we've all had clients who were more interpersonally difficult or who appeared impaired, and we anticipated that we'd see test scores in the more pathological or problematic range. Finally, there are contextual variables at play in how we interpret data. For example, a more powerful or respected treater may refer a client for an evaluation with suspicion of a particular diagnosis. Supervisees (and even supervisors) might be motivated to give that clinician what she or he wants or suspects in order to curry favor or merely because we assume that the clinician is right because he or she is so much more experienced. In all of these cases, supervisors should help supervisees discuss their internal and external pressures and think about how they might impact the interpretation of data and how they write up and present the results.

> **REMEMBER**
>
> Don't ignore how a supervisee *feels* about a client. Encourage supervisees to discuss these feelings openly, as they may affect how data are treated.

SUPERVISION COMPETENCE

As is true for all assessment supervision, supervisors must be skilled at understanding and interpreting assessments, understanding the developmental needs of the supervisee, and understanding the presentation of the client in the context of the referral question. Furthermore, given that assessment is an interaction between a clinician, a client, and a test, supervisors must be aware of the interactions among all of these variables, as well as the interaction between themselves and their supervisees. It is particularly incumbent on the supervisor to maintain a close read of the available literature on all the measures used in order to bring the most robust context to the supervision discussion.

One of the seemingly most common mistakes is that the supervisor does not appreciate how inexperienced the supervisee is. Once a supervisor has been in practice for a number of years, he or she might forget what it is like to be a trainee or to be new at administering a test that the supervisor has administered hundreds of times. Supervisors are encouraged to recall their early assessment experiences and recall how daunting and overwhelming it was to work on a comprehensive report or integrate discrepant forms of data. Recalling the point of view of the supervisee and acknowledging the person's inexperience while encouraging greater independence will help build trust in the supervisee and, in turn, a better experience for the client.

REMEMBER

This part of the assessment process is hard! No matter how good you are at it, your supervisee likely is not yet.

DIVERSITY CONSIDERATIONS

As noted, literature on the supervision of integration in assessment is limited. Thus far, Allen (2007) has proposed a multicultural assessment competency model for assessment supervision that follows the developmental trajectory of a graduate student from being trained to engaging in culturally informed assessment work. This model emphasizes key skills and knowledge needed to provide multiculturally-informed assessment supervision and training, and yet there is a salient lack of focus on the integration process (Allen, 2007). Given that supervisees typically learn how to analyze and integrate assessment data from their supervisors (rather than formally in graduate classes, etc.), it is vital for supervisors to guide and model for students how to consider the role of diversity at every step of the integration process. These diversity-related considerations must be interwoven in the integration process.

Before embarking on the process of assessment integration training, supervisors and supervisees are encouraged to reflect on and attend to their various intersectional identities and biases. As an assessment supervisor, it is important to understand oneself as a "cultural being" with a worldview that will color the relationship with clients, supervisees, and assessment material (APA, 2003, p. 382; Smith & Kent, 2018). By doing so, the supervisor models and guides supervisees to reflect on their identities and to challenge their own assumptions, which can aid in the development of supervisees' multicultural competence and strengthen their working alliance (Ladany, Brittan-Powell, & Pannu, 1997). When cultural and diversity differences exist between supervisors and supervisees, supervisors should consider how their identity and supervisees' identities will impact their working alliance and their approach to the assessment process (Ladany et al., 1997). Even more so, a supervisor's openness to engage in self-reflection may indicate a willingness to be challenged by supervisees, which can be difficult given the power differential in a supervisor–supervisee relationship (Baca & Smith, 2018). Given the complexity of assessment integration, such reflectiveness and openness to feedback are essential.

> **DON'T FORGET**
> ....
> Diversity and cultural differences influence the clinician–client relationship, but they also affect the supervisor–supervisee dyad. When negotiating the integration of data, always consider the potential impact of cultural differences (and similarities, which can lead to "blind spots") on the process and relationship.

Scholars have highlighted how a variety of cultural variables may influence a client's performance on assessments (Brickman, Cabo, & Manly, 2006). In the initial process of integrating assessment data, supervisors and supervisees should examine the normative samples, strengths and limitations, and validity of the assessments available for non-white populations to ensure that they are culturally congruent. For instance, Ardila (2005) noted that in working with Asian American-identified clients, one must consider how values, communication styles, and knowledge will influence assessments outcomes. Others highlight how individuals with collectivistic worldviews may perform differently on tests; for example, on category subtests they may focus on the relationship between objects and details in the background instead of just the object itself (Guo & Uhm, 2014).

In addition to cognitive performance, individuals from communities with collectivistic worldviews may express emotions and relationships differently from those in the dominant culture (Ardila, 2005; Eid & Diener, 2001; Guo & Uhm, 2014; Semrud-Clikeman & Bledsoe, 2014). For example, those within a collectivistic society are often expected to manage extreme emotions, especially when that may negatively impact others; this might encourage clients to avoid selecting points on extreme ends of rating scales (Guo & Uhm, 2014). These cultural differences at the level of test score might increase the likelihood of test inconsistencies, particularly when the normative sample of a test is not representative. Supervisors and supervisees need to be cognizant of how culture-based test approaches might complicate score integration.

Also important to test integration and making sense of inconsistencies, supervisors and supervisees need to consider culture and local context in the process of assessment. The experience of being marginalized is not uniform and depends on larger social context variables such as available social support, community bias, local history relative to particular marginalized groups, and the mechanism of referral (e.g., voluntary versus involuntary, forensic, etc.). These variables, among others, can have a huge impact on test scores, but should also shape the integration of data. Once the first pass of data interpretation is complete, supervisees should review all available information once more with a lens of diversity sensitivity. Finally, supervisors need to remember that culturally-competent test integration is a skill *beyond* mere test integration, so only the most advanced supervisees are ready to grapple with this degree of complexity.

CONCLUSION

Integration of testing and history data represents the most complex task of multifaceted psychological assessment. Thoughtful and client-centered integration shifts the task from mere psychological testing to higher level psychological assessment. Good integration comes with a great deal of clinical expertise and experience coupled with a nuanced command of the available research literature. For these reasons, good and patient supervision of integration is needed to help supervisees reach a greater command of the material and processes. Supervisors need to be sensitive to supervisees' developmental level and growing competence, while also ensuring that clients receive the best assessment experience possible. Having a systematic approach to assessment integration, including consideration of diversity variables, will help both supervisor and supervisee maintain clarity in their work both together and with the client.

🐟 TEST YOURSELF 🐟

1. **True or False: Evidence-based practice in psychology is defined by its flexibility and not only an adherence to research data.**

2. **Krishnamurthy and Yalof (2010) suggest that competence in assessment integration is likely not to come before:**
   (a) Two graduate-level courses in assessment
   (b) A full practicum in assessment
   (c) Predoctoral internship
   (d) Fellowship

3. **True or False: Neuropsychological assessment information can change the meaning of personality assessment data.**

4. **Integration of assessment data should include:**
   (a) Test scores, history information, behavioral observations, cultural information, and reason for referral
   (b) History information and the reports of others
   (c) History information, reason for referral, behavioral observations
   (d) Quantifiable data only
5. **True or False: Supervisors' reflections about their own cultural identity is the first step of culturally responsive supervision.**

Answers: 1. True; 2. c; 3. True; 4. a; 5. True

REFERENCES

Allen, J. (2007). A multicultural assessment supervision model to guide research and practice. *Professional Psychology: Research and Practice*, 38(3), 248–258. https://doi.org/10.1037/0735-7028.38.3.248

American Psychological Association (APA). (2003). Guidelines on multicultural education, training, research, practice, and organizational change for psychologists. *American Psychologist*, 58, 377–402.

APA Presidential Task Force on Evidence-Based Practice. (2006). Evidence-based practice in psychology. *The American Psychologist*, 61(4), 271–285.

Ardila, A. (2005). Cultural values underlying psychometric cognitive testing. *Neuropsychology Review*, 15(4), 185–195. http://dx.doi.org/10.1007/s11065-005-9180-y

Baca, L., & Smith, S. R. (2018). The role of self-reflection and self-assessment in the psychological assessment process. In S. R. Smith & R. Krishnamurthy (Eds.), *Diversity-sensitive personality assessment* (pp. 3–26). New York, NY: Routledge.

Baity, M. R., Hsieh, A. L., & Swanson, S. M. (2018). Assessment contexts. In S. R. Smith & R. Krishnamurthy (Eds.), *Diversity-sensitive personality assessment* (pp. 245–258). New York, NY: Routledge.

Blais, M. A., & Smith, S. R. (2014). Improving the integrative process in psychological assessment: Data organization and report writing. In R. P. Archer & S. R. Smith (Eds.), *Personality assessment (2)* (pp. 433–470). New York, NY: Routledge.

Brickman, A. M., Cabo, R., & Manly, J. J. (2006). Ethical issues in cross-cultural neuropsychology. *Applied Neuropsychology*, 13(2), 91–100. http://dx.doi.org/10.1207/s15324826an1302_4

Eid, M., & Diener, E. (2001). Norms for experiencing emotions in different cultures: Inter- and intranational differences. *Journal of Personality and Social Psychology*, 81(5), 869–885. http://dx.doi.org/10.1037/0022-3514.81.5.869

Estrada, A. (2018). The interpersonal context of assessment. In S. R. Smith & R. Krishnamurthy (Eds.), *Diversity-sensitive personality assessment* (pp. 259–277). New York, NY: Routledge.

Finkelstein, H., & Tuckman, A. (1997). Supervision of psychological assessment: A developmental model. *Professional Psychology: Research and Practice*, 28, 92–95.

Guo, T., & Uhm, S. Y. (2014). Society and acculturation in Asian American communities. In J. M. Davis & R. C. D'Amato (Eds.), *Neuropsychology of Asians and Asian Americans: Practical and theoretical considerations* (pp. 55–76). New York, NY: Springer. doi. http://dx.doi.org/10.1007/978-1-4614-8075-4_4

Handler, L., & Meyer, G. J. (1998). In L. Handler & M. J. Hilsenroth (Eds.), Teaching and learning personality assessment. *The importance of teaching and learning personality assessment* (pp. 3–30). Mahwah, NJ: Erlbaum.

Krishnamurthy, R., & Yalof, J. A. (2010). The assessment competency. In M. B. Kenkel & R. L. Peterson (Eds.), *Competency-based education for professional psychology* (pp. 87–104). Washington, DC: American Psychological Association. http://dx.doi.org/10.1037/12068-005

Ladany, N., Brittan-Powell, C., & Pannu, R. K. (1997). The influence of supervisory racial identity interaction and racial matching on the supervisory working alliance and supervisee multicultural competence. *Counselor Education and Supervision*, 36(4), 284–304. http://dx.doi.org/10.1002/j.1556-6978.1997.tb00396.x

Mayer, J. D. (1998). A systems framework for the field personality. *Psychological Inquiry*, 9(2), 118–144.

Mayer, J. D. (2005). A tale of two visions: Can a new view of personality help integrate psychology? *American Psychologist*, 60(4), 294–307.

Semrud-Clikeman, M., & Bledsoe, J. (2014). Understanding the neuroscience of clients with Asian heritage. In J. M. Davis & R. C. D'Amato (Eds.), *Neuropsychology of Asians and Asian-Americans* (pp. 117–133). New York, NY: Springer.

Smith, S. R. (2007). Integrating neuropsychology and personality assessment with children and adolescents. In S. R. Smith & L. Handler (Eds.), *The clinical assessment of children and adolescents: A practitioner's guide*. Mahwah, NJ: LEA.

Smith, S. R., & Kent, J. (2018). Diversity-focused supervision of psychological assessment. In T. R. Burnes & J. E. Manese (Eds.), *Cases in multicultural clinical supervision: Models, lenses, and applications* (pp. 277–288). San Diego, CA: Cognella Academic Publishing.

Smith, S. R., & Krishnamurthy, R. (2018). Evidence-based practice in diversity-sensitive personality assessment. In S. R. Smith & R. Krishnamurthy (Eds.), *Diversity-sensitive personality assessment* (pp. 363–372). New York, NY: Routledge.

Steele, C. M., & Aronson, J. (1995). Stereotype threat and the intellectual test performance of African Americans. *Journal of Personality and Social Psychology, 6*, 797–811. https://doi.org/10.1037/0022-3514.69.5.797

Sugarman, A. (1991). Where's the beef? Putting personality back into personality assessment. *Journal of Personality Assessment, 56*(1), 130–144.

Wright, A. J. (2018). Improving psychological assessment report writing [Webinar]. In *APA Clinician's Corner Series*. Retrieved from https://apa.content.online/catalog/product.xhtml?eid=8045

Yalof, J. (2018). Supervision and training in personality assessment with multicultural and diverse clients. In S. R. Smith & R. Krishnamurthy (Eds.), *Diversity-sensitive personality assessment* (pp. 349–362). New York, NY: Routledge.

Five

SUPERVISING THE DEVELOPMENT OF TREATMENT RECOMMENDATIONS IN PSYCHOLOGICAL ASSESSMENT

A. Jordan Wright

D evising recommendations as a result of a comprehensive psychological assessment is often the second-to-last stage of the process (before finalizing the written report and providing feedback to the client or other stakeholders). The reason it is the focus of an entire (though brief) chapter in this volume is because the process of coming up with treatment recommendations is generally unaddressed in training (or addressed in a roundabout and quite biased way) and often inherently flawed because of our own (supervisees' and supervisors') biases about different types of treatment. Too often, we rely either on the type of treatment we are trained in or strongly believe in (such as cognitive-behavioral therapy) or rely entirely on research about evidence-based treatments for different diagnoses (e.g., Antony & Barlow, 2011; Fonagy et al., 2014; Jongsma, Peterson, & Bruce, 2014; Nathan & Gorman, 2015; Reichenberg & Seligman, 2016). These can be a good place to start, but they should not be the only determining factors when making ethical, evidence-based recommendations for treatment. In fact, many have worked extensively on improving our understanding of what factors contribute to success in different types of treatment, including but going beyond diagnosis (for example, see Beutler & Clarkin, 2014; Bram & Peebles, 2014; Castonguay & Beutler, 2006; chapter 14 of Groth-Marnat & Wright, 2016; Norcross, 2011).

Essentials of Psychological Assessment Supervision, First Edition.
Edited by A. Jordan Wright
© 2020 John Wiley & Sons, Inc. Published 2020 by John Wiley & Sons, Inc.

As a result of more complicated factors that require attention than may be assumed (by both supervisor and supervisee), developing effective treatment recommendations can be deceptively difficult, and supervising this process can be tricky at times. Specifically, supervisors must check their own biases about treatment, while at the same time challenging supervisees'. This chapter presents a framework with four components for ensuring ethical, evidence-based recommendations that emerge from psychological assessment. It should be noted that this chapter focuses on treatment recommendations that emerge from more traditional clinical assessment. While the general principles will apply to many types of assessment, there are certainly types of assessment that do not culminate in treatment recommendations (e.g., forensic custody evaluations, executive pre-employment evaluations, etc.). Further, it should be noted that the four components discussed in this chapter align strongly with the components listed in the Society for Personality Assessment (2015) framework (also published in Groth-Marnat & Wright, 2016).

RECOMMENDATIONS SHOULD FLOW DIRECTLY FROM ASSESSMENT RESULTS

The first major consideration when developing treatment recommendations as part of a comprehensive psychological assessment has to do with the actual content of the recommendations (as opposed to the style of delivering them). Any reader of an assessment report or receiver of assessment feedback should be able to understand logically how the assessment conclusions lead to the recommendations; one should not have to be a psychologist to understand the link between assessment conclusions (including diagnosis) and recommendations. Supervisees often take for granted how little psychological knowledge many consumers have; it is as easy as it is misguided to assume that those receiving feedback from an assessment come with the same basic knowledge, psychological mindedness and understanding, and general pro-psychology attitudes that the assessor holds. Supervisors need to remain vigilant that supervisees understand that each recommendation should be easily tied to a conclusion (generally, either part of the case formulation or the diagnosis).

Case Formulation

The British Psychological Society's Division of Clinical Psychology (2010) clearly laid out the fact that how one formulates a case "provides the foundation from which actions may derive… Psychological intervention, if considered appropriate, is based upon the formulation" (p. 6). Certainly, how an assessor fits together the information collected from an assessment will drive the recommendations. Theoretical orientation plays heavily into this process (and should—we do not want to ignore theory in our work—it is one of the major things that sets us apart from other mental health disciplines!). For example, if an assessor understands the problematic dynamics of an individual in terms of underlying object patterns (such as dysfunctional object representations), it is likely that psychodynamic treatment will make sense. If a different assessor understands the same problematic dynamics in terms of underlying schemas (such as dysfunctional interpersonal schemas), it is likely cognitive-behavioral treatment will be indicated. This is true even though it is very likely the two different assessors are conceptualizing in a way that is extremely similar (though with different vocabulary and jargon). Supervisors can help supervisees understand not only the theory tied to the case formulation, but also how that theory may overlap with other theories.

Similarly, assessors may conceptualize cases using theories that are not tied as closely to specific psychotherapeutic theoretical orientations, such as traditional psychological models like the diathesis-stress model (see Wright, 2010) or empirical models of personality functioning like the interpersonal circumplex model (see Hopwood, Pincus, & Wright, 2019). These models will also drive specific treatment recommendations. For example, if an assessor uses a diathesis-stress model, such that some aspects of personality functioning are considered the diathesis, some external stressor is considered the stress, and the current emotional functioning is considered the outcome, it is very likely that recommendations will be targeted more toward the personality functioning (and if reasonable the current circumstances), with the expectation that the emotional outcomes will resolve themselves when the underlying dynamics are addressed. (This is of course altered if the emotional outcomes need to be addressed immediately, such as self-harming behaviors or if the assessor feels the client will need a quick and noticeable result in order to continue engaging in treatment.) Generally, though, how an assessor (and thus a supervisor and supervisee) conceptualizes a case will have a direct impact on the type of recommendations for treatment that make sense.

In supervision, the task for the dyad is to be deliberate and explicit in the way they are conceptualizing and formulating the case, which develops from an integration of all available data collected about the individual and his or her culture, context, and history. Once a case formulation has been developed, the supervisor should ask the question of the supervisee: "*What does conceptualizing the client's problems in this way mean for what we will recommend to help?*" The ensuing conversation can encompass both a discussion of theory (theoretical orientation and/or what theory was applied to the data to formulate the case) and a discussion about balancing what that theory means with all of the other data present (such as diagnosis, client preferences, and all the other factors discussed below in the chapter). While it can be tempting to choose a treatment *exclusively* from the case formulation and the theory it relies on, supervisors should ensure that supervisees have considered whether any of the variables presented in this chapter may contraindicate that specific type of treatment. Generally, if none of the below factors contraindicate the specific type of treatment that flows from the case formulation, then that can be the treatment of choice for the client assessed.

> **REMEMBER**
> ....
> How you formulate an assessment case, situating it within a psychological theory, can be a driving force in deciding on treatment recommendations, as long as that treatment is not contraindicated by any other client factors.

Understanding the Problems

Often a great deal of time in supervision is spent on understanding and finalizing psychological *diagnosis* of clients. Regardless of how one feels about diagnosis (including potential for stigma, the *Diagnostic and Statistical Manual of Mental Disorders* (DSM)-5's still-too-meager attention to diversity and cultural issues, etc.; see Corrigan & Watson, 2002; Murphy, 2015), it is the language that our field (and broader fields) use to communicate about problems, as well as to drive much of the research on treatment efficacy and effectiveness. Diagnosis is perhaps our most important way of understanding the mental health/psychosocial problems that are affecting an individual. This should not be minimized. We know a great deal about effective treatments for different diagnoses, though there are very few actual diagnoses that carry only one, clearly superior, research-supported treatment of choice. For example, the research on treating specific phobias has borne out exposure therapies as a clear treatment of choice (Society of Clinical Psychology, 2018a; it should always be noted that this is based on currently available evidence and research support—it is certainly possible that other treatments have simply not yet been devised or evaluated adequately but may be as effective as exposure therapies). However, many common disorders, such as depression, have no such clear, singular guidance on a treatment of choice; for example, even rigorous empirical investigation has not narrowed down a single (or even a few) treatment of choice for depression (Society of Clinical Psychology, 2018b). This is true for many disorders, and is generally when assessors tend to default to their own personal treatments of choice, despite not having considered the many other factors that may affect treatment outcomes (discussed in this chapter). As such, it is the job of a supervisor to help supervisees consider the diagnosis-driven evidence of treatment success, but also to temper that with a theoretical orientation humility to at least consider other factors that may drive success in treatment.

Some of the other, more general factors related to understanding the client's problems have to do with evaluating just how much *functional impairment* and *subjective distress* are being experienced by the client. With the switch from the DSM-IV-TR to the DSM-5 and the loss of the Global Assessment of Functioning (GAF), discussion of global functional impairment and subjective distress have taken a back seat. However, there have been great efforts to link success of different types of therapies and different therapeutic interventions and factors to levels of functional impairment (e.g., Harwood, Beutler, Williams, & Stegman, 2011) and subjective distress (e.g., Harwood et al., 2011; Litz, Gray, Bryant, & Adler, 2002). Supervisors should ensure that supervisees have considered the level of impairment and the stated level of distress the client is experiencing when thinking about treatment recommendations, again focusing on whether either of these variables contraindicates what therapeutic decisions have been made using the clinical formulation and/or diagnosis. To do this, supervisors must often clearly ask supervisees just how impaired the client's functioning is, as well as how much distress the supervisee thinks the client is experiencing. More "extreme" diagnoses do not always come with greater impairment or subjectively felt distress—these are factors that should be considered independent of diagnosis.

The final factor in understanding the problems themselves is determining how *complex* (focused on comorbid conditions) and *chronic* (versus acute) the symptoms are. Meeting criteria for multiple disorders, for example (which would be considered a complex condition), makes using the evidence for what works with single disorders more problematic and difficult. While understanding that a problem is complex or chronic may not be a single determining factor in which treatment modality is likely to be most successful, research has supported that these factors should at least be considered (e.g., Beutler, Clarkin, & Bongar, 2000; Harwood et al., 2011).

Much like with functional impairment and subjective distress, the onus most often falls on the supervisor to engage in the explicit conversation with the supervisee about what comorbidity and chronic diagnoses may mean for treatment

≈ Rapid Reference 5.1

Understanding the Problems

Understanding the problems of the client includes a clear diagnosis (when possible), as well as an understanding of the levels of functional impairment and subjective distress and how complex and chronic the symptoms are.

recommendations. Much like impairment and distress, these conversations may best be focused on whether the treatment recommended by the case formulation and/or diagnosis is in any way *contraindicated* by the complexity and chronicity of the disorders. If not, and if the supervisee has considered this explicitly, then the treatment recommendations from case formulation and/or diagnosis can continue to stand.

If functional impairment, subjective distress, and/or problem complexity and chronicity contraindicate the recommendations that would naturally come from either the case formulation or the diagnosis, the supervisee has three primary options. First, the supervisee can determine that the contraindication simply is not strong enough to affect the chosen recommendation, in which case he or she will keep it. Second, the supervisee can reevaluate the recommendations that come from the case formulation and/or diagnosis to see whether there is an alternative treatment that is equally as empirically supported that would *not* be contraindicated by the other factors. Third, the supervisee can begin to think developmentally about the trajectory of treatment. That is, he or she may recommend a set of treatments *first* that are not contraindicated, then stipulate that when one of the factors changes (e.g., functional impairment is decreased, subjective distress is increased, etc.) the client engage in the original treatment recommendations that emerged from the case formulation and/or diagnosis. Supervisors need to help supervisees navigate this process explicitly, as it is often quite foreign to them.

Understanding Problem Context

Much of the research on how well treatments tend to work with individuals is organized around specific diagnoses and occurs under very controlled conditions. Life, for better or worse, is much more complicated than individual factors (like diagnosis) and optimal conditions. The larger context in which individuals function (or have difficulty functioning) often plays a significant role in the etiology, reinforcement, mitigation, or altering of problems. Because of this, some researchers have focused on how contextual factors affect how well treatments tend to work with different individuals.

One area of focus related to the context in which individuals are struggling and the effect of this context on treatment effectiveness is level of *social support*. While clinical assessments often evaluate (at least informally) level of social support during a clinical interview, it is generally an area that is not formally assessed or discussed in supervision. However, level of social support has been shown to differentially predict what kinds of treatments are likely to be most effective (see

Beutler et al., 2000). What is most important for supervisors to understand is how counterintuitive the findings have been for what most supervisees would expect to be the case. That is, individuals with low social support tend to fare better in cognitive-behavioral therapies that are *not* focused on building relationships, whereas those with a great deal of social support benefit more from treatments aimed at enhancing relationships. Many supervisees implicitly assume that those with low levels of social support need treatments aimed at building more and better relationships. Supervision can address this briefly and even hypothesize or theorize why the counterintuitive finding may make psychological sense, especially within the context of the client being assessed. For example, if an assessment client has a strong and healthy support network, a supervisory discussion may focus on the hypothesis that the client already has strong social skills and the capacity to be close with others, and so treatment should capitalize on and enhance these skills. Primarily, though, as with many of the other contextual and client characteristic factors, the supervisory discussion may be brief and focused on whether this factor (level of social support) somehow contraindicates whatever treatment recommendations emerged from the diagnosis and/or case conceptualization.

While research has not been systematic (for a brief discussion, see chapter 14 of Groth-Marnat & Wright, 2016), supervisors should ensure an explicit consideration of *current life circumstances* and their potential impact on different types of treatment. It may be too ambitious, for example, for someone who has just recently been diagnosed with a significant illness (mental or physical) to engage in treatment targeted at rapid and major behavior change; supportive psychotherapy may be more appropriate in the developmental perspective of treatment. Major life changes or transitions may similarly impact what kind of treatment makes intuitive sense (or what kinds of treatment may not). Because research in this area is sparse, unsystematic, and thus not generally prescriptive (or helpful), the onus is on the supervisory relationship to discuss and consider whether the client's current life circumstances may contraindicate some types of treatment or require a special approach that is independent of the treatment recommendations that emerged from the case conceptualization and/or diagnosis.

Finally, part of the context that is often addressed widely in assessment but less well considered in developing treatment recommendations are *diversity and cultural issues*. Some research has focused on differential effectiveness of different types of treatment on people from different cultural backgrounds (for example, cognitive-behavioral therapy has been found to be more effective for white clients than for people of color [Walling, Suvak, Howard, Taft, & Murphy, 2012; Windsor, Jemal, & Alessi, 2015], while research on psychodynamic treatment with diverse

≡ *Rapid Reference 5.2*

••

Understanding the Problem Context

Understanding the context in which the client is having difficulties includes his or her level of social support, diversity and cultural issues, and the current life circumstances of the client.

clients is woefully inadequate [Watkins, 2012]). However, most of the attention has been paid to understanding how best to *adapt* treatments to address cultural diversity (for just a few examples, see Austin & Craig, 2015; Smith, Domenech Rodriguez, & Bernal, 2011; and Worthington, Hook, Davis, & McDaniel, 2011). Too few assessment reports include any information on the potential for adapting specific treatments (especially empirically supported ones) based on the specific cultural background of the client who was assessed. Supervisors should encourage supervisees to look into research on how treatments may be adapted to better suit the cultural background of the client. Once a treatment recommendation has been decided (such as based on the diagnosis or case formulation), a supervisor should encourage the supervisee to be deliberate and explicit in considering whether or not cultural adaptations to that treatment recommendation are likely to improve the outcomes. Supervisors can reinforce the behavior of considering cultural adaptations, even if in the end no adaptations are recommended. Modeling the behavior of explicitly considering culture and diversity, though, at this stage of an assessment when diversity is less often considered, helps supervisees internalize how important this information can be in the ultimate treatment recommendations.

Treatment-Specific Client Characteristics

There are multiple client characteristics that have been the focus of research related to differentially predicting success in different treatment modalities. It should be noted that there are infinite other client characteristics that may affect how well one fares in different types of treatment; the ones presented here are just ones that have research programs dedicated to them and have borne out some helpful results. The first client characteristic that has been shown to differentially predict success by theoretical orientation and treatment characteristics is *coping style*. Beutler, Harwood, Kimpara, Verdirame, and Blau (2011a) examined internalizers (those who cope with emotional difficulty by internalizing, constricting, withdrawing from others, somaticizing, and otherwise turning inward on themselves) versus externalizers (those who cope by blaming others, being aggressive, acting out behaviorally, seeking stimulation, and otherwise turning outward toward others). These two primary coping styles will likely be intimately tied to the case formulation, as it should be clear from a clinical assessment, for example, if the client is anxious or depressed and feeling that in his or her subjective experience (internalizing) or if the client is anxious or depressed and acting out behaviorally, using alcohol to cope, or otherwise blaming others (externalizing). Still, supervisors should discuss the research around more effective treatments for each style, as insight-oriented therapy, for example, may be contraindicated for externalizers, who tend to be more successful in skills-based and cognitive and behavioral treatments.

Another client characteristic that is specifically relevant to treatment recommendations is level of *resistance* (also called *reactance* in the literature). Some individuals are quite open to feedback and direction, while others have an innate reaction to resist being told what to do. This information may not be highly obvious in the context of a clinical assessment (though many of our more popular self-report inventory measures now include a scale or index related to potential for treatment rejection, openness to feedback and suggestion, or some similar construct). However, it can be extremely important when thinking about what treatments are likely to be effective, independent of diagnosis (Beutler, Harwood, Michelson, Song, & Holman, 2011b). With more information, especially about those clients high in resistance/reactance, treating therapists may be less frustrated with the therapy behaviors that seem to block progress. Regardless of the case conceptualization, if a client is highly resistant to suggestion or direction, he or she likely needs nondirective, supportive, and self-directed interventions (or for braver clinicians, paradoxical techniques). Knowing this going into a treatment relationship can minimize the likelihood for major therapeutic alliance ruptures and frustration on both sides. Supervisors should again be explicit with their supervisees about considering level of resistance. All evidence may be pointing toward cognitive-behavioral therapy as the treatment of choice for a particular client with a particular diagnosis, but high resistance/reactance will make their acceptance of suggestions (to evaluate their own automatic thoughts, to do homework, etc.) very unlikely.

Another client characteristic that is uniquely applicable to psychotherapeutic treatment is the client's *stage of change* related to his or her difficulties. Supervisors and supervisees should be familiar with this transtheoretical model (e.g., Prochaska & DiClemente, 2005) and what it means for treatment recommendations (Norcross, Krebs, & Prochaska, 2011). As a dynamic (developmental and cyclical) model, it allows supervisors to encourage supervisees to think developmentally about treatment. That is, while a diagnosis or case formulation may point toward a directive, behavioral treatment, the client being in a precontemplation stage of change (when the client has little to no intention of changing him- or herself) will make it less likely that directive interventions will be taken and used effectively. However, supervisees do not have to "throw out" the ideas of directive and behavioral treatments. Rather, developmentally, the supervisee may suggest beginning treatment with motivational interviewing (in order to help the client move to a more change- or action-oriented stage of change), at which point the directive, behavioral treatment can be utilized. Unfortunately, stage of change is rarely (at this point) formally evaluated in a typical clinical assessment. There may be indicators that a supervisor and supervisee can identify as proxies to help identify where the client is *likely* located in the stages of change (for example, those in greater subjective distress are more likely to be beyond a precontemplation stage), and a supervisory discussion can help illuminate these ideas more informally. A supervisory dyad may also feel it is important enough (for example, in an assessment related to addictions) to evaluate formally in the course of an assessment. Like most of the other factors presented, simply modeling that this client characteristic *should be considered* is an important supervisory technique; supervisees are more likely to internalize the fact that they need to be more inclusive in their considerations when their supervisors model such behavior.

Finally, another client characteristic that is specifically relevant to psychotherapeutic intervention is related to the *preferences and expectations* of the client related to treatment. The client's preferences have for too long been deemed less important than the assessor's "expertise," but they have been found to be hugely important for keeping individuals in treatment (Swift, Callahan, & Vollmer, 2011). Clients have preferences about who their therapist is (e.g., race, ethnicity, gender), what they do (e.g., theoretical orientation, modality of treatment), and how they work (e.g., directiveness, collaborativeness). These are not questions or variables we often evaluate in a typical clinical assessment, but they may be important additions to the process (perhaps in the clinical interview, or in a collaborative or therapeutic feedback session). Supervisors who address the question of client preferences model not only the inclusion of potentially important information, but also a respect for the client that can be easily lost in the assessment process (or at least can be generally secondary when assessors are, in a short period of time, collecting data). The importance of client expectations (Constantino, Glass, Arnkoff, Ametrano, & Smith, 2011), specifically how effective they expect a therapy to be, may apply more to how feedback is delivered. That is, the recommendations should be convincing, such that clients are more likely to have faith in them. The supervisory responsibility here is ensuring that the supervisee understands the rationale behind the recommendations clearly, buys into their likelihood of improving the client's functioning, and can communicate aspects of

Rapid Reference 5.3

Understanding Treatment-Specific Client Characteristics

Multiple client characteristics have been identified and studied as relating to treatment success in different forms of treatment. Among these are the client's coping style, level of resistance, stage of change, and preferences in and expectations for therapy.

the recommendations clearly (answering any questions clients may have). Supervisors may want their supervisees to practice answering nitpicky questions about the treatments they have recommended in a way that clients are likely to understand and agree with. Supervisors should make clear that supervisees cannot control every aspect of what happens after the assessment is completed (i.e., whether or not clients follow through with recommendations), but that their confidence in the recommendations may play a specific role in the expectations of clients that the recommendations are likely to be helpful.

A Model for Supervising Therapeutic Recommendation Decision-making

Larry Beutler and his colleagues (Beutler, 2011; Beutler et al., 2000; Beutler & Clarkin, 2014; Beutler, Forrester, Holt, & Stein, 2013; Beutler, Harwood, Bertoni, & Thomann, 2006; Harwood & Williams, 2003) did quite a bit of the heavy lifting in pulling together the research on most of the client-related variables listed above and their relation to success in different types of treatment. They funneled much of the above information into their InnerLife (innerlife. com) method, in which you can input a great deal of information about yourself (as a client) or your client (as a therapist or assessor) and get information on treatment matching. A similar model is presented here, with suggested questions and decisions for the supervisor to guide the supervisee through. When the primary determining factor for choosing a treatment recommendation is either case formulation or diagnosis (or the combination of the two), the supervisor can help the supervisee be explicit in at least considering whether other client variables may contraindicate (or call for some modification of) the selected treatment. The supervisor can use the checklist to make sure the supervisee has at least considered each of these variables (at least the ones that are known), even if they ultimately do not affect the treatment recommendations.

≡ Rapid Reference 5.4

A Checklist for the Model for Supervising Therapeutic Recommendation Decision-making

Questions for Your Supervisee

What treatment would your case formulation naturally lead to?

What treatment(s) would your diagnosis lead to?

Can you reconcile these two factors into a specific set of treatment recommendations? If so, what are they?

For the above set of treatment recommendations, have you considered if any of the following *contraindicate* your decision? If so, how will you reconcile this?

☐ Functional Impairment; Reconciliation: _____
☐ Subjective Distress; Reconciliation: _____
☐ Problem Complexity/Chronicity; Reconciliation: _____
☐ Coping Style; Reconciliation: _____
☐ Social Support; Reconciliation: _____
☐ Current Life Circumstances; Reconciliation: _____
☐ Diversity Issues; Reconciliation: _____
☐ Resistance; Reconciliation: _____
☐ Stage of Change; Reconciliation: _____
☐ Preferences/Expectations; Reconciliation: _____
☐ Other (specify)_____ ;
Reconciliation: _____

Ultimate Recommendations

_____

RECOMMENDATIONS SHOULD BE CLEAR

Once treatment recommendations have been decided, supervisees have the responsibility to communicate those recommendations to clients or other stakeholders (parents, guardians, schools, courts, etc.) in a way that ensures that the recommendations are understood. The first criterion in evaluating whether treatment recommendations are being appropriately communicated is whether or not they are clear (for discussions on this, see Allyn, 2012; Groth-Marnat & Davis, 2014; Groth-Marnat & Wright, 2016; and Wright, 2010). Supervisors should work with supervisees to ensure that all recommendations are clear (this applies to the written report, as well as to verbal feedback communicated to clients and other stakeholders). Stating that a client needs "treatment" is not clear—it is unclear what kind of treatment (medication, therapy, vitamins, electroconvulsive therapy [ECT], etc.). Vagueness can be unclear; however, so can too much detail and specificity. For example, if a supervisee creates a beautifully detailed recommendation for treatment that includes components from 12 different theoretical modalities, all under the umbrella framework of a contemporary psychoanalytic orientation, the reader will have very little clarity on what he or she actually needs to do. Supervisors need to ensure that clients will know exactly what their next steps are in order to receive the help or treatment they need.

REMINDER

Recommendations should be *clear*. The reader should understand exactly what he or she should do as a next step.

RECOMMENDATIONS SHOULD BE SPECIFIC

After evaluating whether or not treatment recommendations are clear, supervisors must ensure that recommendations are sufficiently specific to meet the needs of the client. A thorough clinical assessment can be really well written and informative, but vague recommendations can leave clients, stakeholders, and treating clinicians without a roadmap for treatment. For example, while stating that a client "should consider psychotherapy" is clear, it is likely too vague to be useful. A good assessment should provide at least enough information to indicate that a specific modality of treatment and theoretical orientation is advised. The level of specificity, however, is up to the supervisor. For example, one supervisor may believe that a recommendation for cognitive-behavioral therapy to treat a client's anxiety is sufficiently specific. Another supervisor, however, may feel that the supervisee should include specific interventions, such as relaxation training, mindfulness, cognitive evaluation of worry, and problem-solving training (for example, see Leahy, Holland, & McGinn, 2012).

REMINDER

Recommendations should be *specific*. The reader should know that the recommendations are not generic and apply directly to the client assessed.

It is important not to sacrifice clarity for specificity—there is a sweet spot in the middle between too vague and too specific that aids in clarity. Supervisees should be clear who the audience for the recommendations actually is; for some recommendations, even if feedback is given to a client or parents, the actual recommendations are for a treating clinician or a school (in terms of accommodations). The recommendations should be specific enough to be directly useful to the actual audience, even if that is not the client him- or herself.

RECOMMENDATIONS SHOULD BE REASONABLE

Highly related to the previously presented material on current life circumstances, supervisors and supervisees should explicitly discuss whether the recommendations developed for a client are reasonable, given the many constraints and potential roadblocks that exist when clients want or need treatment. The primary question in evaluating whether or not a treatment recommendation is reasonable is about access. Supervisors should always ask: *Will the client have access to the treatment you are recommending?* Access encompasses many components, with multiple factors determining whether or not a client will have access to a specific treatment. First is availability. All signs (case formulation, diagnosis, context, client characteristics) may be pointing to a specific treatment, but if that treatment does not exist geographically near the client, it is an unreasonable recommendation. For example, while Dialectical Behavior Therapy (DBT) is one treatment of choice for a client struggling with Borderline Personality Disorder, if the client lives in a rural area that has no clinicians specifically trained in DBT (and otherwise no access), then that recommendation may not be reasonable. Even when certain treatments are available, clients may still not have access to them. Another consideration is financial. Again, a specific treatment may be the best fit for the struggles of a client, but if he or she cannot afford the only available treatment of that type, it is not a reasonable recommendation. Supervisors and supervisees should be vigilant about ensuring that whatever treatment is recommended, the client will have access to it.

The other consideration related to whether or not treatment recommendations are reasonable has to do with treatment fitting into the client's life. For example, an assessment may reveal that a client will likely benefit most from a specific form of intensive treatment that includes multiple groups per week in addition to individual therapy. However, a client who is working full time and could not possibly fit that amount of treatment into his or her schedule is unlikely to follow through on such a recommendation, making it unreasonable. Another example is when assessors recommend multiple treatments (without prioritizing them) for a child client, whose parents do not have the freedom or flexibility to follow through on all of them. Supervisors should help supervisees understand what is likely to be logistically feasible for clients when developing and communicating treatment recommendations.

> **REMINDER**
> ....
> Recommendations should be *reasonable*. The client should have access (geographical and financial) to the recommended services, and they should be feasible logistically within the context of the client's real life.

CONCLUSION

Supervisors have multiple issues to contend with when supervising the development of treatment recommendations within the context of a psychological assessment. The first hurdle is challenging one's own biases about different modalities of treatment, in order to make the most evidence-informed decisions possible. Very often, though, a supervisor's biases are shared by a supervisee (as many supervisees end up in placements that align with their own theoretical orientations). Supervisors should model a deliberate, explicit decision-making process when determining the best treatment recommendations for each individual client. This methodical, deliberate decision-making process is a specific skill that psychologists in practice should have and use in their everyday clinical work, and supervision is the best place for psychologists to learn it and see it in action.

☰ Rapid Reference 5.5
....

Questions for Supervisors to Ask Explicitly of Treatment Recommendations

Do the treatment recommendations flow logically and directly from the conclusions of the assessment: ☐ Yes ☐ No
Are the treatment recommendations clear: ☐ Yes ☐ No
Are the treatment recommendations specific: ☐ Yes ☐ No
Are the treatment recommendations reasonable: ☐ Yes ☐ No

TEST YOURSELF

1. Because case formulations in a psychological assessment should generally be completely independent from theoretical orientation, they rarely dictate what orientation of treatment will be recommended. True or False?

2. All of the following should be explicitly considered when developing treatment recommendations, **EXCEPT**
   (a) Client ethnicity
   (b) Client preferences
   (c) Client resistance
   (d) Client relationship with the assessor
   (e) Client diagnosis

3. Supervisors should evaluate every single treatment recommendation to ensure that they are:
   (a) Clear
   (b) Reasonable
   (c) Consistent with the conclusions of the report
   (d) Specific
   (e) All of the above

4. If you've adequately addressed cultural and diversity issues throughout the assessment process, you don't need to explicitly address them when developing treatment recommendations. True or False?

Answers: 1. False; 2. d; 3. e; 4. False.

REFERENCES

Allyn, J. B. (2012). *Writing to clients and referring professionals about psychological assessment results: A handbook of style and grammar.* New York, NY: Routledge.

Antony, M. M., & Barlow, D. H. (2011). *Handbook of assessment and treatment planning for psychological disorders (2).* New York, NY: Guilford Press.

Austin, A., & Craig, S. L. (2015). Empirically supported interventions for sexual and gender minority youth. *Journal of Evidence-Informed Social Work,* 12(6), 567–578.

Beutler, L. E. (2011). Prescriptive matching and systematic treatment selection. In J. C. Norcross, G. R.VandenBos, & D. K. Freedheim (Eds.), *History of psychotherapy: Continuity and change (2)* (pp. 402–407). Washington, DC: American Psychological Association.

Beutler, L. E., & Clarkin, J. F. (2014). *Systematic treatment selection: Toward targeted therapeutic interventions.* New York, NY: Routledge.

Beutler, L. E., Clarkin, J. F., & Bongar, B. (2000). *Systematic guidelines for treating the depressed patient.* New York, NY: Oxford University Press.

Beutler, L. E., Forrester, B., Holt, H., & Stein, M. (2013). Common, specific, and cross-cutting psychotherapy interventions. *Psychotherapy, 50(3),* 298–301.

Beutler, L. E., Harwood, T. M., Bertoni, M., & Thomann, J. (2006). Systematic treatment selection and prescriptive therapy. In G. Striker & J. Gold (Eds.), *A casebook of psychotherapy integration* (pp. 29–41). Washington, DC: American Psychological Association.

Beutler, L. E., Harwood, T. M., Kimpara, S., Verdirame, D., & Blau, K. (2011a). Coping style. In J. C. Norcross (Ed.), *Psychotherapy relationships that work: Evidence-based responsiveness (2)* (pp. 336–353). New York, NY: Oxford University Press.

Beutler, L. E., Harwood, T. M., Michelson, A., Song, X., & Holman, J. (2011b). Reactance/resistance level. In J. C. Norcross (Ed.), *Psychotherapy relationships that work: Evidence-based responsiveness (2)* (pp. 261–278). New York, NY: Oxford University Press.

Bram, A. D., & Peebles, M. J. (2014). *Psychological testing that matters: Creating a road map for effective treatment.* Washington, DC: American Psychological Association.

Castonguay, L. G., & Beutler, L. E. (Eds.) (2006). *Principles of therapeutic change that work: Integrating relationship, treatment, client, and therapist factors, Vol. I.* New York, NY: Oxford University Press.

Constantino, M. J., Glass, C. R., Arnkoff, D. B., Ametrano, R. M., & Smith, J. Z. (2011). Expectations. In J. C. Norcross (Ed.), *Psychotherapy relationships that work: Evidence-based responsiveness (2)* (pp. 354–376). New York, NY: Oxford University Press.

Corrigan, P. W., & Watson, A. C. (2002). Understanding the impact of stigma on people with mental illness. *World Psychiatry, 1(1),* 16–20.

Division of Clinical Psychology (2010). *Clinical psychology: The core purpose and philosophy of the profession.* Leicester, England, UK: British Psychological Society.

Fonagy, P., Cottrell, D., Phillips, J., Bevington, D., Glaser, D., & Allison, E. (2014). *What works for whom? A critical review of treatments for children and adolescents.* New York, NY: The Guilford Press.

Groth-Marnat, G., & Davis, A. (2014). *Psychological report writing assistant.* Hoboken, NJ: Wiley.

Groth-Marnat, G., & Wright, A. J. (2016). *Handbook of psychological assessment (6).* Hoboken, NJ: Wiley.

Harwood, T. M., Beutler, L. E., Williams, O. B., & Stegman, R. S. (2011). Identifying treatment-relevant assessment: Systematic Treatment Selection/InnerLife. In T. M. Harwood, L. E. Beutler, & G. Groth-Marnat (Eds.), *Integrative assessment of adult personality (3)* (pp. 61–79). New York, NY: Guilford Press.

Harwood, T. M., & Williams, O. (2003). Identifying treatment relevant assessment: The STS. In L. E. Beutler & G. Groth-Marnat (Eds.), *Integrative assessment of adult personality* (pp. 65–81). New York, NY: Guilford Press.

Hopwood, C. J., Pincus, A. L., & Wright, A. G. (2019). The interpersonal situation: Integrating personality assessment, case formulation, and intervention. In D. Samuel & D. Lynam (Eds.), *Using basic personality research to inform personality pathology.* New York, NY: Oxford University Press.

Jongsma Jr, A. E., Peterson, L. M., & Bruce, T. J. (2014). The complete adult psychotherapy treatment planner: Includes DSM-5 updates (Vol. 296). Hoboken, NJ: Wiley.

Leahy, R. L., Holland, S. J. F., & McGinn, L. K. (2012). *Treatment plans and interventions for depression and anxiety disorders (2).* New York, NY: Guilford.

Litz, B. T., Gray, M. J., Bryant, R. A., & Adler, A. B. (2002). Early interventions for trauma: Current status and future directions. *Clinical Psychology: Science and Practice, 9,* 112–134.

Murphy, D. (2015). "Deviant deviance": Cultural diversity in DSM-5. In S. Demazeux & P. Singy (Eds.), *The DSM-5 in perspective: Philosophical reflections on the psychiatric babel* (pp. 97–110). Heidelberg, Germany: Springer, Dordrecht.

Nathan, P. E., & Gorman, J. M. (Eds.) (2015). *A guide to treatments that work.* New York, NY: Oxford University Press.

Norcross, J. C. (Ed.) (2011). *Psychotherapy relationships that work: Evidence-based responsiveness (2).* New York, NY: Oxford University Press.

Norcross, J. C., Krebs, P. M., & Prochaska, J. O. (2011). Stages of change. In J. C. Norcross (Ed.), *Psychotherapy relationships that work: Evidence-based responsiveness (2)* (pp. 279–300). New York, NY: Oxford University Press.

Prochaska, J. O., & DiClemente, C. C. (2005). The transtheoretical approach. In J. C. Norcross & M. R. Goldfried (Eds.), *Handbook of psychotherapy integration (2)* (pp. 147–171). New York, NY: Oxford University Press.

Reichenberg, L. W., & Seligman, L. (2016). *Selecting effective treatments: A comprehensive, systematic guide to treating mental disorders.* Hoboken, NJ: Wiley.

Smith, T. B., Domenech Rodriguez, M., & Bernal, G. (2011). Culture. In J. C. Norcross (Ed.), *Psychotherapy relationships that work: Evidence-based responsiveness (2)* (pp. 316–335). New York, NY: Oxford University Press.

Society for Personality Assessment (SPA). (2015). Personality Assessment Proficiency: Report Review Form. Retrieved from: http://storage.jason-mohr.com/http://www.personality.org/General/pdf/Proficiency%20Report%20Review%20Form%202015.pdf

Society of Clinical Psychology. (2018a). Research-supported psychological treatments for specific phobias. Retrieved from https://www.div12.org/diagnosis/specific-phobias

Society of Clinical Psychology. (2018b). Research-supported psychological treatments for depression. Retrieved from https://www.div12.org/diagnosis/depression

Swift, J. K., Callahan, J. L., & Vollmer, B. M. (2011). Preferences. In J. C. Norcross (Ed.), *Psychotherapy relationships that work: Evidence-based responsiveness (2)* (pp. 301–315). New York, NY: Oxford University Press.

Walling, S. M., Suvak, M. K., Howard, J. M., Taft, C. T., & Murphy, C. M. (2012). Race/ethnicity as a predictor of change in working alliance during cognitive behavioral therapy for intimate partner violence perpetrators. *Psychotherapy, 49*(2), 180–189.

Watkins Jr, C. E. (2012). Race/ethnicity in short-term and long-term psychodynamic psychotherapy treatment research: How "White" are the data? *Psychoanalytic Psychology, 29*(3), 292–307.

Windsor, L. C., Jemal, A., & Alessi, E. J. (2015). Cognitive behavioral therapy: A meta-analysis of race and substance use outcomes. *Cultural Diversity and Ethnic Minority Psychology, 21*(2), 300–313.

Worthington Jr, E. L., Hook, J. N., Davis, D. E., & McDaniel, M. A. (2011). Religion and spirituality. In J. C. Norcross (Ed.), *Psychotherapy relationships that work: Evidence-based responsiveness (2)* (pp. 402–422). New York, NY: Oxford University Press.

Wright, A. J. (2010). *Conducting psychological assessment: A guide for practitioners.* Hoboken, NJ: Wiley.

Six

SUPERVISING PSYCHOEDUCATIONAL ASSESSMENT

Michael R. Hass
Annmary S. Abdou

The supervision of psychoeducational assessments is challenging because competent psychoeducational assessments require an extraordinarily broad set of knowledge and skills, which can include, but are not limited to, knowledge of typical and atypical child development, models of cognitive and academic development, child and adolescent psychopathology, theories of instruction and learning, and legal definitions of disability found in educational law and regulations. In addition, practitioners must have a thorough understanding of psychometrics, including validity, reliability, the meaning of different scores, and test interpretation. Last, it requires that practitioners understand how to integrate information from various assessment methods and sources to come to an understanding of a child's strengths and limitations, as well as how to develop, implement, and evaluate interventions.

WHAT IS A COMPREHENSIVE AND USEFUL PSYCHOEDUCATIONAL ASSESSMENT?

Given the complexities inherent to assessment processes, it is important to first understand what a useful and comprehensive psychoeducational assessment might look like. Understanding this helps both supervisors and supervisees make

Essentials of Psychological Assessment Supervision, First Edition.
Edited by A. Jordan Wright.
© 2020 John Wiley & Sons, Inc. Published 2020 by John Wiley & Sons, Inc.

decisions as to whether an assessment is sufficiently comprehensive to meet legal and ethical standards, as well as if it is useful to stakeholders.

In general, assessment can be defined as the process of gathering information that leads to decisions (Salvia, Ysseldyke, & Bolt, 2007). More specifically, psychological assessments seek to gather information to make decisions about the nature of a person's behavior, abilities, or personality. Psychoeducational assessments, as the name implies, are a type of psychological assessment that focuses on the relationship between variables we consider psychological (e.g., intelligence, abilities in a variety of specific cognitive abilities, social skills, emotional functioning, etc.) and the acquisition of academic skills and classroom performance (e.g., difficulty completing work, following classroom routines, or relating positively to peers). Given the focus on acquisition of academic skills and classroom performance, psychoeducational assessments are typically done with children and adolescents.

Although we consider psychoeducational assessment to be a type of psychological assessment, with its focus on individual characteristics or variables, it is important to understand that a useful psychoeducational assessment does not solely focus on the characteristics of the individual and should take a broader ecological perspective (Gutkin, 2012). Using Bronfenbrenner's (1976) ecological model of human development as a framework, this means that information is gathered from and about children's immediate environments, or microsystems (e.g., families, schools, classrooms), and this information is interpreted in the context of the system of connections among the various microsystems in a child's life (e.g., home-school communication, links between school and community agencies) and the broader system of government agencies, local systems of transportation, and social networks outside of the school and family, as well as the larger systems of laws governing education, economic conditions that influence employment, and changing regulations concerning access to health care. This perspective represents a shift from a medical model of assessment (e.g., within-child disabilities) to an ecological model of assessment (i.e., consideration of internal and external environments; Jacob, Decker, & Lugg, 2016). The ecological model of assessment minimizes the risk of misdiagnosis and over-identification by considering curricular and environmental risks and limitations.

Looking at assessment from an ecological perspective also allows us to better meet the federal laws and regulations that mandate that evaluations to determine whether a child has an educational disability are comprehensive (Individuals with Disabilities Education Act [IDEA], 2004). This mandate can be divided into two parts. The first states that it is necessary to assess in all areas of suspected disability, and the second states that it is necessary to assess in all areas of suspected need (Hass & Carriere, 2014a). These are related but distinct mandates. The first is related to the criteria for determining whether a disability per IDEA exists, such as a specific learning disability, autism, etc. The second focuses on unique areas of need that may or may not be directly related to the definition of the disability. To illustrate the difference, let us consider the legal definition of autism in IDEA:

> Autism means a developmental disability significantly affecting verbal and nonverbal communication and social interaction, generally evident before age three, that adversely affects a child's educational performance. Other characteristics often associated with autism are engagement in repetitive activities and stereotyped movements, resistance to environmental change or change in daily routines, and unusual responses to sensory experiences. (Department of Education, Assistance to States for Education of Children with Disabilities Program and the Preschool Grants for Children with Disabilities Program, 2006, Sec. 300.8 (c) (1))

We have the legal obligation to assess in the areas relevant to the identification of autism—i.e., communication and social interaction, sensory experiences, repetitive and stereotyped movements, and resistance to change—because information about these areas of functioning help us determine whether a child has autism or not. At the same time, children suspected of having autism often have difficulties beyond what is included in the definition of autism. For example, it is common that children suspected of having autism have challenges related to anxiety, self-care, or organization of their school materials. These are not part of the definition of autism, but the legal mandate of assessing all areas of related need would also obligate us to include these areas in a comprehensive psychoeducational assessment.

In addition to legal mandates, all professions have standards for what is considered good practice for assessment, and one of the important functions of supervision is to model and encourage use of these practices (National Association of School Psychologists, 2014). These practices have legal and ethical implications, as we are ethically obligated to provide competent care, which implies following what is considered good practice in the field. These standards also have consequences, because if our practice of psychoeducational assessment is called into question, it is important to show that we (and our supervisees) have followed accepted practices in our field. As such, having a clear understanding and rationale for choosing assessment models is an important quality for supervisors to have and convey to their trainees. Assessment approaches often differ between districts and professionals, particularly for Specific Learning Disabilities (e.g., discrepancy model versus patterns of strengths and weaknesses [PSW]), the most common disability addressed by psychoeducational assessment, as there is not a scholarly consensus on the most valid or reliable method (McGill, Styck, Palomares, & Hass, 2016).

As psychoeducational assessments should comprise information that accounts for both individual and environmental factors that impact learning and behavioral functioning (Christo & Ponzuric, 2017), supervisors can facilitate the process of making connections among context, tool selection, and general assessment approaches. However, there are a few key elements of good practice in psychoeducational assessment that are important to consider for training and supervision.

Good practice in framing a comprehensive psychoeducational assessment can be understood using different models. One approach to understanding this is the acronym R.I.O.T., or (a) *record review*, (b) *interviews*, (c) *observations*, and (d) *tests* or sometimes standardized behavior rating scales (Leung, 1993). Leung argues that each method of gathering information has strengths and limitations and that the only way to compensate for the limitations of one approach is to supplement it with other methods of assessment. One function of both training programs and supervision of psychoeducational assessment is to ensure that supervisees understand good practices for each of these methods, as well as their respective strengths, limitations, and role in a comprehensive psychoeducational assessment.

Merrell suggests a complementary metric for judging the comprehensiveness of an assessment with the *rule of two* (Merrell, 2008). Like R.I.O.T., the *rule of two* focuses on the principle that a comprehensive assessment must gather information using different *methods*, but it goes on to suggest that it should also include information from multiple *settings* and from different *informants*. The *rule of two* suggests that a reasonable standard for judging comprehensive assessment would be two methods, two informants, and two settings. In their discussion of a social-emotional assessment of bilingual/bicultural youth, Hass and Kennedy (2014b) propose a matrix that combines these two approaches:

≡ *Rapid Reference 6.1*

Matrix for a Comprehensive Psychoeducational Assessment

Informant	Record review/ history	Interview	Observation	Test/rating scale
Student				
Teacher				
Parent				
Assessor				
Other				

Although it is important for supervisees to conduct comprehensive psychoeducational assessments, being comprehensive alone will not assure that a psychoeducational assessment will be useful. Hass and Carriere (2014a) argue that useful assessments: (a) respond to the concerns of those who initiated the referral; (b) focus on strengths as well as needs; (c) provide useful and feasible recommendations; and (d) are presented to stakeholders in a way that is clear and understandable. A second matrix for making judgments about the usefulness of a psychoeducational assessment can be a useful supervision tool, as well:

≡ Rapid Reference 6.2

Matrix for Judging the Usefulness of a Psychoeducational Assessment

Standard	Not at all met	Partially met	Fully met
Concerns of consumers are responded to, and their questions are answered			
Assessment addresses strengths as well as needs			
Concludes with useful and reasonable recommendations			
Results are explained orally and in writing in a way that is understandable by all consumers			

In addition to understanding what a comprehensive and useful psychoeducational assessment is, it is also important to understand the process of conducting an assessment, as each phase or step in the assessment process requires different skills and knowledge. One approach, drawn from the Consultative Referral Assessment/Report Writing Model (Batsche, 1983; Hass & Carriere, 2014a), proposes seven steps to the assessment process, including: (a) reviewing existing background data on the student, (b) consultation with the referring person to clarify concerns, (c) collaborative development of assessment questions, (d) selection of assessment procedures to answer the assessment questions, (e) integration of assessment data for different procedures to answer the referral questions, (f) developing recommendations in response to the assessment results, and (g) presenting the assessment results and recommendations orally and in writing to key stakeholders.

≡ Rapid Reference 6.3

Seven Steps in the Psychoeducational Assessment Process

1. Reviewing existing background data
2. Consulting with the referring person to clarify concerns
3. Collaborative development of assessment questions
4. Selection of assessment procedures to answer the assessment questions
5. Integration of assessment data to answer referral questions
6. Developing recommendations based on assessment results
7. Presenting the assessment results and recommendations orally and in writing to key stakeholders

This model and the matrices discussed above can be useful to supervisors and supervisees as tangible tools for explaining the process of assessment and the skills needed, as well as what is meant by a comprehensive and useful psychoeducational assessment. They can also be useful ways to facilitate discussions and make judgments about the performance of supervisees.

KEY CONSIDERATIONS IN SUPERVISION OF PSYCHOEDUCATIONAL ASSESSMENT

What Is Supervision?

Supervisor roles and responsibilities for psychoeducational assessments have been delineated into two distinct categories: clinical supervision and administrative supervision (Jacob et al., 2016). These roles may overlap or can be carried out by distinct professionals. For example, administrative supervisors may take on responsibilities related to organizing professional development for the supervisee related to psychoeducational assessment, delegating assignments and tasks, and overseeing the legal aspects of assessment. Clinical supervision, the primary focus of this chapter, generally involves modeling, guiding, and monitoring the various components of the psychoeducational assessment process from start to finish. Unfortunately, once psychologists are in the field, few of them receive clinical supervision (Harvey & Pearrow, 2010), especially related to psychoeducational assessment.

☰ Rapid Reference 6.4

Supervisor Functions and Responsibilities

Clinical supervisor	Administrative supervisor
• Direct teaching to promote skill development	• Providing effective leadership and management of school psychological services
• Modeling assessment procedures	
• Reviewing results and providing feedback	• Hiring
• Assisting with case conceptualization and conclusions	• Delegating work assignments
	• Evaluation of job performance
• Reviewing reports and providing detailed feedback	• Contract renewal or nonrenewal

Professional Standards for Supervision

While supervision competencies may not significantly differ across various types of assessment supervision, there are several important considerations in the development of effective and competent supervision skillsets. The quality of supervision during critical developmental periods of emerging practitioners sets the foundation for professional identity, later competent service delivery, and meeting ethical, legal, and professional standards (Sullivan, Svenkerud, & Conoley, 2014). As increased competence in psychoeducational assessment is the primary goal of supervision, it is important that supervisor competence be a precursor to matching supervisors and supervisees. Scholars of school psychology supervision, the field that conducts the majority of psychoeducational assessments, have identified supervision skills as a "distinct professional competency that requires competency-based training, development, and support similar to other core professional functions" (Simon & Swerdlik, 2017, p. 1).

Despite the fact that many practitioners will serve as a supervisor at some point in their careers, most report that they do not receive explicit or adequate training in supervision skills (Harvey & Struzziero, 2008). Supervision skills, as they specifically apply to psychoeducational assessment, are even more specialized as the variability of eligibility models and ambiguity of eligibility criteria require the development of complex decision-making skills and professional judgment (Sullivan et al., 2014).

Ethical and Legal Knowledge

A clear and comprehensive understanding of legal and ethical guidelines that are central to psychoeducational assessment practices is an important requirement for both novice and expert practitioners. For psychologists who take on the responsibility of supervision activities, an additional layer of ethical, professional, and legal knowledge should be acquired prior to accepting a supervisee. Regardless of training or perceived competence of a trainee, the supervisor is responsible for the work of his or her supervisees and ultimately their client welfare (Jacob et al., 2016). However, for supervisees who hold preliminary credentials, the level of supervisor control and intensity of supervision may vary.

In order to minimize the risk of ethical conflicts and to respect the rights of both the supervisor and supervisee to make informed choices prior to entering a supervisory relationship, Cobia and Boes (2000) argue that professional disclosure statements can be a helpful tool. Also known as an individualized learning contract, the purpose of this written document is to ensure that there is a mutual understanding and explicit statement of the parameters of supervision, methods of evaluation, desired outcomes, and potential risks and benefits of the supervision experience. Using clear and straightforward language in such agreements can remove ambiguity about roles and responsibilities, as well as what can be expected from each party. It is also important that intentional time is dedicated in supervision to review and process the agreements, in order to ensure that both the supervisor and supervisee have read all parts and have had an opportunity to ask questions and express potential concerns or needs. It may also be helpful to include specific information regarding types of psychoeducational assessment the trainee will be participating in, the process for training, and perhaps how many assessments will be expected of them. For interns and practicum students, parallel types of agreements should also exist between universities and supervisors to ensure clarity regarding supervisory roles of both parties regarding the practicum student or intern's field experience (NASP, 2014). While these types of documents are typically prepared and provided by associated university supervisors, it is important for site supervisors to ensure that they thoroughly review the contracts and communicate any disagreements or areas for individualization or improvement. Nine components have been enumerated that may be included in a supervision professional disclosure statement (Jacob et al., 2016, p. 297).

≡ Rapid Reference 6.5

Possible Components of a Professional Disclosure Statement

1. Description of the supervision site, clientele, and types of services typically provided
2. Credentials of the supervisor
3. General goals and approaches of supervision and how specific objectives will be selected
4. Time frame, frequency, length of supervision contacts, and type of supervision provided (individual versus group supervision)
5. Rights and responsibilities of supervisor and supervisee
6. Potential risks and benefits of supervision
7. Parameters of confidentiality
8. Record keeping
9. Methods of evaluation

In addition to ensuring that supervisors, supervisees, and university affiliates are adequately informed of all parameters and roles and responsibilities in the training experience, parents/guardians and caregivers should be afforded the same opportunity for informed consent. While there are not specific guidelines requiring written consent for supervisees to provide assessment and/or services to a minor, NASP supervision standards indicate that "any service provision by interns, practicum students, or other trainees is explained and agreed to in advance, and the identity and responsibilities of the supervising school psychologist are explained prior to the provision of services" (Jacob et al., 2016, p. 299). A simple way to do this is through passive consent in assessment packets with an opportunity for parents/guardians to call and request that a supervisee not work with their child. Supervisors should take adequate steps to ensure that notes are visible and clear and that parents understand the information and their rights (e.g., by providing translation or clarification, if needed). Further, while the provision of services by a supervisee does not necessarily need written consent beyond verbal agreement, any video or audio recording as part of the training process does

DON'T FORGET!

Parents/guardians should be informed and allowed the opportunity to accept or reject psychoeducational assessment services from a practicum student, trainee, or intern. Transparency in the process is your ethical responsibility!

require written consent, including the purpose of the recordings and how long they will be kept.

Supervisor vigilance to ethical guidelines and responsibilities as a guide and mentor is important for both issues of liability and preserving the quality and integrity of the practice of psychology in school-related matters. By attending to the various ethical and legal issues discussed in this section, supervisors may enhance their own practice as well as the future service delivery and potential impact on student welfare through the subsequent work of their trainees.

Cultural Competence

The supervisor's skillsets surrounding culturally competent supervision can be viewed in parallel to culturally competent assessment practices and service delivery. Supervisors should have adequate knowledge of culturally competent assessment practices, including culturally responsive interviewing practices, ability testing across cultures, assessment of English-language learners, and achievement testing for culturally diverse groups (Suzuki & Ponterotto, 2007). While supervision is only one part of comprehensive cultural competence development, helping a supervisee make connections between theories of multicultural competence in assessment and the relevant population and individual circumstances they are assessing is a key supervisor responsibility. Supervisors who do not feel they have adequate cultural competence skills should seek resources and training through university supervisors or other legitimate professional organizations (Newell et al., 2010). Continued professional development opportunities for both supervisors and supervisees in this area is critical.

Despite limited research in multicultural supervision and "cross-racial supervision," this consideration in training is significant for both effectiveness and ethical practice (Eklund, Aros-O'Malley, & Murrieta, 2014). Specifically, regarding linguistic, racial, and ethnic differences between supervisor and supervisee, cultural factors that should be considered in the supervisor–supervisee dynamic include cultural match, White privilege, differing communication styles, supervisor training and supervision experience in culturally competent practices, and the impact on the supervisee's cultural competency development on the welfare of future clients. Eklund et al. (2014) summarized best practice considerations for multicultural supervision.

≋ Rapid Reference 6.6

Best Practice Considerations in Multicultural Supervision

1. Discuss cultural similarities and differences
2. Show genuine interest in and respect for each other's unique cultures
3. Create a safe and inclusive setting
4. Model and impart multicultural competencies
5. Value ongoing professional development opportunities

When it comes to supervision of psychoeducational assessment skills, the skills surrounding interviewing practices, testing decisions, and case conceptualization are most salient to the issue of cultural competence. When considering the ethical issues of parent/guardian involvement and consent (Jacob et al., 2016), supervisors must pay special attention to how they model appropriate and culturally responsive family communication and collaboration skills. Although supervisors should lead supervisees through the entire assessment process during all cases, from first parent/guardian contact for assessment consent to communication of results and recommendations, this close guidance becomes especially important in situations where many standard procedures have to be modified or reconsidered in light of culture and language. Considerations of personal biases and balancing the cultural dynamics of other assessment team members should also be transparent and addressed throughout. Explicit guidance surrounding the core considerations and steps in this process, as well as how it should be individualized based on cultural and linguistic differences, is important for a novice psychoeducational assessor's development. Open and respectful discussions about diverse characteristics and needs of clients and supervisees should be commonplace within supervision in efforts to increase both knowledge and skills needed to work effectively with diverse populations (NASP, 2014).

INTERPERSONAL SUPERVISION SKILLS

While supervision, for assessment and other practices, can be manifested in different ways, most definitions start with acknowledging the interpersonal aspect of supervision. For example, McIntosh & Phelps (2000) define supervision of school psychological services as:

> An interpersonal interaction between two or more individuals for the purpose of sharing knowledge, assessing professional competencies, and providing objective feedback with the terminal goals of developing new competencies, facilitating effective delivery of psychological services, and maintaining professional competencies. (pp. 33–34)

The National Association of School Psychologists (2018) also emphasized the collaborative nature of supervision in defining it as an "ongoing, positive, systematic, collaborative process between the school psychologist and the school psychology supervisor" (p. 1) that promotes competence and benefits all parties involved. Based on the key concepts discussed in this section, it is clear that supervision is fundamentally a collaborative interpersonal process. While professional standards for supervision activities are somewhat concrete, they are less specific about what interpersonal skills are needed to accomplish the supervisory goals. Furthermore, while there are common themes regarding interpersonal relations within the supervisory relationship, it is important to be aware of some key factors that may be unique to supervision within the psychoeducational assessment training process. For example, feedback and critique on assessment activities are often surrounding more concrete skills and competencies, such as accurate administration and scoring. As an area where mistakes are usually more common, especially in the beginning stages of training, supervisors are advised to be very intentional about how feedback is structured. Constructive feedback should be communicated in a non-judgmental tone and normalized as a natural part of the training process. Balancing feedback about technical mistakes with feedback about areas of supervisee strength and growth (often not as concrete) can be helpful in maintaining a positive supervision relationship and a safe learning environment.

NASP (2014) guidelines for best practices in supervision include specific skills surrounding the establishment of a strong working relationship with school psychology supervisees as a critical feature. Examples of recommended strategies to foster a healthy working relationship include transparency in requirements and expectations, providing appropriate structure and support, open and frequent communication, establishing trust and boundaries, collaboration with university supervisors, and fostering opportunities for collaboration with other school professionals. Within the context of supervision for psychoeducational assessments, communication about the process and expectations about the training experience (e.g., scaffolding, feedback, expectation of making mistakes) can help set the stage for a positive and productive working relationship. As supervisee competencies in assessment continue to grow, supervisors should continue to communicate how the process and expectations evolve with their skillsets. For example, a supervisor may choose to have a supervisee do more observations or record reviews at the start of their training to provide opportunities for refining these skills. However, as the supervisee continues to develop his or her assessment skills, a collaborative conversation about expanding on these skills and trying out more complex assessment activities (with scaffolding and frequent feedback) may help create smooth transitions between developmental stages.

> **REMEMBER**
>
> Fostering a positive working relationship between yourself as the supervisor and your supervisees is *critical* to their professional development.

As we briefly discussed in the context of culturally competent supervision, various individual and cultural characteristics may impact the relationship and dynamic between supervisor and supervisee (e.g., cultural match, White privilege, differing communication styles; Eklund et al., 2014). The complexity of this dynamic increases as supervisor and supervisee collaborate on assessments for culturally and linguistically diverse students and families. While each supervisor may have a unique interpersonal style, adapting and attending to the needs of the supervisee is important to optimize training and preparedness (Crespi & Fischetti, 1997). Using reflective and relationship-based supervision approaches, where supervisors regularly facilitate non-judgmental reflective activities with their supervisees while consistently fostering a positive relationship, are key elements to both effective and culturally responsive supervision (Wu, 2013). Mirroring the value and skills needed for relationship building in counseling, family collaboration, and consultation relationships, effective supervisors understand the value of interpersonal connection within a teaching and learning relationship. For supervision of psychoeducational assessment specifically, many different activities require supervisors to correct, critique, and advise supervisees throughout the learning process. Creating a supervision environment that feels supportive and safe to take risks in learning is an important investment for a positive experience for both the supervisor and supervisee.

Know Your Supervisees, and Let Them Know You

There are two aspects to getting to know supervisees. The first has to do with supervisees' formal training. Although training programs often respond to similar state or national standards, leading them to have similar courses and types of fieldwork experiences, they can also vary in how they meet these standards, including varied emphasis on topics, even in courses with very similar sounding titles.

These differences reflect the background, interests, and theoretical viewpoints of the faculty members, as well as the goals of the institutions where programs are housed. It is important for supervisors to begin by trying to understand what their supervisees know about psychoeducational assessment and what they have been taught to value as the "way to go about things." Whether it is inquiry about supervisee comfort level with the overarching assessment process (e.g., RIOT) or experience with specific tests, it's important to get a baseline of competence and comfort in the various assessment skills. This can also open a valuable dialogue between supervisors and supervisees about the program's goals and, more importantly, what the supervisee understands about conducting an effective psychoeducational assessment and what it means to be a competent professional.

Supervisees also bring a myriad of individual differences to the formal experiences of coursework and fieldwork. These include prior experiences other than those associated with a formal training program, competing life demands of health or family, and differences in temperament or disposition. Taken together, this means that, in addition to being familiar with supervisees' training, supervisors must also know them as individuals. For example, supervisors might ask supervisees questions like, "What do you think are your strengths and needs relative to psychoeducational assessment?"; "What parts of your training in psychoeducational assessment have made the most sense to you?"; "What have you found confusing or unclear?"; and "Given this, what kinds of experiences would be most helpful to you?" (Hass & Carriere, 2008). Asking supervisees what they think their strengths and needs are will encourage an individualizing of supervisory experiences. Supervisees are, of course, not always aware of their needs, but encouraging them to think through their answers to these questions can help them and supervisors arrive at a clearer understanding of what these needs might be. As Hass and Carriere put it, "This dialogue also allows students to see that supervisors genuinely want to know and help them... ." (2008, p. 8).

Establish Clear Expectations

Clinicians become supervisors for different reasons. They may be leaders in their districts or agencies and/or have a sincere wish to play a role in developing the future of the field. They may also need help with their workloads, and they are often motivated by a combination of these and other factors. Once they become supervisors, they are then responsible for balancing the needs of the agency or school district, supervisees, and perhaps a university training program. It is important for supervisors to understand their motivations and expectations for the supervisory relationship.

This self-assessment will help frame the initial communication and interactions with supervisees. Supervisors might ask themselves: "What are your expectations, needs, and vision for the supervisory relationship?" and "How do these relate with supervisees' expectations and program requirements?" Once these expectations have been clearly identified, a thoughtful plan based on mutual needs and a shared vision can be created. For example, a supervisee may need experience interpreting tests, conducting clinical interviews, or writing reports. He or she may also need or want experience with certain populations. Fieldwork or work sites may need someone to help with non-English speaking children and parents, or they may need to provide more assessments with preschool children suspected of having autism. The needs of supervisee, supervisor, and site can be met by making expectations clear from the beginning.

Set Goals

The process of setting expectations implies goal setting. Setting goals keeps both supervisee and supervisor focused on what is important and prevents them from becoming lost in the demands of day-to-day practice. Supervisees can end up doing a large number of psychoeducational assessments without having gained the specific experiences or skills they need or having their expectations met.

We have found certain questions useful for goal setting. These include: (a) scaling questions, (b) relationship questions, and (c) future-focused questions (De Jong & Kim Berg, 2013; Murphy, 2014). Future-focused questions are directed at how supervisees imagine their future and can be the first step toward the development of goals. Examples include:

- "How will you know when you have started to get better at this?"
- "If things go well, down the road, how will your assessments be different?"
- "If our supervisor/supervisee relationship works well for you, how will you be different in six months?"

Future-focused questions like these can not only initiate a discussion about goals but often can engender a more hopeful perspective in supervisees (Pedrotti, Edwards, & Lopez, 2008).

Scaling questions are similar to self-anchored scales, which are individualized scales created for specific individuals and situations (Nugent, 2004). Examples from clinical work include the strategy of *subjective units of distress* in the behavioral or cognitive behavior treatment of anxiety (Creed, Reisweber, & Beck, 2011; Wolpe, 1990). Scaling questions are very flexible and can help supervisees make judgments about how difficult something is or how much progress they have made toward a goal. For example, rather than asking a supervisee, "How comfortable are you with…?," supervisors can ask, "On a scale from 1 to 10, with 10 being mastery and 1 being you have no idea, how well do you think you can express your assessment results to families and teachers?" If a supervisee says 4 on this 1 to 10 scale, then the supervisor can help goal setting by asking, "What would be different if you were a 5 by next week? What would you be doing differently or what might I observe that was different?" Scaling questions can be helpful because they help supervisees be specific about their next steps.

Relationship questions widen the conversation between supervisor and supervisee by bringing in the perspective of someone who is important to the situation being discussed, if only through imagination. An example might be: "If I asked that parent what she thought of how you explained things, what do you think she would say?" Another example might be: "What do you think that kid experienced while you were giving her the test you just gave her?" or "If your English teacher were here, what would she say about how you are doing in class?" Relationship questions are especially useful for supervisees who feel defensive or who are struggling to gain insight into a difficult situation.

Model Reflection, and Help Supervisees Think Like Professionals

The process of conducting a comprehensive and useful psychoeducational assessment is not simply a process of learning a set of discrete facts and skills, although these things are necessary. More importantly, it involves learning to think like a professional. In our fieldwork seminars, students often discuss difficult situations that arise at their fieldwork sites. They can usually describe in some detail what test their supervisors suggested or how many classroom observations they conducted, but they often have no sense of *why* their supervisors did the things they did. Thus, they learn certain discrete assessment activities or skills, but often do not learn from their supervisors how to define a problem and choose what actions to take in response to that problem. This process of learning to think like a professional (or a more expert professional if one is already in practice) involves learning how to frame the problem that a psychoeducational assessment is trying to solve.

Research on how experts in various fields think and make decisions suggests that they should have a flexible cognitive framework that allows them to organize and evaluate complex information. They think deductively, operating from a working theory of the situation to a specific hypothesis that incorporates elements of both the general framework and the uniqueness of the situation. Novices, on the other hand, tend to think inductively and approach problems by searching for patterns in a trial-and-error manner (Horn & Blankson, 2005). Supervisors can help their students learn these frameworks by making their thinking about a situation more transparent and explicit, such as by "thinking aloud" as they go through the problem-solving process. This process helps supervisees build up a repertoire of ideas, images, strategies, and theories that help them "think through" a problem (Schön, 1983). An added benefit is that it will also help supervisors be more explicit in thinking more critically about their own practice.

THE DEVELOPMENTAL/ECOLOGICAL PROBLEM-SOLVING (DEP) MODEL OF SUPERVISION

Beyond the cultivation of a positive working relationship with supervisees, supervisors are encouraged to be systematic and intentional about how to structure supervision. Good practices for supervisors include the use of goal-directed and problem-solving approaches both for modeling practice as well as supervising (NASP, 2014). The Developmental/Ecological/Problem-Solving (DEP) Model provides a comprehensive framework for supervisors to consider that addresses the relevant aspects of the psychoeducational assessment supervision process that have been discussed in this chapter, as well as the diverse professional roles that most practitioners of psychoeducational assessments play (Simon, Cruise, Huber, Swerdlik, & Newman, 2014). Each component of the DEP model includes various tasks and considerations for supervisors to use for structuring their supervision approach in a reflective and purposeful way. Rapid reference 6.7 provides a summarized outline of the DEP components, along with the specific tasks and actions associated with each, as outlined by Simon et al. (2014). While these steps can be specifically applied to psychoeducational assessment skills, they can be beneficial to apply to all aspects of supervisor and skill development.

Supervisors using the DEP model to guide their supervision processes can view these strategies as sequential, cyclical, and overlapping. For example, upon beginning the psychoeducational assessment training process, a supervisor might use scaling questions to determine the supervisee's development of knowledge and comfort with the assessment process as a whole (e.g., the RIOT matrix). This may then inform the supervisor as to how detailed or explicit to be in explanations of this aspect of assessment. This same process can be used when training supervisees on specific assessment tools. Gauging the supervisee's experience and comfort with an assessment tool should guide the supervisor's decisions regarding how much time to spend on that instruction. Ideally, supervisors would take some time at the beginning of a supervisory relationship to assess supervisee skills across all domains of a fieldwork plan (Simon et al., 2014). There should also

⇛ Rapid Reference 6.7

DEP Model of Supervision

Developmental component	a. Begin supervision process with assessment of practicum student or trainee's current skills and needs across all domains outlined in fieldwork plan (usually aligned with NASP domains) b. Explicitly specify supervisee's needs, strengths, and goals c. Using needs assessment information, engage in dialogue regarding appropriate levels of independence and challenge d. Consider development continuum and adjust depending on stage of training (e.g., directive to less directive, individual to systemic focus, direct observation to intern reports) e. Provide guided opportunities for supervisees to supervise less advanced trainees or other school staff with specific tasks or projects
Ecological component	a. Evidence-based interventions are taught and modeled in ways that involve and influence each context of the student (e.g., internal, classroom, home). b. Supervisor provides opportunities for trainee to participate in systems change efforts and guidance on how to navigate • New initiatives • Garnering stakeholder support • Resistance to change • Systems-level consultation c. Trainees are taught to assess systemic resources for and barriers to positive change (i.e., implementation science) d. Supervisors provide leadership training through modeling, direct instruction, and practice e. Supervisors model, teach, and reflect on inclusive and culturally responsive practices
Problem-solving component	a. Training and guidance in data-based decision making uses systemic analyses of both individual and contextual factors b. Supervisors guide integration and implementation of the entire problem-solving process c. Supervisees receive coaching and feedback regarding participation in problem-solving teams d. Supervisors model and teach collaborative problem-solving skills and strategic response to resistance to change from any stakeholder

e. Supervisee has opportunities to systematically teach problem-solving skills to students, teachers, and parents

f. Supervisors obtain feedback from supervisees about the effectiveness of joint problem-solving efforts in supervision

be several natural points throughout the training experience (often facilitated through the supervisee's university) to monitor progress across these domains to which supervisors may adjust accordingly. Through this intentional process, supervisors can scaffold their training appropriately and avoid spending too much or too little time on guidance for various skill sets.

As novice practitioners must expend a lot of energy learning foundational skills and knowledge bases, the ecological component of the DEP model emphasizes the importance of contextual and systems-thinking approaches to supervision (Simon et al., 2014). For example, supervisors can help guide supervisees through the assessment process with questions and discussions that consider the client's various contexts and identities in the assessment and decision-making process. The ecological lens in supervision for assessment is particularly important for assessment of culturally, economically, and linguistically diverse clients, as well as subsequent culturally responsive decision-making. The provision of opportunities for supervisees to engage in systems-level work in the contexts related to assessment processes (e.g., student study team [SST] meetings, multi-tiered system of supports [MTSS], program evaluation) can help them deepen their understanding of assessment from an ecological lens.

The problem-solving component of the DEP model is perhaps the most familiar to most supervisors in its emphasis on systematic and data-based decision-making, which links identified problems with evidence-based interventions (Simon et al., 2014). The integration of supervisee developmental stages and the orientation to ecological components strengthen the problem-solving component of supervision for assessment in several ways. This integrated perspective can help supervisors take a developmentally appropriate and holistic approach in their guidance of supervisees throughout the entire assessment process. Not only do these strategies result in high quality training, but supervisors using a DEP approach model best practices that prepare supervisees to be well-rounded and systems-oriented practitioners (Simon et al., 2014). While adopting a DEP approach to supervision for assessment may take some investment from supervisors to learn and establish within their embedded practices (like any new skillset), the goal is for these components to become more automatic and natural elements to one's supervision style.

CONCLUSION

Supervision of psychoeducational assessment presents unique challenges. We believe that a foundation for effective supervision of psychoeducational assessment begins with a shared understanding of what a comprehensive and useful assessment looks like. In addition, it requires an understanding of the different skills needed to facilitate a quality supervisor–supervisee relationship. The DEP model provides one useful and comprehensive framework for understanding the process of supervising psychoeducational assessments.

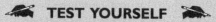

TEST YOURSELF

Case Study

Jorge is an experienced school psychologist who has recently decided to supervise an intern, Briana, at his elementary and middle school sites. His supervisee is a younger, White female who has had minimal experience in schools prior to her practicum year. Briana appears to have a strong assessment knowledge base but lacks confidence in translating her knowledge to assessment planning and interpretation. Jorge is struggling to find the best way to support Briana's development and orientation to the *process* of assessment without being too directive or prescriptive. What are some strategies that Jorge can consider in his supervision approach with Briana to meet her individual needs? Are there any cultural considerations that he should be aware of in this supervisory relationship?

Quiz

1. **Comprehensive assessments include at least two different tests for every area of academic and social-emotional functioning. True or false?**

2. **Supervisors should NOT disclose to parents that a supervisee is providing assessment services if the case is considered "high profile." True or false?**

3. **Choose two examples of culturally competent supervision practices:**
   (a) Modeling culturally responsive practice
   (b) Encouraging supervisees to learn the languages of their clients
   (c) Having respectful and open conversations regarding cultural similarities and differences
   (d) Disregarding one's own culture over those of supervisees and clients

Answers: 1. False; 2. False; 3. a and c

REFERENCES

Batsche, G. (1983). The referral oriented, consultative assessment report writing model. In *Communicating psychological information in writing*. Retrieved from ERIC database (ED 240775).

Bronfenbrenner, U. (1976). The experimental ecology of education. *Teachers College Record*, 78(2), 157–204.

Christo, C., & Ponzuric, J. (2017). CASP position paper: Specific learning disabilities and patterns of strengths and weaknesses. *Contemporary School Psychology*, 21(1), 7–9. https://doi.org/10.1007/s40688-016-0099-5

Cobia, C. D., & Boes, S. R. (2000). Professional disclosure statements and formal plans for supervision: Two strategies for minimizing the risk of ethical conflicts in post-master's supervision. *Journal of Counseling and Development*, 78(3), 293–296. https://doi.org/10.1002/j.1556-6676.2000.tb01910.x

Creed, T. A., Reisweber, J., & Beck, A. T. (2011). *Cognitive therapy for adolescents in school settings*. New York, NY: Guilford Press.

Crespi, T. D., & Fischetti, B. A. (1997). Clinical supervision for school psychologists: Bridging theory and practice. *School Psychology International*, 18(1), 41–48. https://doi.org/10.1177/0143034397181004

De Jong, P., & Kim Berg, I. (2013). *Interviewing for solutions*. Belmont, CA: Brooks/Cole.

Department of Education. (2006). Assistance to States for the Education of Children with Disabilities and Preschool Grants for Children with Disabilities. Retrieved from https://www.gpo.gov/fdsys/granule/FR-2006-08-14/06-6656

Eklund, K., Aros-O'Malley, M., & Murrieta, I. (2014). Multicultural supervision: What difference does difference make? *Contemporary School Psychology*, 18(3), 195–204. https://doi.org/10.1007/s40688-014-0024-8

Gutkin, T. B. (2012). Ecological psychology: Replacing the medical model paradigm for school-based psychological and psychoeducational services. *Journal of Educational and Psychological Consultation*, 22(1–2), 1–20. https://doi.org/10.1080/10474412.2011.649652

Harvey, V. S., & Pearrow, M. (2010). Identifying challenges in supervising school psychologists. *Psychology in the Schools*, 47(6), 567–581. https://doi.org/10.1002/pits.20491

Harvey, V. S., & Struzziero, J. A. (2008). *Professional development and supervision of school psychologists: From intern to expert*. Thousand Oaks, CA: Corwin Press.

Hass, M., & Carriere, J. A. (2008). Tools for working with school psychology practicum students and interns. *CASP Today*, 58(2), 8–10.

Hass, M., & Carriere, J. A. (2014a). *Writing useful, accessible, and legally defensible psychoeducational reports.* Hoboken, NJ: Wiley.

Hass, M., & Kennedy, K. (2014b). Integrated social-emotional assessment of the bilingual child. In A. Clinton (Ed.), *Assessing bilingual children in contex: An integrated approach* (pp. 163-187). Washington, DC: American Psychological Association.

Horn, J. L., & Blankson, N. (2005). Foundations for understanding cognitive abilities. In D. P. Flanagan & P. L. Harrison (Eds.), *Contemporary intellectual assessment: Theories, tests, and issues (2)* (pp. 41–68). New York, NY: The Guilford Press.

Individuals with Disabilities Education Act, 20 U.S.C. § 1400 (2004)

Jacob, S., Decker, D. M., & Lugg, E. T. (2016). *Ethics and law for school psychologists.* Hoboken, NJ: Wiley.

Leung, B. (1993). Back to basics: Assessment is a R.I.O.T.! *NASP Communiqué, 22*(3), 1–6.

McGill, R. J., Styck, K. M., Palomares, R. S., & Hass, M. R. (2016). Critical issues in specific learning disability identification: What we need to know about the PSW model. *Learning Disability Quarterly, 39*(3), 159–170. https://doi.org/10.1177/0731948715618504

McIntosh, D. E., & Phelps, L. (2000). Supervision in school psychology: Where will the future take us? *Psychology in the Schools, 37*(1), 33–38. https://doi.org/10.1002/(SICI)1520-6807(200001)37:1<33::AID-PITS4>3.0.CO;2-F

Merrell, K. W. (2008). *Behavioral, social, and emotional assessment of children and adolescents (3).* London, UK: Taylor and Francis/Routledge.

Murphy, J. J. (2014). *Solution-focused counseling in schools (2).* Alexandria, VA: American Counseling Association.

National Association of School Psychologists (2014). *Best practices guidelines for school psychology intern field supervision and mentoring.* Bethesda, MD: Author.

National Association of School Psychologists (2018). *Supervision in school psychology [position statement].* Bethesda, MD: Author.

Newell, M. L., Nastasi, B. K., Hatzichristou, C., Jones, J. M., Schanding, G. T., & Yetter, G. (2010). Evidence on multicultural training in school psychology: Recommendations for future directions. *School Psychology Quarterly, 25*(4), 249–278. https://doi.org/10.1037/a0021542

Nugent, W. R. (2004). A validity study of scores from self-anchored-type scales for measuring depression and self-esteem. *Research on Social Work Practice*, 14(3), 171–179.

Pedrotti, J. T., Edwards, L. M., & Lopez, S. J. (2008). Promoting hope: Suggestions for school counselors. *Professional School Counseling*, 12(2), 100–107.

Salvia, J., Ysseldyke, J. E., & Bolt, S. (2007). *Assessment in special and inclusive education*. Boston, MA: Houghton Mifflin.

Schön, D. (1983). *The reflective practitioner. How professionals think in action*. London, UK: Temple.

Simon, D. J., Cruise, T. K., Huber, B. J., Swerdlik, M. E., & Newman, D. S. (2014). Supervision in school psychology: The developmental/ecological/problem-solving model: Developmental/ecological/problem-solving model. *Psychology in the Schools*, 51(6), 636–646. https://doi.org/10.1002/pits.21772

Simon, D. J., & Swerdlik, M. E. (2017). *Supervision in school psychology: The developmental, ecological, problem-solving model*. New York: NY. Routledge.

Sullivan, J. R., Svenkerud, N., & Conoley, J. C. (2014). Best practices in the supervision of interns. In P. L. Harrison & A. Thomas (Eds.), *Best practices in school psychology: Foundations* (pp. 527–540). Bethesda, MD: National Association of School Psychologists.

Suzuki, L. A., & Ponterotto, J. G. (2007). *Handbook of multicultural assessment: Clinical, psychological, and educational applications*. Hoboken, NJ: Wiley.

Wolpe, J. (1990). *The practice of behavior therapy*. Oxford, UK: Pergamon Press.

Wu, T. C. (2013). Fostering self-reflection in multicultural school psychology supervision. *Communique*, 42(3), 14.

Seven

SUPERVISING FORENSIC ASSESSMENT

Richart L. DeMier
Carol E. Holden

Over the past 50 to 60 years, forensic psychology has grown from the occasional duty of the odd psychologist to a well-established specialty (Grisso, 1987; Heilbrun & Otto, 2003). Today, students can choose graduate schools that offer specialty training in forensic psychology, and graduates can attend formal postdoctoral fellowships to develop their skills in the specialty. Psychologists can join a division of the American Psychological Association (APA) devoted to psychology and the law, and they can seek board certification in forensic psychology by the American Board of Professional Psychology.

Heilbrun (2001) defined forensic assessment as: "evaluation that is performed by mental health professionals as part of the legal decision-making process, for the purpose of assisting the decision-maker or helping one of the litigants in using relevant clinical and scientific data" (p. 3). It is difficult to overstate the importance of such evaluations. Whether in the criminal or civil realm, results can have profound impacts on the person being evaluated. Few issues are more life-altering than proceeding through the criminal justice system or losing custody of one's children. While all would agree that psychologists in every specialty should have appropriate training and demonstrable competencies, the stakes in forensic psychology are especially high. Because forensic psychologists are often

Essentials of Psychological Assessment Supervision, First Edition.
Edited by A. Jordan Wright
© 2020 John Wiley & Sons, Inc. Published 2020 by John Wiley & Sons, Inc.

involved in capital cases, it is not overly dramatic to say that these evaluations can be matters of life and death.

It is incumbent on practicing forensic psychologists to train the next generation of forensic practitioners. Competent supervision is essential for trainees, postdoctoral fellows, novice psychologists seeking supervision for licensure or gaining expertise in their chosen field, and even seasoned psychologists who seek to expand their practices to include forensic evaluation.

In addition to the APA ethical mandate to undertake specific education and training in a specialty area (APA Ethics Code, 2.01c), the APA ethics code also addresses forensic matters specifically: "When assuming forensic roles, psychologists are or become reasonably familiar with the judicial or administrative rules governing their roles" (APA Ethics Code, 2.01f). Additionally, the APA's Specialty Guidelines for Forensic Psychology state, "Forensic practitioners planning to provide services, teach, or conduct research involving populations, areas, techniques, or technologies that are new to them are encouraged to undertake relevant education, training, supervised experience, consultation, or study" (Specialty Guidelines, 2.02; APA, 2013a, 2013b).

Supervision can occur in a wide variety of contexts, including practica, internship, and postdoctoral residency settings. Much of this training occurs in settings that devote many resources to forensic assessment, such as forensic evaluation units in state hospitals, the Federal Bureau of Prisons, and court clinics that offer services in specific jurisdictions. Some states have specific requirements and offer specialized training for psychologists who wish to become forensic examiners. A growing number of practitioners have independent practices limited to forensic psychology, and some of those psychologists provide supervision services.

In addition to technical and clinical competence, an important aspect of forensic psychology involves communication to legal professionals and juries in the form of testimony. Learning to testify effectively is a skill that is unique and essential for forensic psychologists. According to the Federal Rules of Evidence (n.d.), opinions can be offered during courtroom testimony only by a "person qualified as an expert by knowledge, skill, experience, training, or education" (Federal Rules of Evidence, Rule 702). This rule, and its many state equivalents, necessitates that psychologists who perform forensic evaluations have the skills necessary to help judges and juries understand psychological issues via effective courtroom testimony. Learning these skills therefore falls under the rubric of forensic assessment supervision.

CONSIDERATIONS SPECIFIC TO FORENSIC ASSESSMENT SUPERVISION

Supervisees learning forensic assessment need to attain competence in a wide variety of skills. Some of those skills—like interviewing, testing, and report writing—overlap significantly with traditional clinical skills. However, there are aspects of even those traditional skills that are unique to forensic psychology. For example, there are numerous specialized tests specific to forensic psychology, and some rely on methodologies that are rarely employed outside of forensic psychology or neuropsychology (e.g., forced-choice paradigms to assess response style). Testifying, as noted, is a skill that is almost unique to forensic psychologists.

In addition to learning new skills, there is sometimes a need to "unlearn" old skills, or to learn to apply old skills in new ways. For example, the differences between a traditional clinical role and a forensic role are stark (Greenberg & Shuman, 1997, 2007). Graduate students and interns often approach their work from the perspective of a helping professional, and it can require deliberate effort and careful supervision to learn to establish rapport while maintaining a strictly neutral stance. Similarly, graduate students and interns most often learn to write for other mental health professionals, but they have little experience writing for a legal or lay audience. One of the most common criticisms of forensic reports is that they tend to contain clinical jargon which would be foreign to a judge or jury.

Clinicians in forensic settings are more likely to encounter rare forms of psychopathology (e.g., delusional disorder) or individuals who, absent involvement in a forensic evaluation, would rarely present for treatment (e.g., individuals with antisocial personality disorder or psychopathy). All psychologists need to be culturally competent, but people in forensic systems may encounter a wider range of race and ethnicity. (For example, the "catchment area" for the federal prison system is all states and US territories, and evaluees include individuals from around the globe.) Moreover, clinicians encounter systems that are often not taught in graduate school; in addition to interfacing with hospital or clinic settings, forensic psychologists must be able to navigate juvenile courts, criminal courts, civil courts, and correctional systems. People who work in forensic settings may need to pay more attention to issues of personal safety, and they may encounter other unique stressors, such as rigid deadlines set by courts.

More than in any other specialty in psychology, forensic practitioners and their supervisees must confront issues of response style. Some individuals referred for forensic evaluation may be highly motivated to generate a positive, socially favorable presentation. For example, a person who is facing potential restrictions in his or her parenting time will be at increased risk for such dissimulation. In contrast, individuals facing criminal prosecution may go to great lengths to convince forensic practitioners that they are mentally ill, when, in fact, they are not. It is paramount for supervisees to learn to adequately assess response style, and it is incumbent upon the supervisor to help place those skills in the proper context.

Many less experienced practitioners of forensic psychology are easily enamored with the idea of "catching a faker." They also grapple with other issues of countertransference, especially when working with individuals accused or convicted of heinous crimes. Supervisors should be alert to—and should help supervisees negotiate—voyeuristic tendencies and feelings of anger, rage, or disgust. Noting that these reactions occur even among seasoned forensic psychologists can decrease supervisees' shame around having them.

> **DON'T FORGET**
> ....
> Supervisors should always be alert to, and should help supervisees negotiate, personal reactions in their work, including voyeuristic tendencies and feelings of anger, rage, or disgust.

Supervisees in forensic settings are likely to feel pressures not usually felt in other realms of psychological practice. Supervisees may feel pressured by the priorities of the agency in which they work (imagine a novice's response to a memo that reads, "The state attorney general asked why our rate of findings of incompetency increased last month"), political movements, or media scrutiny. Forensic psychologists experience heightened critical scrutiny of their work, and that scrutiny may sometimes be unfair. Nobody is immune to bias, and forensic clinicians may be especially vulnerable to issues related to bias. Recent research on allegiance issues (Blair, Marcus, & Boccaccini, 2008; Murrie et al., 2009; Murrie, Boccaccini, Guarnera, & Rufino, 2013) shows that even the most careful and ethical forensic practitioners may be influenced to offer opinions helpful to the side that hired them.

The high stakes of forensic work and the increased scrutiny experienced by forensic practitioners underscores the importance of excellent documentation. Forensic practitioners should be prepared to produce the bases for their opinions. The Specialty Guidelines for Forensic Psychology (APA, 2013a, 2013b) indicate:

> Forensic practitioners are encouraged to recognize the importance of documenting all data they consider with enough detail and quality to allow for reasonable judicial scrutiny and adequate discovery by all parties. This documentation includes, but is not limited to, letters and consultations; notes, recordings, and transcriptions; assessment and test data, scoring reports and interpretations; and all other records in any form or medium that were created or exchanged in connection with a matter. (p. 16)

Supervisees may need supervision to ensure that they are producing, maintaining, and *appropriately* disclosing such data.

While APA and many state laws mandate that records be kept for seven years (APA, 2007), there are reasons that forensic practitioners may wish to retain their records for longer than the time period required by law or take special steps to ensure that they remain accessible. The Specialty Guidelines for Forensic Psychology (APA, 2013a, 2013b) suggest, for example, that the extent of the rights, liberties, and properties that may be at risk, the complexity of the case, the amount and legal significance of unique evidence in the care and control of the forensic practitioner, and the likelihood of future appeal might prompt special handling of records (p. 16).

> **N O T E**
>
> Given the ease and affordability of digital storage systems, some forensic practitioners have adopted the policy of simply keeping all their records, forever.

MODEL OF FORENSIC ASSESSMENT SUPERVISION

The supervisor's ultimate goal is to shift gradually from the role of teacher to that of a consultant. The ease of this transition will vary based on a number of factors, including the experiences and skills of the supervisee. Obviously, a graduate student completing his or her first practicum experience will require a different sort of supervision than a postdoctoral resident or a licensed professional seeking to expand his or her area of practice. In both cases, however, the goal is to move the supervisee in the direction of becoming a colleague. To that end, we offer a model of forensic assessment supervision that comprises six elements: (a) modeling, (b) preparation for the evaluation, (c) live supervision of the evaluation, (d) feedback, (e) supervision of writing, and (f) preparation for testimony. In this section, the word "dyad" refers to the supervisor and supervisee.

≋ Rapid Reference 7.1

Mode of Forensic Assessment Supervision

1. Modeling
2. Preparation for the evaluation
3. Live supervision of the evaluation
4. Feedback
5. Supervision of writing
6. Preparation for testimony

Modeling

Modeling is a key part of the learning process, and ideally it is the first step in supervision. Especially with inexperienced supervisees, an invitation to observe the types of evaluations she or he is seeking to master offers two opportunities. First, the supervisee will observe a seasoned professional ply the craft at a high level. Second, and even more importantly, the shared experience of the assessment provides context for discussion. The supervisor should explain what he or she was attempting to accomplish, what techniques were employed and why, what worked well, and what did not. This involves modeling a critical analysis of one's own work, as well as communicating that the ability to objectively examine one's own work (as far as that is really possible) is essential for continued improvement. Additionally, acknowledgement of the supervisor's lack of perfection has the potential to reduce the supervisee's performance anxiety.

Preparation for the Evaluation

Prior to completing an evaluation, there are several preparatory steps to be completed, and each provides the opportunity to learn a skill relevant to forensic evaluation. Forensic referral questions can be clear and consistent with controlling statutes, or they can be muddled, confused, and confusing. Many forensic psychologists have received referrals that say something like this: "Take a look at this person and tell me what you think." Some attorneys simply do not know what to ask, and to best serve them—and the justice system as a whole—forensic practitioners may have to help the attorney determine what she or he really wants to know. During a conversation with the referral source, the assessor may need to discuss relevant legal standards, and in doing so, it should become evident whether a clinical evaluation or a forensic one is being sought. Even when the referral question is clear, the supervisee should practice speaking to attorneys; this underscores the importance of being facile with legal concepts and of being able to communicate about forensic psychological issues with non-mental health professionals.

> **REMEMBER**
> ....
> Forensic referral questions can be clear and consistent with controlling statutes, or they can be muddled, confused, and confusing.

Supervisees should also be prepared to discuss legal issues with the person being evaluated. Supervisees should have some familiarity with the concepts of assent and consent, but the application of those concepts in a forensic context is especially important, given that the person being evaluated may have much to lose (or, conversely, that another entity has much to lose, like an employer who is duped for bogus workers' compensation payments). Much has been written about the importance of notifications (DeMier, 2013; Heilbrun & Collins, 1995; Otto, DeMier, & Boccaccini, 2014). Discussion of this process ahead of time provides the supervisor with an opportunity to confirm that the supervisee has an adequate grasp of these oft-thorny issues.

An explicit discussion of the materials to be sought and reviewed will help the supervisee consider material from a broad range of sources, only some of which are commonly used in non-forensic clinical assessment. Records might be gathered from schools, clinics, hospitals, law enforcement, and correctional facilities. Interviews might be conducted with collateral sources of information, such as coworkers, family members, and previous providers. Some supervisors may be tempted to rely on the supervisee to review the material and conduct any collateral interviews independently, but this is a mistake. Not only is the supervisor ultimately responsible for the finished product, but the supervisor needs to be familiar with the records or other information obtained to determine whether the supervisee was able to extract the relevant information.

Following such a review, the dyad should discuss the anticipated areas of inquiry, the appropriate psychological tests, and the other tasks that might be necessary for a competent evaluation. The supervisee should be encouraged to anticipate areas of difficulty and to discuss potential ways to combat those difficulties. While it is never possible to anticipate all such areas, it is a good exercise in critical thinking and self-preparation to try to think through such problems prior to the evaluation. This approach can also go far in alleviating a supervisee's anxiety.

Live Supervision

In our view, direct observation of the evaluation is the most important aspect of supervising forensic assessment. There are two primary reasons for this. First, a forensic evaluation often occurs in a single session, even if the examiner might prefer otherwise. For example, an examiner's request for a second appointment will almost certainly be refused by a jail that must free up a deputy to drive hours to bring a defendant to an evaluation center. There may be no additional

DON'T FORGET
....
Direct observation of the evaluation is the most important aspect of supervising forensic assessment.

opportunity to remedy any deficiencies in the evaluation, and vital interests are at stake. Although most evaluations are not "high profile" (that is, most attract little attention or publicity), each evaluation is extremely high profile in the eyes of the person being evaluated. The quality of the evaluation is ultimately the supervisor's responsibility, and it is imperative that the supervisor be present to ensure that adequate information is gathered.

Second, in other types of psychological supervision, it is sometimes adequate to rely on the supervisee's perceptions and recollections of an evaluation or therapy session. But there is a lot going on in a forensic evaluation, and the data obtained in and conclusions drawn from the evaluation are likely to be more heavily scrutinized than within the context of a traditional, non-forensic psychological assessment. The best way to monitor it is live and in-person.

Observing the evaluation allows the supervisor to see the supervisee's subtle interactions, such as things that make the evaluee more or less forthcoming. For example, one supervisee sometimes put down her pencil and made direct eye contact when listening to an evaluee's responses about difficult topics; for her, this was remarkably effective. Another took notes only when, as he explained later, the evaluee "said something relevant," clearly signaling to the evaluee what was and was not of interest to the supervisee. The supervisors would never have known had they not been there in person.

The way questions are asked can be as important as the questions themselves. Live observation offers the supervisor the opportunity to see exactly how questions are being phrased, and that leads to an opportunity for the dyad to work together to improve future questions. Countertransference issues (like avoiding difficult topics, becoming overly allied with the evaluee, nonverbally signaling negative [or positive] reactions, or becoming argumentative) are less likely to be reported by supervisees, because supervisees are unlikely to be consciously aware of them. And when a supervisee *is* conscious of error, there is a good chance that the issue will not be raised due to fear or embarrassment.

> **REMEMBER**
> ....
> The way questions are asked can be as important as the questions themselves.

We recommend that the supervisor's goal in these sessions is to be an observer, rather than a co-interviewer. At the outset of the evaluation, the supervisee should introduce the supervisor and carefully explain the nature of the supervisory relationship. Then, ideally, the supervisor will be able to focus on all elements of the interaction.

No matter how carefully the dyad prepared for the evaluation, there will be stumbling blocks. The dyad should have an explicit plan for how to address them.

One potential solution might be for the supervisor to step in momentarily with a few questions. Sometimes, this is a helpful way to model a particular approach that the supervisee has not yet observed. If chosen, this approach should be approached tactfully. The supervisor should ask the supervisee for permission to ask a few questions (i.e., "May I follow up with a couple of quick questions?"). This communicates to the person being evaluated that the interruption is temporary, and that the supervisee/assessor remains the person in charge. Another approach, if practical, is for the dyad to remove themselves from the evaluation room for a brief consultation. If the dyad plans to use this approach, the evaluee should be so informed at the beginning of the evaluation.

> **REMEMBER**
>
> There will be stumbling blocks in the process of forensic evaluations. The supervisor and supervisee should have an explicit plan for how to address them.

Feedback

For many supervisors, the most rewarding part of the experience is the dyad's discussion of what went well and what could have gone better. These discussions are where much of the learning takes place, so supervisors should allow plenty of time for in-depth explorations. Before the supervisor provides feedback, the supervisee should be asked to comment on what she or he saw as the positive and negative aspects of the evaluation. Supervisors should then balance their feedback between the positive and the critical, and supervisees should be encouraged to respond to critical feedback with their own suggestions for how to improve. Supervisors should attend to both the nuts and bolts of the evaluation process (e.g., were the right questions asked?), as well as to the more subtle aspects (e.g., how the supervisee stiffened when the defendant discussed a prior sexual offense).

After a discussion of the dynamics of the interview, the supervisor should help the supervisee focus on the next tasks at hand. Is a follow-up interview necessary (in settings where that is possible)? Are there new collateral contacts to be interviewed? Did the evaluee say something that necessitates another examination of the police reports or medical record?

Testing, which is discussed in more detail below, should be scored, and the supervisor should carefully check the supervisee's scoring and interpretation. Scoring errors are both surprisingly common and easily avoided (Allard & Faust, 2000; Simmons, Goddard, & Patton, 2002; Tyner & Frederick, 2013). Interpretation of forensic assessment instruments, and incorporation of that information into the overall case formulation, requires careful thought, and the supervisee should take the lead in this endeavor.

Discussions of case formulation will likely combine traditional clinical supervision with forensic assessment supervision. Assuming the supervisee has clinical abilities commensurate with her or his level of training, the supervisor should focus on ways to apply the information gathered to the legal issue at hand. In forensic assessment, it is particularly important to explicitly consider alternative hypotheses, and the supervisee should be asked to generate hypotheses and articulate exactly why one hypothesis is preferred over the alternatives.

> **DON'T FORGET**
> ....
> In forensic assessment, it is particularly important to consider alternative hypotheses explicitly, and supervisees should be tasked with generating hypotheses and articulating exactly why one hypothesis is preferred over the alternatives.

Supervision of Writing

Developing professionals generally requires extensive supervision of their written work, to ensure that their findings are supported by the assessment data and are clear to the reader. Supervisees are often accustomed to writing for professors, clinical supervisors, and other mental health professionals, all of whom share professional jargon and clinical reasoning heuristics. However, the intended readers of forensic assessment reports are generally judges, attorneys, employers, insurance investigators, and other non-mental health professionals. Close supervision is necessary to ensure that the data and conclusions will be communicated in a manner these readers will understand. Supervisees often struggle with a style that differs from what they learned in clinical training. It is therefore important to emphasize the rationales for such differences. It is not enough to say, "This is how it's done in forensic psychology." The lessons will stick when the supervisee knows *why* the report is written in a particular way.

Before a supervisee begins writing, it is often helpful to offer a reminder about the purpose of the report: forensic reports should help their readers understand technical or scientific matters that they might not otherwise understand. Reports are tools for teaching people who are not psychologists.

It is beyond the scope of this chapter to offer detailed advice about forensic report writing, and there are numerous sources available for such guidance (DeMier, 2013; Grisso, 2010; Karson & Nadkarni, 2013; Otto et al., 2014; Witt, 2010). Supervisors should help supervisees recognize the many differences between a report written for clinical or therapeutic purposes and one intended for a lay or legal audience, and they should discuss elements of effective forensic report-writing.

Forensic referral questions tend to be specific, and relevance should guide what information is included in (and excluded from) the report. Although supervisees may understand the difference among facts, inferences, and opinions, they will probably not be accustomed to making these distinctions as explicitly as forensic reports require. Such distinctions, however, make it easier for the reader to understand the opinions and their bases.

Supervisees are likely to include jargon in their reports, even when urged to avoid it. This is understandable: jargon is a useful tool for communication among professionals who share a common, technical vocabulary, and supervisees may be itching to use the words that signal they are part of the club. Supervisors often need to remind supervisees that the legal or lay readers will not understand the jargon; they are not part of the group that uses this particular shorthand. Even when lay readers are familiar with psychological terms, the terms may be misunderstood (e.g., multiple personality disorder, I.Q., defensive, correlation); and certain terms are likely to leave a non-psychologist reader bewildered or misguided. For example, as DeMier and Otto (2017) noted, "There may be no better example of jargon than test scores. Lay readers are likely to misinterpret an IQ score, [and] they will likely have no idea whatsoever regarding the meaning of a T-score" (p. 223).

Supervisors should remind supervisees that language is both subtle and powerful. As Otto et al. (2014) point out, "It takes much more care to guard against subtle forms of bias. Certain words carry positive or negative connotations that are quite subtle, and some of those words are frequently used without regard to their implications"(pp. 46–47). Consider, for example, the word "admit." Psychologists often use this word when a person acknowledges an element in his or her history. However, there is a perception that people "admit" only to things that are problematic; nobody "admits" to being a college graduate. Supervisors should help supervisees detect and avoid unintended implications of the words they choose.

> **DON'T FORGET**
> Supervisors should remind supervisees that language is both subtle and powerful.

Finally, supervisors can help supervisees understand the advantages of including hypotheses other than the one they ultimately endorse. Individuals in all fields often feel a press to provide the "right" answer; that is how academic achievement is rewarded. They may not realize that a report will be more powerful if it acknowledges that alternative explanations exist and explains the reasons the supervisee thinks her or his explanation is the most compelling in a particular case.

Preparation for Testimony

Finally, supervisors should prepare supervisees to share their findings orally, via testimony. This should be routine, with such a discussion accompanying every case, regardless of whether the case is likely to require testimony. This prepares the supervisee to keep potential testimony in mind throughout the evaluation process, and it will lead to better work overall. For example, supervisees are likely to be more thoughtful about test selection when they ask themselves, "How would I defend these choices in court? What would I say if asked why I administered this test but did not administer that one?" Awareness of the challenges of cross-examination will also lead to the production of better written reports.

> **REMEMBER**
>
> Preparation for testimony should be routine, with such a discussion accompanying every case, regardless of whether the case is likely to require testimony.

Here is an area in which most psychologists are not formally trained. Supervisees need to be continually educated about the role of an expert witness. Supervisors can direct them to the seminal works in the area (e.g., Brodsky, 2013; Brodsky & Gutheil, 2016; Faust, 2012). Moreover, they can highlight some universal truths regarding testimony.

Testimony is often an anxiety-provoking experience, especially for the novice forensic psychologist, but familiarity with the role and its purpose can ease that anxiety. Make sure the supervisee understands that although he or she may have important information to offer the fact finder, the case probably does not pivot on this testimony. An important lesson for the supervisee is, "It's not about you."

As noted, there is a natural (but largely avoidable) pull to provide helpful opinions to the referral source. Supervisors should help supervisees understand that they will be the most useful when telling the whole truth, including aspects that might be disappointing to the referral source. Supervisors should stress that the supervisee's loyalty should be to her or his opinion, not a party in a case.

CONSIDERATIONS RELATED TO TESTS AND MEASURES

Test Selection

As all competent forensic supervisors know, the hallmark of forensic assessment is the use of multiple sources of information. As the Specialty Guidelines for Forensic Psychology (APA, 2013a, 2013b) state, "Forensic practitioners ordinarily avoid relying solely on one source of data, and corroborate important data whenever feasible" (p. 15). Colloquially, this approach is often referred to as "multiple sources and multiple methods." Psychological testing, of course, is one such method.

Supervisees will typically enter supervision with a global understanding of psychometrics. It will likely be incumbent upon supervisors to explain the nuances of testing as applied within forensic assessment. There are strictly clinical measures (e.g., Beck Depression Inventory-II [Beck, Steer, & Brown, 1996]) that can have an appropriate role in forensic work. There are clinical measures that have specific scales that are particularly important in forensic assessment. Examples include the validity scales of the Minnesota Multiphasic Personality Inventory, Second Edition, Restructured Form (MMPI-2-RF; Ben-Porath & Tellegen, 2008), or the Digit Span subtest of the Wechsler Adult Intelligence Scale, Fourth Edition (WAIS-IV; Wechsler, 2008), if one is using the reliable digit span measure to assess response style (Greiffenstein, Baker, & Gola, 1994). There are numerous measures designed specifically for assessment of response style (e.g., Validity Indicator Profile [Frederick, 1997], Test of Memory Malingering [Tombaugh, 1996], Inventory of Legal Knowledge [Musick & Otto, 2010], and the Structured Interview of Reported Symptoms, Second Edition [Rogers, Sewell, & Gillard, 2010]). While those measures assess abilities directly relevant to forensic assessment, they do not directly measure psycholegal abilities. Measures within a final category do, however. For example, the MacArthur Competency Assessment Tool-Criminal Adjudication (MacCAT-CA; Poythress et al. 1999) is specifically designed to measure abilities related to trial competency, and Goldstein, Zelle, and Grisso's (2014) Miranda Rights Comprehension Instruments are specifically designed to measure an individual's ability to waive those rights. Novices in forensic psychology may fail to recognize such distinctions.

A thorough understanding of these distinctions will lead the supervisee to the understanding that there are no "magic tests" which will, by themselves, resolve a forensic question. The supervisor's guidance will likely be necessary in test selection, especially earlier in training. Several questions can help guide an assessor toward measures that will be most helpful.

First, is the measure appropriate for forensic work in general? Any measure used should meet the appropriate evidentiary standards in a jurisdiction (i.e., *Frye* or *Daubert*). General acceptance of the measures is particularly important (Archer, Buffington-Vollum, Stredny, & Handel, 2006; McLaughlin & Kan, 2014). Moreover, measures should be normed on an appropriate sample. How close the normative sample should match the person being evaluated is an open question and a compelling supervision topic. Ultimately, the assessor who selects the measures should understand the level of scrutiny that might be applied to her or his decision. Supervision activities could include role-playing exercises in which the supervisee explains the rationale for the choice to the supervisor/judge in an evidentiary hearing, or in which the supervisee explains the purpose and interpretation of the test to the supervisor/juror.

Obviously, after it is determined that the measure is appropriate for forensic work in general, it should be determined that it is also appropriate for the specific forensic question at hand. Topics for supervision could include whether measures of response style are always necessary (spoiler alert: they are not), as well as the limitations of specific forensic assessment instruments under consideration. Finally, supervisors should ensure that supervisees become aware of the literature regarding the strengths and weaknesses of clinical, actuarial, and structured professional judgment measures.

Finally, supervision will offer the opportunity for the supervisee to consider how results are conveyed. Assessors should be aware of the literature that discusses the impact of presenting risk assessment results as percentages, percentiles, or frequencies (Monahan et al., 2002; Slovic, Monahan, & MacGregor, 2000), and they should follow the best practice of reporting results in multiple ways, to decrease the chance of misinterpretation.

Allegiance Effects

Does the referral source affect the outcome of a forensic evaluation? Assessors may assert that they would not be swayed by the party who is footing the bill, and most supervisors might have agreed until recently. Supervisees may be unaware of impor-

≡ Rapid Reference 7.2

Questions to Consider When Selecting Tests in Forensic Assessments

1. Is the measure appropriate for forensic work in general?
2. Does it meet the appropriate evidentiary standards (i.e., *Frye* or *Daubert*)?
3. Is it generally accepted among forensic psychologists?
4. Is it normed on an appropriate sample?
5. Is it appropriate for the specific forensic question at hand?
6. Can you explain the rationale for your choice of the particular test?
7. What are its strengths and limitations?
8. Can you explain the purpose and interpretation of the test?
9. Can you describe the test results in multiple ways?

tant empirical research from the last several years that demonstrates that even honest, competent clinicians may be swayed—at least to some extent—by the fact that they were hired by one side or the other in a dispute (Blair et al., 2008; Murrie et al., 2009, 2013). These allegiance effects may occur even in court-ordered evaluations for which neither party pays, as clinicians become committed to an opinion that supports one side or the other. Supervisees should be directed toward systematic methods for addressing one's own biases, and they should have a plan for doing so routinely (see, for example, Lilienfeld & Jones, 2008; Meehl, 1973; Neal & Grisso, 2014). Proper treatment of this important issue is clearly beyond the scope of this chapter, but such issues should be forefront during supervision of forensic assessment.

SUPERVISION COMPETENCE AND THE SUPERVISORY RELATIONSHIP

As noted in earlier chapters, supervision is a special skill, distinct from the other skills shared by psychologists. Historically, little attention was paid to the qualities that make a good supervisor, and the only requirement for supervising others was that one had been supervised in the past. We now know (and probably always did know) that not all good clinicians make good supervisors.

To state the obvious, a supervisor must be competent in the areas in which she or he is supervising. In forensic assessment, this means the person should have a sophisticated understanding of the psycholegal issues in question, be a skilled interviewer, be facile with the types of psychological measures discussed above, be a competent writer for a legal or lay audience, and be able to testify effectively. (It is worth noting that teaching a person to testify [and supervising mock or actual testimony] is radically different from what most psychologists do.) Moreover, supervisors need a thorough understanding of ethical issues that may arise in the course of both forensic assessment and in supervision.

The American Board of Forensic Psychology has compiled a list of core competencies in forensic psychology (available at https://abpp.org/BlankSite/media/Forensic-Psychology-Documents/ABFP-Core-Competencies.pdf). According to that document, forensic supervisors should be able to "translate relevant and current forensic knowledge and skills to provide high-quality supervision and mentoring to trainees and colleagues" (p. 4). They recommend a variety of behavioral anchors, which include:

> … describing a sound theoretical foundation for the supervisory role; articulating the manner in which that theory is applied in specific supervisory situations; identifying potential ethical conflicts which can arise in the

supervisory relationship; and explaining ways in which those conflicts could be resolved. (p. 4)

Translating those ideals into practice can be tricky. Paying special attention to decision points may offer particular opportunities to do so. How are tests selected? How much information is enough? How does one determine whether a piece of information is relevant or irrelevant? Is a particular bit of information probative or prejudicial? How are alternative hypotheses considered, and to what extent are they discussed in written forensic reports? Each of these areas contains ample fodder for supervision, and to the extent that the supervisee sees the supervisor grapple with such issues, he or she will learn that such struggles are both routine and necessary.

> **REMEMBER**
>
> To the extent that the supervisee sees the supervisor grapple with tough issues, he or she will learn that such struggles are both routine and necessary.

Supervision of forensic assessment shares much in common with competent supervision of other clinical aspects in psychology. A competent supervisor should be flexible in her or his style. Moreover, he or she should be able to employ a range of supervisory techniques (e.g., observation, Socratic questioning, role playing). Supervisors should have a style that is genuine and reflective of their own personalities and professional values (in other words, if you are not warm and fuzzy, do not try to be warm and fuzzy; it will not work). Just as different psychologists would approach an assessment in different ways, supervisors approach supervision in different ways. Remember, however, that the goal is not to make the supervisee just like the supervisor. The goal is for the supervisee to find a style of practice that suits his or her personality, and the supervisor's task is to ensure that the supervisee's choices are within the parameters of competent practice.

Finally, supervisors should be comfortable with a gatekeeping role. In an ideal world, all practitioners at this level of training would be competent and ethical. Unfortunately, some students, for example, are not able to acquire the skills (or the professional and ethical behavior) required to practice competently, and the particular challenges of real-world forensic assessments may make this apparent. Supervisors should embrace that just as they have an obligation to their supervisees, they have an obligation to society to safeguard the quality and reputation of the profession. Sometimes, that obligation means that supervisees must be confronted about inadequate work or that schools, internship directors, or licensing boards must be made aware of significant problems. It is a great disservice to "look the other way" when a supervisee is practicing at an inadequate level or engaging in unethical behaviors. This most unpleasant aspect of supervision is arguably one of the most important.

To be effective—in both routine supervision and when confronting particularly thorny issues—a supervisor must have a solid relationship with the supervisee. As in all supervisory relationships, the dyad must confront issues of trust, power, and control. These should be acknowledged directly and with transparency. It is important for the supervisee and supervisor to be aware of the limits on what a supervisee can and cannot do, and there should be a frank discussion about the supervisor's ability to take over an interaction or a case if that becomes necessary.

Regardless of the supervisor's interpersonal style, there are several keys to a productive supervisory relationship. They can be divided into two broad categories of transparency and respect. Within the realm of transparency, supervisors must strive to recognize the supervisee's strengths, even when they are not readily apparent. Supervisors should readily acknowledge those strengths and discuss in an honest manner what the supervisee does well. Those positive strokes should be balanced by straightforward and constructive comments on weaknesses. Even seasoned clinicians will benefit from the observations of a supervisor, provided those observations come from a place of integrity and a genuine desire to help the supervisee improve his or her practice.

For constructive feedback to be received, it must be delivered with respect. Fairness is paramount. Supervisors should phrase critical feedback in a manner that emphasizes the reason it is being delivered—to help the recipient improve forensic practice. Fairness demands that supervisors monitor their own reactions to supervisees. Supervisors must remain aware of the fundamental attribution error when difficulties arise and keep the goals of supervision in mind. When tempted to throw her or his hands up and conclude, "This intern is hopeless," the supervisor should take a step back and ask, "What can I do to help this intern improve?" Such reframing requires both humility and compassion, which, fortuitously, are attributes supervisors should be modeling.

DIVERSITY

As a group, psychologists tend to believe that they are better at addressing issues of diversity than they actually are (Hansen et al., 2006). Although supervisors report that they routinely discuss diversity issues in supervision, students have reported that, in practice, issues regarding diversity are typically not addressed unless the student raises them (Duan & Roehlke, 2001). It is imperative that these issues be discussed explicitly with supervisees, including issues of diversity that might affect the relationship between the supervisee and supervisor. Addressing such issues directly and honestly helps establish a relationship wherein the supervisee is comfortable bringing them up in future interactions.

While issues of diversity are important in all areas of psychology, they merit particular attention in forensic assessment. Depending on the jurisdiction in which one works, there may be frequent contact with people who differ in important ways from the assessor. It is crucial to understand disparate cultures and subcultures, as well as the ways culture may affect an evaluee's clinical presentation or reaction to the assessor. In addition to the clinical or interpersonal differences, in forensic psychology, one may encounter people who are familiar with legal systems quite different from those about which the assessor is knowledgeable. Forensic psychologists working in the criminal realm may evaluate people in connection to crimes (for example, the killing of a family member who has brought shame to the family) that would not have been prosecuted in their homelands.

As noted earlier, forensic psychologists frequently evaluate people who would likely not come to the attention of a mental health professional if it were not for the pertinent psycholegal issue. Similarly, practitioners are likely to encounter people with unusual belief systems (such as "sovereign citizens," i.e., people who believe they are not under the government's jurisdiction; for more information, see Pytyck & Chaimowitz, 2013). Differentiating an unusual belief system shared by a subculture from a delusional system can be a difficult task for a seasoned professional; supervisors need to monitor a supervisee's thinking closely through this forensic briar patch.

Working with interpreters poses special challenges. Assessors must learn the importance of emphasizing direct and accurate translations from an interpreter, even when the subject matter is graphic or uncomfortable. (One of the authors struggled with an interpreter of a rare dialect. She would only say that the defendant "sounds very angry." Only after much work was the psychologist able to get the interpreter to disclose that the defendant was repeating a single phrase: "Fuck you.")

It is imperative to pay attention to issues of diversity in test selection. Assessors may not attend closely enough to issues that would bear on the reliability and validity of psychological measures. A discussion of differences between the person being evaluated and the normative group—and whether or how those differences matter—can make for a memorable supervision session, not to mention a useful tool in testimony later on.

Finally, the issue of racism within the criminal justice system should be addressed directly and honestly by the supervisor. While there may be many cases which are not tainted by overt racism, there is ample evidence of systemic racism in the criminal justice system. For example, incarceration rates vary by ethnicity in a manner that is disproportionately advantageous to the majority culture (Nellis, 2016). Black people are more likely than white people to be wrongfully convicted (Gross, Posely, & Stephens, 2017). Additionally, legal cases about the differences between penalties for powder versus crack cocaine can easily be framed as racist (Fellner, 2009). While such systemic injustices are clearly lamentable, many assessors need guidance regarding their own internalized biases and their responses when confronted with such. Supervisors should note the unintended possibility of supervisees' having internalized some of the systemic injustices when assessing, for example, people of color. Further, supervisees may be inclined to comment about systemic issues in a report about an individual; however, the forensic assessment report is not the place for judicial activism.

ASSESSMENT, EVALUATION, AND FEEDBACK

If a supervisor only provides feedback via a written evaluation at the end of a supervisory relationship, he or she is doing it wrong. Clear and timely feedback is essential for supervisees at any level of training. As noted above, a feedback session should be scheduled immediately after any forensic assessment, if that is possible. However, every supervision should involve constructive feedback that balances praise with suggestions for improvement. Suggestions for improvement should be clear and, to the extent possible, concrete. Ideally, supervision is a constant cycle of suggestions for improvement, opportunity for practice, and ongoing feedback.

> **REMEMBER**
>
> If you only provide feedback via a written evaluation at the end of a supervisory relationship, you're doing it wrong.

Feedback is better received when it is provided orally and immediately. Indirect feedback is not associated with good outcomes (Hoffman, Hill, Holmes, & Freitas, 2005). To the extent possible, feedback should reflect measurable goals with behavioral anchors, and the supervisor should follow up explicitly on the supervisee's subsequent progress toward these goals. APA (2012) has developed benchmarks for various levels of practice (i.e., readiness for practicum, readiness for internship, and readiness for entry-level practice) that can be adapted for supervision of forensic assessment. Similarly, the core competencies developed by the American Board of Forensic Psychology could be similarly adapted (as noted above, they are available at https://abpp.org/BlankSite/media/Forensic-Psychology-Documents/ABFP-Core-Competencies.pdf).

ETHICAL, LEGAL, AND REGULATORY CONSIDERATIONS

The very nature of forensic assessment is such that knowledge of the law is essential. Forensic assessment provides an essential service to civil courts, criminal courts, and other legal and regulatory consumers, such as insurance companies. Competent provision of those services requires that the forensic practitioner understand the law and remain abreast of changes in the law (changes which often go unannounced). It is critical for forensic assessors to understand and internalize this value of forensic psychology. While supervisees' understanding is important, it is the supervisor, most often as the licensed member of the dyad, who retains ultimate responsibility for the quality of the evaluation. Whether there are liability protections associated with court-ordered evaluations varies by jurisdiction; supervisees should be able to depend upon the supervisor's facility with the intricacies of such laws.

Issues that sometimes receive limited coverage in graduate school are forefront in forensic assessment. Assessors need to understand the difference between confidentiality (likely covered well in graduate school) and privilege (perhaps never mentioned in graduate school). In the context of a forensic assessment of a demonstrably or potentially dangerous individual, assessors may find real-life opportunities to consider issues of duty to warn or protect. A student's or psychologist's first real confrontations with such issues may occur under forensic assessment supervision.

When confronted with ethical issues, assessors should be aware of various sources of guidance. In addition to the Ethical Principles and Code of Conduct (APA, 2010) and the Specialty Guidelines for Forensic Psychology (APA, 2013a, 2013b), supervisees can be directed to many other authoritative sources, including (but not limited to):

- Code of Medical Ethics (American Medical Association, 2016),
- Principles of Medical Ethics with Annotations Especially Applicable to Psychiatry (American Psychiatric Association, 2013),
- Ethics Guidelines for the Practice of Forensic Psychiatry (American Academy of Psychiatry and the Law, 2005),
- Guidelines for Child Custody Evaluations (APA, 2010),
- Professional Practice Guidelines for Occupationally Mandated Psychological Evaluations (APA, 2017a, 2017b), and
- Guidelines for Psychological Evaluations in Child Protection Matters (APA, 2013a, 2013b).

Many assessors are unaware of the majority of these sources.

CONCLUSION

Many practitioners of forensic psychology look forward to their first "high-profile" case. But as noted, every case is high-profile for the people involved. For some, it is a literal matter of life and death. Most psychologists work in areas in which their performance can have profound impacts on people's lives. In forensic psychology, those impacts may include, for example, under what circumstances a person can see his or her children, whether a person is allowed to make his or her own decisions about money, whether a person is involuntarily committed to a psychiatric hospital, whether a person goes to prison, and whether he or she lives or is executed. These are matters of tremendous importance, and supervisors must communicate to supervisees the gravity of the work. Given this backdrop, the importance of effective supervision is clear. It is incumbent upon forensic supervisors to prepare the next generation of psychologists for this vital work.

 TEST YOURSELF

1. **True or False: To protect the privacy of clients, records should be destroyed soon after the forensic assessment report is generated.**

2. **Why is it essential that the supervisor directly observe the forensic evaluation?**
   (a) The supervisor can be sure that the student obtains adequate information.
   (b) The supervisor can observe how the student asks important questions.
   (c) The supervisor can observe subtle interactions between the student and the person being evaluated.
   (d) Ultimately, the supervisor is responsible for the quality of the evaluation.
   (e) All of the above.

3. **True or False: The supervisor should always prepare the student to provide court testimony, even if testimony is not likely in a particular case.**

4. **Which of the following is *not* true about the use of psychological testing in forensic assessment?**
   (a) The tests used should be generally accepted by forensic psychologists.
   (b) Test results should always be presented in percentile form.
   (c) Some clinical measures are appropriate in forensic assessment.
   (d) A number of tests have been developed to assess response style.
   (e) Students should be prepared to defend the rationale for their selection of tests.

Answers: 1. False; 2. e; 3. True; d. b.

REFERENCES

Allard, G., & Faust, D. (2000). Errors in scoring objective personality tests. *Assessment*, 7, 119–129.

American Academy of Psychiatry and the Law. (2005). Ethics guidelines for the practice of forensic psychiatry. http://www.aapl.org/ethics-guidelines

American Medical Association. (2016). Code of medical ethics. https://www.ama-assn.org/delivering-care/ama-code-medical-ethics

American Psychiatric Association (APA). (2013). *Principles of medical ethics with annotations especially applicable to psychiatry.* Arlington, VA: American Psychiatric Association.

American Psychological Association (APA). (2007). Record keeping guidelines. *American Psychologist*, 62(9), 993–1004.

American Psychological Association (APA). (2010). Guidelines for child custody evaluations in family law proceedings. *American Psychologist*, 65(9), 863–867.

American Psychological Association (APA). (2012). Benchmarks evaluation system. https://www.apa.org/ed/graduate/benchmarks-evaluation-system.aspx

American Psychological Association (APA). (2013a). Specialty guidelines for forensic psychology. *American Psychologist*, 68(1), 7–19.

American Psychological Association (APA). (2013b). Guidelines for psychological evaluations in child protection matters. *American Psychologist*, 68(1), 20–31.

American Psychological Association (APA). (2017a). *Ethical principles of psychologists and code of conduct.* Washington, DC: American Psychological Association.

American Psychological Association (APA). (2017b). Professional practice guidelines for occupationally mandated psychological evaluations. http://www.apa.org/practice/guidelines/occupationally-mandated-psychological-evaluations.pdf

Archer, R. P., Buffington-Vollum, J. K., Stredny, R. V., & Handel, R. W. (2006). A survey of psychological test use patterns among forensic psychologists. *Journal of Personality Assessment*, 87(1), 84–94.

Beck, A. T., Steer, R. A., & Brown, G. K. (1996). *Beck Depression Inventory–II (BDI-II) [Assessment instrument].* San Antonio, TX: Pearson.

Ben-Porath, Y. S., & Tellegen, A. (2008). *Minnesota Multiphasic Personality Inventory – 2 – Restructured Form (MMPI-2-RF) [Assessment instrument].* Minneapolis, MN: University of Minnesota Press.

Blair, P. R., Marcus, D. K., & Boccaccini, M. T. (2008). Is there an allegiance effect for assessment instruments? Actuarial risk assessment as an exemplar. *Clinical Psychology: Science and Practice*, 15(4), 346–360.

Brodsky, S. L. (2013). *Testifying in court: Guidelines and maxims for the expert witness* (pp. 2). Washington, DC: American Psychological Association.

Brodsky, S. L., & Gutheil, T. G. (2016). *The expert expert witness: More maxims and guidelines for testifying in court* (pp. 2). Washington, DC: American Psychological Association.

DeMier, R. L. (2013). Forensic report writing. In R. K. Otto & I. B. Weiner (Eds.), *Handbook of psychology: Forensic psychology* (2nd ed., Vol. 11, pp. 75–98). Hoboken, NJ: Wiley.

DeMier, R. L., & Otto, R. K. (2017). Forensic report writing: principles and challenges. In R. Roesch & A. N. Cook (Eds.), *Handbook of forensic mental health services* (pp. 216–234). New York, NY: Routledge.

Duan, C., & Roehlke, H. (2001). A descriptive "snapshot" of cross-racial supervision in university counseling center internships. *Journal of Multicultural Counseling and Development, 29,* 131–146.

Faust, D. (2012). *Coping with psychiatric and psychological testimony* (pp. 6). New York, NY: Oxford University Press.

Federal Rules of Evidence (n.d.). https://www.rulesofevidence.org

Fellner, J. (2009). Race, drugs, and law enforcement in the United States. *Stanford Law and Police Review, 20*(2), 257–292.

Frederick, R. I. (1997) Validity indicator profile (VIP) [Assessment instrument]. San Antonio, TX: Pearson.

Goldstein, N. E. S., Zelle, H., & Grisso, T. (2014). Miranda Rights Comprehension Instruments (MRCI) [Assessment instrument]. Sarasota, FL: Professional Resource Press.

Greenberg, S. A., & Shuman, D. W. (1997). Irreconcilable conflict between therapeutic and forensic roles. *Professional Psychology: Research and Practice, 28*(1), 50–57.

Greenberg, S. A., & Shuman, D. W. (2007). When worlds collide: Therapeutic and forensic roles. *Professional Psychology: Research and Practice, 38*(2), 129–132.

Greiffenstein, M. F., Baker, W. J., & Gola, T. (1994). Validation of malingered amnesia measures with a large clinical sample. *Psychological Assessment, 6*(3), 218–224.

Grisso, T. (1987). The economic and scientific future of forensic psychological assessment. *American Psychologist, 42*(9), 831–839.

Grisso, T. (2010). Guidance for improving forensic reports: A review of common errors. *Open Access Journal of Forensic Psychology, 2,* 102–115. http://www.forensicpsychologyunbound.ws

Gross, S., Posely, M., & Stephens, K. (2017). Race and wrongful convictions in the United States. Irvine, CA: National Registry of Exonerations.

Hansen, N. D., Randazzo, K. V., Schwartz, A., Marshall, M., Kalis, D., Frazier, R., … Norvig, G. (2006). Do we practice what we preach? An exploratory survey of multicultural psychotherapy competencies. *Professional Psychology: Research and Practice, 37,* 66–74.

Heilbrun, K. (2001). *Principles of forensic mental health assessment.* New York, NY: Kluwer Academic/Plenum Publishers.

Heilbrun, K., & Collins, S. (1995). Evaluations of trial competency and mental state at time of offense: Report characteristics. *Professional Psychology: Research and Practice, 26*(1), 61–67.

Heilbrun, K., & Otto, R. (2003). Forensic psychology and board certification. *American Psychologist, 58*(1), 80.

Hoffman, M. A., Hill, C., Holmes, S. E., & Freitas, G. F. (2005). Supervisor perspective on the process and outcome of giving easy, difficult, or no feedback to supervisees. *Journal of Counseling Psychology, 52*(1), 3–13.

Karson, M., & Nadkarni, L. (2013). *Principles of forensic report writing.* Washington, DC: American Psychological Association.

Lilienfeld, S. O., & Jones, K. (2008). Allegiance effects in assessment: Unresolved questions, potential explanations, and constructive remedies. *Clinical Psychology: Science and Practice, 15*(4), 361–365.

McLaughlin, J. L., & Kan, L. Y. (2014). Test usage in four common types of forensic mental health assessment. *Professional Psychology: Research and Practice, 45,* 128–135.

Meehl, P. E. (1973). *Psychodiagnosis: Selected papers.* Minneapolis, MN: University of Minnesota Press.

Monahan, J., Heilbrun, K., Silver, E., Nabors, E., Bone, J., & Slovic, P. (2002). Communicating violence risk: Frequency formats, vivid outcomes, and forensic settings. *International Journal of Forensic Mental Health, 1*(2), 121–126.

Murrie, D. C., Boccaccini, M. T., Guarnera, L. A., & Rufino, K. A. (2013). Are forensic experts biased by the side that retained them? *Psychological Science, 24*(10), 1889–1897.

Murrie, D. C., Boccaccini, M. T., Turner, D. B., Meeks, M., Woods, C., & Tussey, C. (2009). Rater (dis)agreement on risk assessment measures in sexually violence predator proceedings: Evidence of adversarial allegiance in forensic evaluation? *Psychology, Public Policy, and Law, 15*(1), 19–53.

Musick, J., & Otto, R. (2010). *The Inventory of Legal Knowledge (ILK)* [Assessment instrument]. Lutz, FL: Psychological Assessment Resources.

Neal, T. M. S., & Grisso, T. (2014). The cognitive underpinnings of bias in forensic mental health evaluations. *Psychology, Public Policy, and Law, 20*(2), 200–211.

Nellis, A. (2016). *The color of justice: Racial and ethnic disparity in state prisons.* Washington, DC: The Sentencing Project.

Otto, R. K., DeMier, R. L., & Boccaccini, M. T. (2014). *Forensic reports and testimony: A guide to effective communication for psychologists and psychiatrists.* Hoboken, NJ: Wiley.

Poythress, N., Nicholson, R., Otto, R., Edens, J., Bonnie, R., Monaha, J., & Hoge, S. (1999). The MacArthur Competence Assessment Tool – Criminal Adjudication (MacCAT-CA) [Assessment instrument]. Lutz, FL: Psychological Assessment Resources.

Pytyck, J., & Chaimowitz, G. A. (2013). The Sovereign Citizen movement and fitness to stand trial. *International Journal of Forensic Mental Health*, 12(2), 149–153.

Rogers, R., Sewell, K. W., & Gillard, N. D. (2010). *Structured Interview of Reported Symptoms, 2 (SIRS-2)* [Assessment instrument]. Lutz, FL: Psychological Assessment Resources.

Simmons, R., Goddard, R., & Patton, W. (2002). Hand-scoring error rates in psychological testing. *Assessment*, 9, 292–300.

Slovic, P., Monahan, J., & MacGregor, D. G. (2000). Violence risk assessment and risk communication: The effects of using actual cases, providing instruction, and employing probability versus frequency formats. *Law and Human Behavior*, 24(3), 271–296.

Tombaugh, T. N. (1996). Test of Memory Malingering (TOMM) [Assessment instrument]. North Tonawanda, NY: Multi-Health Systems.

Tyner, E. A., & Frederick, R. I. (2013). Rates of computational errors for scoring the SIRS primary scales. *Psychological Assessment*, 25(4), 1367–1369.

Wechsler, D. (2008). Wechsler Adult Intelligence Scale – Fourth Edition (WAIS-IV) [Assessment instrument]. San Antonio, TX: Pearson.

Witt, P. H. (2010). Forensic report checklist. *Open Access Journal of Forensic Psychology*, 2, 233–240. http://www.forensicpsychologyunbound.ws

Eight

SUPERVISING NEUROPSYCHOLOGICAL ASSESSMENT

Catherine L. Leveroni

The American Psychological Association (APA) (2010) stipulates that competence in clinical neuropsychology requires the acquisition of specific knowledge and skills; the ability to integrate findings with medical, psychological, behavioral, and scientific knowledge; and the ability to interpret these findings within the context of social, cultural, and ethical issues. Comprehensive and explicit guidelines related to neuropsychology education, training, and credentialing have been put forth. Specifically, the Houston Conference (Hannay et al., 1998) provides an integrated model for education and training in clinical neuropsychology that defines programmatic and competency-based guidelines and serves as training standards. Its ultimate goal is to promote quality and consistency in the field of neuropsychology.

So how do we use these guidelines in practice, ensuring that supervision meets the noted training goals? Practical experience is a crucial component in the education and training of neuropsychologists, yet, until recently, little attention has been paid to the specific methods of supervision (Shultz, Pedersen, Roper, & Rey-Casserly, 2014; Stucky, Busch, & Donders, 2010). There are multiple methods by which supervisors can foster and monitor the development of specific neuropsychological assessment competencies in their supervisees.

Essentials of Psychological Assessment Supervision, First Edition.
Edited by A. Jordan Wright
© 2020 John Wiley & Sons, Inc. Published 2020 by John Wiley & Sons, Inc.

MODEL OF SUPERVISION

The goal of supervision in neuropsychology is to foster the development of competency. Competency is defined as follows: "the individual is qualified, capable, and able to understand and do things in an appropriate and effective manner" (Rudolfa et al., 2005). Specialized knowledge and skills are not in and of themselves sufficient for competence. The clinician must also possess judgment, critical thinking, and decision-making capacities, as these are the foundations for effective performance and optimal outcomes in neuropsychology. Various frameworks have been provided to define competencies. Rudolfa and colleagues presented a conceptual framework to guide the training of specific competencies in clinical psychology. They designed a three-dimensional matrix that describes the foundations of competency as it develops through stages of training. On the x-axis are what they term *foundational competencies*. These competencies are defined as the knowledge, attitudes, and values that underlie all of a psychologist's activities. They include scientific knowledge and method, relationships, and ethical standards. On the y-axis are the *functional competencies*. These are the specific functions that comprise the work activities of the psychologist. For the neuropsychologist, these include assessment, intervention, consultation, teaching, and research. These two sets of competencies interact with the stages of professional development, which comprise the z-axis (Rudolfa et al., 2005).

> **REMEMBER**
>
> Knowledge and skills aren't enough to ensure competency. Supervisees must also be able to use adequate judgment, critical thinking, and decision-making to implement these skills for optimal neuropsychological assessment outcomes.

Stucky et al. (2010) present a model to support the acquisition of these competencies for the clinical neuropsychologist. They promote a model of supervision that is developmental and process-based. They stipulate that the overarching supervisory goals are not only to develop knowledge and skills, but also to develop critical thinking and decision-making abilities that lead to high quality care. Additionally, supervision promotes ethical practice and life-long learning.

These goals promote a model of supervision that is developmental and process-based. Preparation starts at the pre-doctoral level with specialized education and practicum experiences. Trainees further their development through internship training and complete formal training at the postdoctoral level. Stucky et al. (2010) emphasize, however, that life-long learning is essential for evidence-based practice: ideally, the neuropsychologist continues to develop his or her competencies by

⟰ Rapid Reference 8.1

Goals of Supervision (Stucky et al., 2010)

1. Advance knowledge and skill
2. Develop critical thinking and decision-making abilities
3. Promote high quality clinical care
4. Promote life-long learning
5. Enhance patient outcomes
6. Develop attitudes conducive to ethical practice

keeping up with the scientific literature, attending rounds and seminars, and participating in continuing education/professional development. Development progresses through defined stages that relate to the trainee's attainment of knowledge, skill, and expertise (Nelson et al., 2015; Stucky et al., 2010).

A recent paper (Nelson et al., 2015) delineated basic competency expectations for graduate students entering and exiting clinical practica in neuropsychology. The authors also set the stage for the development of specific competency expectations for more advanced levels of training, but explicit guidelines have yet to be published. Still, the article offers enough guidance about (a) explicating relevant areas of competence necessary for the practice of clinical neuropsychology and

⟰ Rapid Reference 8.2

Definition of Competency Expectations (Nelson et al., 2015)

- *Novice*: possesses beginning skill related to general psychology practice; needs intensive supervision in neuropsychology
- *Basic*: has exposure to neuropsychology and some experience; ongoing supervision needed
- *Intermediate*: has intermediate exposure and experience in neuropsychology with gaps in knowledge and skill; ongoing supervision as needed
- *Advanced*: has solid experience, handles typical situations well; requires supervision in complex situations
- *Proficient*: functions autonomously, knows limits of ability; seeks supervision and consultation as needed
- *Expert*: serves as a resource to others; is recognized as having expertise

(b) providing a description of the expectations of trainees at different stages of development. Supervisors should engage in supervision practices that are appropriate for the developmental level of need of the supervisee.

Supervision is tailored to meet the needs of the individual at his or her level at a given point in time. Supervision needs to be flexible, such that guidance is appropriate to the supervisee's developmental level. As such, supervisors should assign responsibilities that are consistent with the supervisee's established and emerging abilities, and gradually increase responsibilities and independence. In this way, supervisors maximize what the supervisees gain from the experience. The supervising neuropsychologist prepares supervisees to function in multiple roles, including clinician, teacher, consultant, and administrator. Through modeling, observation, and direct teaching, the supervisor teaches skills, furthers knowledge and its application, and encourages the development of the critical thinking abilities necessary for competence in neuropsychology practice (Stucky et al., 2010).

SETTING UP A TRAINING PROGRAM

Program Training Plan

Supervision starts even before supervisees arrive, with the development of a detailed and explicit training plan. Training sites should devote considerable thought to the types of experiences they can offer and how these experiences will foster the development of competencies in supervisees. The first step is to determine whether the training site has the necessary elements to foster growth in individuals at differing levels of training (Nelson et al., 2015). Many training sites work with supervisees with varying levels of experience, from the beginning practicum student to the postdoctoral fellow. While the supervisees most often engage in the same clinical activities with patients, supervisees at various levels of development will have very different supervisory needs, capacities for independent functioning, and training goals. It is critical that supervisors determine whether their site has any inherent limitations that would make it less than ideal for supervisees at certain stages of development. For example, some settings do not have the infrastructure to provide beginning practicum students with the intensive time and training surrounding test administration and scoring. It is best for supervisors in these settings to offer the training experience only to supervisees who have previously acquired these skills, rather than take beginning students and fail to train them adequately to a level of proficiency in testing. On the other end of the spectrum, supervisors also need to consider whether their training site provides the proper breadth and depth of opportunities to prepare more advanced supervisees for competent independent practice and board certification. Thoughtful self-assessment at the time when the training plan is

> **DON'T FORGET**
> ....
> Clarity is key! The training plan should be explicit in terms of logistics, details, and expectations.

developed can help to ensure that the supervisors can meet the needs of the supervisees and guide decisions regarding the kinds of experiences to offer.

An optimal training plan is specific about the time commitment, including the duration of the experience (i.e., start and end dates), the number of hours per week, and the plan for vacation/time off. Sites should be explicit regarding how the trainees' time will be allotted across various activities (e.g., number of cases/reports per week or month, participation in didactics, supervisory and/or administrative responsibilities). This provides the basis of the supervisory contract. The plan for supervision needs to be predetermined. The site should delineate who will be providing supervision, the format for supervision (e.g., individual, group, on a case-by-case basis), and the number of hours of supervision that will be provided per week or per case. When determining the amount of supervision provided, attention should be paid to national and state guidelines, so that supervisees receive adequate supervision to meet their goals (e.g., graduation, qualifications for internship, state licensure, board certification; Stucky et al., 2010). Perhaps most important, the training plan should delineate the overarching goals for supervisees in the program, framed in terms of the competencies that they can expect to acquire. It also should delineate how the specific experiences offered will provide a breadth and depth of experience and move trainees toward various competencies. For example, many training sites stipulate that supervisees will participate in interdisciplinary rounds, didactic rounds, journal groups, case conferences, and seminars as a way to foster growth and move them toward increased competency. If such types of experiences are not available at the training site, supervisors may seek out joint rounds at nearby institutions or participate in case reviews and literature review exercises one-on-one to ensure that supervisees are able to round out their learning experiences.

Orientation

Once the supervisees arrive, they need be oriented to policies governing training that are institution- and site-specific (Nelson et al., 2015). The responsibilities of all parties involved in the supervisory relationship should be made explicit. Stucky et al. (2010) promote the idea of developing a supervisory contract at this stage.

The responsibilities of the supervisee to the training program include behaving in an ethical manner, completing the predetermined hours of work, attending required meetings, coming prepared for supervision, seeking supervision and extra help when needed, keeping up with paperwork demands, and being punctual (Stucky et al., 2010). The more explicit the expectations are the better. It is helpful to provide supervisees with written materials in the form of either a contract or a policy handbook, so they have something to refer to over the course of the training experience. Supervisors should also make their own responsibilities and commitment to the training process as explicit as possible. They should agree to provide sufficient and appropriate cases to foster development, monitor supervisees' progress and development of specific skills, provide adequate hours of supervision to meet their needs, and communicate effectively with trainees and, if relevant, their programs of origin (Nelson et al., 2015; Stucky et al., 2010).

Trainee-Specific Plan Development

The pace and timing of training activities will vary based on characteristics of each individual supervisee. Supervisors should work hard not to make assumptions that an individual at a certain level of training (e.g., practicum, intern, postdoctoral fellow) has achieved certain competencies based only on their education and prior experience. Regardless of their level of training, individual supervisees come in with varied types of clinical experiences, gaps in knowledge, and areas of personal strength and weakness. These factors need to be assessed at the outset of the training experience in order to generate a training plan that is specific to the individual's competencies and goals. It is a good idea to meet with each supervisee individually to gain an understanding of his or her specific prior experiences and current goals. Supervisees should provide insights into the kinds of clinical activities they have mastered, can engage in with supervision and guidance, or have not yet experienced. It is also important to get a sense of the types of settings in which they have worked, the populations they have seen, and the ways in which they would like to grow over the training period.

> **WARNING**
>
> Don't be overly swayed by a supervisee's previous training and experience. Coming up with an individual plan for approaching training and supervision in neuropsychological assessment requires more data, as each supervisee comes in with personal strengths and weaknesses, different learning curves, and specific needs that can affect the level and types of support he or she will need in supervision.

Based on your joint assessment, the supervisee's developmental level for specific clinical tasks, the program requirements, and the supervisee's goals, come up with an initial plan. This plan should include the specific training and supervision methods and timeframes for the acquisition of various competencies. For example, for novice practicum students, an early goal is often the development of proficiency with test administration and scoring. The supervisor can estimate the amount of time to be spent on training in test administration based on prior experience working with novice students. They should build in some flexibility because individuals have various levels of prior exposure to testing and learn at different rates. Some students may have had exposure and practice through coursework, and others may not. Based on their prior experience, the experience might begin with time to review test manuals, direct instruction in test administration and scoring, and a period of practice. Once they are skilled enough to work with patients, they will need to be observed by a qualified individual (e.g., the neuropsychologist, a proficient intern/fellow, a trained research assistant, a psychometrist) for a period of time. The supervisee's progress should be monitored. For example, supervisors and affiliated trainers can log the specific tests they have observed and the student's performance in a notebook or document and track progress toward independence for each test. It is best to explicitly state the criteria used to determine proficiency (e.g., the specific test will be administered without error a certain number of times). The supervisor should set aside time to review and discuss the student's progress and address any questions that arise. Once the student is determined to be independent for test administration and scoring, the supervisor should monitor their continued performance. For example, they can sit in and observe testing at random intervals and spot check scoring for accuracy.

Assessments

Over the course of the training, the supervisor and supervisee should meet at predetermined intervals to monitor the supervisee's progress toward meeting training benchmarks and to adjust the training plan accordingly. A schedule for written assessment also should be determined. Written assessment tools should explicitly describe the supervisee's progress toward the development of specific competencies in neuropsychology. Progress should be tracked. Forms should be kept on file, as they will likely be needed to document hours and competencies for licensure, employment, and board certification.

Ideally, assessment in clinical neuropsychology training is a two-way process. Supervisees should be encouraged to provide feedback to their supervisors, and supervisors should be thoughtful about using this information to enhance their own skills. It is an opportunity for continued growth. Stucky et al. (2010) stress that supervisors should be self-reflective and open to feedback from their supervisees. Such feedback from supervisees helps to refine the process by which supervisors foster skill development. It is also an important part of encouraging and maintaining collaborative relationships. It allows the supervisor to be responsive to the needs of supervisees, and to identify and remediate any problems that may arise (Stucky et al., 2010). Many supervisors set aside a specific time to learn about their supervisees' experiences. This information can be invaluable, and the feedback can be incorporated into future training plans.

Remediation

Even highly qualified supervisees can struggle to acquire a specific competency. Structured assessment helps supervisors identify and respond to problems that can arise. It is crucial to provide feedback to prevent the supervisees from forming bad habits that will later be difficult to break. Corrective feedback should be timely and explicit (Stucky et al., 2010). It should be delivered in a manner that is respectful of the individual, specific to the skills in question, and couched in terms of the training goals. Feedback should be constructive and provide concrete strategies the supervisee can put in practice to improve. In this way, an area of weakness becomes the focus of more intensive attention during supervision and ultimately leads to the development of greater skill.

At times, a supervisee's difficulties are more significant in nature. They are intractable, despite effort on the part of the supervisee and supervisor. In these cases, the supervisee's skill deficit can become a roadblock to the development of autonomy and competency. Supervising neuropsychologists should be prepared for this scenario and give forethought for how significant lags in skill development will be addressed and remediated. For more serious issues, oral feedback may be insufficient, and a formal written remediation plan will be required. Supervisors may wish to consult with peers, other training centers, and/or institutional human resources for guidance. A training plan should be developed that provides a rationale for the need for remediation, sets concrete and measurable goals, explicates the specific means by which the goals will be achieved (including responsibilities of both the supervisor and supervisee), and specifies the timeframe and endpoint for the period of remediation (Stucky et al., 2010). In very rare cases, despite intensive efforts at remediation, a supervisee is unable to acquire the core competencies and meet the exit criteria for the training experience. In these cases, communication with the supervisee and, when applicable, the training program is crucial. It is better to identify serious deficiencies early, so that the supervisee can address omissions in their training or choose an alternate specialization or career path, if and when remediation is not possible.

METHODS OF SUPERVISION

Supervision in neuropsychology is frequently informal and flexible. It does not lend itself solely to scheduled weekly meetings. That said, scheduled meetings are certainly helpful when it comes to case preparation, case formulation, discussions about recommendations, and planning feedback. These meetings also provide an opportunity to disseminate knowledge and discuss ethical issues relevant to cases. However, supervision also needs to occur in real time when patients are present. On the date of an evaluation, supervisors and supervisees typically need to touch base multiple times not only to process the case, but also to adjust the assessment plan in response to the case's specifics (Marcopulos, 2015). The intensity of supervision typically varies according to both the complexity of the case and the supervisee's specific competencies. Supervision needs be flexible, because a supervisee might be proficient with one type of case or clinical population, but be relatively inexperienced with a second type of case and therefore require more hands-on supervision with it. The supervisor can use multiple techniques to impart knowledge, teach skills, and reinforce standards of practice. These include modeling, practice exercises, constructive critique following direct observation, feedback on oral and written communications, and direct teaching.

Modeling

It is common for neuropsychology supervisees to sit in on interviews, testing, feedback sessions, and interdisciplinary meetings for the purposes of observation. This is especially true at the outset of the training experience, but should occur periodically throughout, so that trainees can observe ways in which adjustments are made based on factors such as referral questions, timeframes, and patient characteristics. Prior to any period of observation, it is best to meet to discuss the goals of the interaction and structure the interaction accordingly. While observing, supervisees learn ways to establish rapport, communicate compassion, and encourage open communication. Supervisors model ways to organize, prioritize, and guide the interaction. When performing an interview, they can observe how to follow up when more information is needed and redirect when the interaction goes off track. Supervisees can see how the information and observations from an interview inform the initial hypotheses and help guide battery selection. It can be especially beneficial for supervisees to sit in on feedback sessions that are more complex or challenging. Prior to feedback sessions, supervisors should share strategies to best convey results to patients who vary with regard to their insight, attention span, level of comprehension, and interest in the results. Supervisors can model different strategies to convey results (e.g., the use of charts, graphs, pictures, and other visuals to help patients and families understand the results and impressions).

> **REMEMBER**
>
> When modeling interviews, feedback, or other sessions for supervisees, explicitly discuss ahead of time your plans in the sessions, then follow up afterward with a discussion about adjustments you made in the moment.

Direct Observation

As supervisees gain autonomy and take on more responsibility for clinical activities, supervisors have the opportunity to observe their level of skill for various tasks. Even for more experienced supervisees, periodic direct observation is important, as it allows the supervisor to gauge the supervisee's development and adjust goals going forward. Supervisors should offer constructive feedback on organizational strategies, techniques to improve efficiency and flow, ways to communicate, and ways to hone observational abilities.

Teaching

An important goal of supervision is to foster the development of knowledge as it applies to practice. This is often a major difference between supervision of neuropsychological assessment and other clinical activities, such as counseling, which tend to use less actual teaching during supervision. Life-long learning is a fundamental in competent neuropsychology practice and a value that needs to be modeled and reinforced by mentors. Advancements in scientific understanding of brain-behavior relationships, disease processes, effective treatments, and patient outcomes inform evolution in evidence-based practice. Knowledge is disseminated in multiple formats, including direct teaching in supervision, selected readings/journal groups, clinical conferences, and formal didactics (Stucky et al., 2010). To some extent, the knowledge gained in supervision is guided by specific cases. The supervisory dyad meets to discuss referral issues, scientific evidence that guides clinical decision making, and at times relevant literature to inform case conceptualization. Many settings offer the opportunity for supervisees to participate in interdisciplinary or interdepartmental rounds and seminars. These are excellent forums to increase the breadth of experience, introduce new concepts, and deepen knowledge. For training sites that do not have such opportunities on site, it is sometimes possible to arrange for supervisees to attend rounds or didactics at nearby or affiliated institutions. Formal or informal journal groups also provide opportunities to explore issues relevant to clinical practice. If possible, supervisors should also provide the opportunity for supervisees to teach, lecture, supervise, and present in meetings and provide feedback to encourage them to develop skills as teachers.

Case Conceptualization Exercises

The ability to formulate cases aloud is essential for supervisees who plan to take the neuropsychology board examination, and it is a strong training tool regardless. It is never too early to teach supervisees to organize and summarize information quickly, synthesize results with respect to brain-behavior relationships, make diagnostic decisions, and come up with comprehensive and relevant recommendations. Case conceptualization exercises reinforce core clinical skills—the ability to organize, prioritize, and form hypotheses based on a patient's history, gather data to evaluate hypotheses, and make meaning out of the information gathered. Doing all of this orally with immediate feedback also helps supervisees develop confidence in their skills and boost their report writing efficiency. Case conceptualization exercises also increase the breadth of exposure to both typical and complex cases. In many settings, such exercises are completed in group format, so that supervisees can learn from one another. Supervisors can also practice case formulation one-on-one with a supervisee using active and past cases.

Review of Communications

Much of neuropsychology supervision is delivered through the review of supervisees' written reports. Supervisors should teach flexibility in writing, so that reports can be tailored to be effective and appropriate for varied referral questions and audiences. Supervisors can provide models, templates, or sample reports, but the ultimate goal is to help supervisees develop a framework for comprehensive and professional written products in their own style of expression. Reviewing reports offers supervisors the opportunity to examine the ways in which supervisees prioritize, organize, and conceptualize material, as well as to help them enhance the clarity of their written communication. Ideally, supervisors will also have the opportunity to observe their supervisees' skills at presenting cases to referral sources (e.g., in rounds, case conferences, team meetings, school meetings). Some supervisors give their supervisees the opportunity to practice professional communications to help them learn to prioritize salient information for the setting, organize and structure what they want to say, and do so in a timely manner.

FOUNDATIONAL COMPETENCIES

Rodolfa et al. (2005) define foundational capacities as "the building blocks of what psychologists do" (p. 350). They incorporate attitudes, values, and professionalism. They encompass a basis in scientific knowledge and how it can be applied to practice in varied settings and systems (Marcopulos, 2015; Stucky et al., 2010).

Reflective Self-Practice

Supervisors reinforce attitudes that are the underpinnings of professional and ethical practice through direct teaching, thoughtful guidance, and modeling. The goal is to promote a self-evaluative process. Competency is fluid. An individual can be competent in one type of activity yet be at a basic or novice level for another. A person's level of competence can also vary over time: as changes in the scientific foundation of our knowledge evolve, the neuropsychologist must keep up and adjust. Competence in neuropsychology thus requires reflection, insight, and humility. Knowledge and skill acquisition in neuropsychology is a life-long and fluid process due to advances in science. It is crucial that practicing neuropsychologists are self-aware and challenge the bases and status of their knowledge and skills on a regular basis, and supervisors should be willing to do this in front of their supervisees. Individuals can be harmed through evaluation by a clinician who is not competent to answer the referral question or work with the specific population. Supervisees also should be taught to think critically about the basis of their knowledge as it relates to cases. This includes their level of experience with and

≡ Rapid Reference 8.3

Foundational Competency Domains (Rodolfa et al., 2005)

- Reflective practice-self-assessment
- Scientific knowledge and methods
- Relationships
- Ethical and legal standards
- Individual/cultural diversity
- Interdisciplinary systems

exposure to similar cases and knowledge of how neuropsychological data relate to relevant outcomes. They also need to understand the limitations of that knowledge. Self-reflective practice involves examination of what a person does not know about in a given case, including an understanding of the strengths and weaknesses of our measures and normative samples, the status of knowledge in the field, and controversies related to conceptualization, diagnosis, or treatment. Supervisors model reflective practice when preparing for cases, refining referral questions, triaging patients, familiarizing themselves with relevant knowledge (through scientific literature, participation in didactics, continuing education), and peer consultation.

> **DON'T FORGET**
>
> Appropriately questioning your own knowledge in front of supervisees can encourage self-reflective practice in them.

Scientific Knowledge and Methods

In neuropsychology, a foundation in scientific knowledge is the basis of evidence-based practice. The Houston Conference guidelines stipulate the clinical neuropsychologist needs to possess a general education in psychology and clinical psychology, including an understanding of statistics, methodology, individual and cultural diversity, psychometric theory, assessment techniques, and professional ethics (Hannay et al., 1998). Upon this solid foundation, the clinical neuropsychologist builds a base of knowledge of the nature of brain-behavior relationships and how this can be applied to the understanding of individuals. Per the APA, this includes "functional neuroanatomy, principles of neuroscience, brain development, neurological disorders and etiologies, neuro-diagnostic techniques, normal and abnormal brain functioning and neuropsychological and behavioral manifestations of neurological disorders" (APA, 2010).

≡ Rapid Reference 8.4

Domains of Specialized Knowledge in Clinical Neuropsychology (Hannay et al., 1998)

Foundations for Study of Brain-Behavior Relationships

a. Functional neuroanatomy
b. Neurology and related disorders including etiology, pathology, course, and treatment
c. Non-neurological conditions affecting CNS functions

d. Neuroimaging and other diagnostic techniques
e. Neurochemistry of behavior
f. Neuropsychology of behavior

Foundations for the Practice of Clinical Neuropsychology

a. Specialized neuropsychological assessment techniques
b. Specialized neuropsychological intervention techniques
c. Research design and analysis in neuropsychology
d. Professional issues and ethics in neuropsychology
e. Practical implications for neuropsychological conditions

Knowledge acquisition typically begins with coursework, but it is reinforced, furthered, and solidified through supervised experience. Through direct teaching, guided readings, discussion of reports, case conferences, and didactics, supervisees expand the scope of their knowledge base and come to appreciate how it evolves through scientific advancement. Supervisors model and encourage ways to integrate research findings into clinical practice, including evaluating effectiveness of clinical activities through the scientific literature, determining best evidence and clinical expertise, and employing best practices based on scientific evidence (Nelson et al., 2015; Rey-Casserly, Roper, & Bauer, 2012). Encourage supervisees to not only review any materials you provide for them, but also to independently review the scientific literature when faced with questions about a case. Take time to review materials they find together and to discuss ways to integrate the information into the case formulation. This will increase supervisees' ability to integrate knowledge in their own clinical decision-making. It also will reinforce an attitude that embraces the importance of life-long learning.

Relationships

The competent clinical neuropsychologist needs to develop and maintain effective relationships with supervisees, patients, caregivers, colleagues, referral sources, and team members. Supervisors model and encourage clear and effective styles of communication in the various settings in which they practice (Nelson et al., 2015). Supervisors also teach approaches to problem solving in response to any relationship issues that arise, be it with a supervisee, a patient, a peer, or a colleague (Stucky et al., 2010). Provide a framework for trainees to approach relationship challenges. Without compromising privacy, share relationship issues that have arisen in your experience. Have the supervisee generate possible ways to address the situation. Brainstorm together possible pitfalls to different solutions. Discuss how you chose to approach the situation, your plan of action, and the outcomes. Most important, even if your actions did not have the desired results, share how the experience has informed your practices going forward.

The mentoring relationship itself is a vehicle for the development of a supervisee's professional identity, values, and self-esteem. Supervisors foster positive growth through investment of more than just their time and knowledge. Ideally, supervisors are flexible, supportive, and collaborative. They are committed to open and honest communication, which in turn fosters trust. They are genuinely interested in training and are committed to the development of their supervisees' careers. Supervisors should be sensitive to the power differential that exists between themselves and supervisees. Communicate respect and an atmosphere of collaboration and collegiality. Do not take on the role of venerated and all-knowing mentor; be respectful of supervisees' ideas and be open to reciprocal learning.

Ethical Practice

Ethical practice is a cornerstone of competency in clinical neuropsychology. Through supervision, clinicians enhance their understanding of ethical and legal standards and learn how to apply these standards in day-to-day practice. In particular, it is important for supervisees to gain experience with the ethical issues that are particularly relevant to the practicing neuropsychologist. These include informed consent, test security, protection and release of health information, and mandatory reporting (AACN Board of Directors, 2007; Nelson et al., 2015). It is best to review institutional policies relating to these issues directly with supervisees at the outset of the training experience, ideally during orientation. Also provide supervisees with access to any forms, guidelines, or online resources that your institution provides. Prepare supervisees to navigate issues with their patients (e.g., obtain informed consent, determine patient safety, manage and store patient files). It is also important to discuss the ways in which our ethical code touches everyday clinical decision-making. Ethics guide everything from our use of valid and reliable measures, our choice of appropriate normative groups for comparison, our interpretation of data in the context of individual differences and cultural factors, and the bases of the conclusions we draw.

Discuss ways to identify and approach ethical dilemmas. Teach a problem-solving approach to resolving ethical dilemmas and evaluating outcomes, as this helps prepare supervisees not only to respond to the situation at hand but also provides a framework from which to approach situations in the future.

Individual and Cultural Diversity

One of the most salient challenges facing clinical neuropsychologists is the provision of culturally competent care. The demographic of our community is evolving in the direction of increased diversity, yet education and training in culturally competent care lag behind the clinical need. As cultural competence is critical for ethical practice in neuropsychology, it is a priority in the education of the next generation of clinicians. It is important to discuss the ways in which the very basis of our opinions depends on assumptions about test results that do not always mean the same thing in diverse populations. Issues related to test reliability and validity are paramount. Contextual factors, including health-related beliefs and level of acculturation, also influence behavior and test performance.

Supervisors provide supervisees with a framework from which to approach work with diverse individuals. Training should include discussion of appropriate normative data and threats to reliability and validity of testing when appropriate norms are not available. Supervisees should be taught how to work with interpreters, with the recognition that we are responsible for their competence. Most importantly, supervision should include discussion about how to challenge assumptions so as not to misinterpret or misconstrue the meaning of test data, while also making meaningful statements and recommendations for the individual being assessed.

Interdisciplinary Systems

It is important that supervisees develop an understanding of the ways in which neuropsychological assessments can be applied in different professional contexts, as well as the neuropsychologist's roles in these contexts (Nelson et al., 2015; Rey-Casserly et al., 2012). Moreover, trainees benefit from exposure to different types of referrals, as case formulation and clinical decision-making may differ based on setting and role (e.g., between clinical and medicolegal settings). Through modeling and direct teaching, supervisees learn to effectively communicate the nature of their roles. This can include clarifying referral issues (e.g., identifying who the client is), educating clients regarding the neuropsychologist's role and responsibilities, and clearly explicating limitations of confidentiality (Nelson et al., 2015; Rey-Casserly et al., 2012).

Particularly relevant for consultation are the neuropsychologists' oral communication skills. Colleagues are best able to comprehend neuropsychological data, utilize the results, and commit to recommendations when we communicate in a clear, concise, and professional manner. Our comportment can engender the trust and respect that is the basis of collaborative partnerships. Ideally, supervisees have the opportunity to observe supervisors in a variety of consulting settings, including team meetings, conferences, rounds, and, if appropriate, legal proceedings. They also can have the opportunity to deliver results to other professionals and receive constructive feedback on their delivery. If the training setting does not lend itself to interdisciplinary collaboration or professional presentation, supervisors can engage in informal or formal exercises aimed at giving trainees experience presenting cases and opinions in a clear, concise, and effective manner. This will not only hone their skills as consultants, but also increase their comfort level with oral presentation and professional confidence.

With training and experience, supervisees develop awareness of the unique role of the neuropsychologist and how our data complement those of our interdisciplinary colleagues. Additionally, supervisors working in multidisciplinary settings need to model and encourage the development of the professionalism, collaborative spirit, and self-confidence that are necessary for effective consultation (Marcopulos, 2015; Rey-Casserly et al., 2012; Stucky et al., 2010). Supervisees should be taught to manage professional relationships, respect others, and resolve conflict in a way that promotes communication and moves the team toward positive change (Stucky et al., 2010). This can be achieved through modeling, discussion, and feedback following observation.

FUNCTIONAL COMPETENCIES: ASSESSMENT

Functional competencies are the knowledge, skills, and values needed for the day-to-day practice of the psychologist (Rudolfa et al., 2005).

≡ *Rapid Reference 8.5*

Functional Competency Domains (Rodolfa et al., 2005)

- Assessment-diagnosis-case conceptualization
- Intervention
- Consultation
- Research-evaluation
- Supervision-teaching
- Management-administrative

≡ *Rapid Reference 8.6*

Components of Assessment

- Clarification of referral
- History taking
- Battery selection
- Administration and scoring
- Interpretation and diagnosis
- Treatment planning
- Report writing
- Provision of feedback

For the neuropsychologist, these skills include assessment; specialized treatments and interventions; research analysis in neuropsychology; the ability to integrate assessment findings with medical, psychosocial, and behavioral data; and the ability to interpret findings within the context of social, cultural, and ethical issues (APA, 2010; Hannay et al., 1998). When discussing the assessment competency, there are multiple components of a neuropsychological examination.

Clarifying Referral Question and Generating Testable Hypotheses

The assessment process begins before the patient enters the clinician's office, as the neuropsychologist refines the referral question based on the context of the evaluation, the examiner's professional role, and the patient's presentation (Nelson et al., 2015; Rey-Casserly et al., 2012). Supervisees initially need be taught to gather information relevant to the referral from various sources, including the referring individual, medical charts and other records, and conversations and interviews with patients and families. Set aside time to meet with supervisees to review data in order to generate specific hypotheses to be addressed via interview and testing. Touch base at points during the evaluation to refine hypotheses and revise the test battery accordingly. As supervisees grow in their autonomy, they become increasingly more competent in their ability to clarify referral questions and plan the evaluation.

History Taking

Skill in interviewing is crucial for competent neuropsychologists. The clinical interview serves multiple purposes. It is an opportunity to establish rapport, gather information relevant to the referral questions, perform an initial assessment of a patient's presentation, and obtain collateral information. In many training settings, supervisees initially observe supervisors' interview techniques and gradually increase their participation in the interview process to the point at which they are directing the interview under observation. Supervisees often utilize structured or semi-structured templates to ensure that all domains are covered and that the information they gather is complete. Typically, as the supervisee grows in experience, supervisors work with them to hone their interview skills and rely more on internal rather than external templates to structure the interview. Supervisees learn to set goals for the interview and prioritize topics that are most relevant to the referral questions. Through modeling, planning, and practice, they can become strategic in their use of open- and closed-ended questions. They integrate the data learned from patients and families with clinical observations of the patient's mental status, comportment, and insight. They learn to guide the tempo of the discussion to manage time and the flow of information, all without sacrificing rapport. Ultimately, supervisees become able to gather information and observations, refine initial hypotheses, prioritize focus of the interview, and establish a relationship with the client in an efficient yet comprehensive manner. It is at this point that they are competent in clinical interviewing.

Battery Selection

Novice supervisees will need guidance to generate a testing battery that has adequate breadth and depth with regard to cognitive and emotional domains. In discussing the battery, have the supervisee articulate why he or she chose the specific measures. Ask questions about the choices. For example, are there problems with the use of certain measures for specific types of patients (e.g., normative issues, reliability and validity issues, ease of administration and scoring)? Do the tests measure overlapping versus unique aspects of processing? As supervisees' skills develop, they learn to choose measures based on best practices for specific referral questions and exam contexts, including assessment of effort, if relevant (Nelson et al., 2015; Rey-Casserly et al., 2012). As supervisees become more experienced, they should be able to discuss psychometric issues that influence test selection, including reliability, validity, repeatability, and appropriate normative groups. This is especially true when working with special populations, such as children, older adults, very disabled individuals, and individuals from multicultural backgrounds. Finally, they learn to maximize efficiency in a way that is in line with best practices in neuropsychology.

Test Administration and Scoring

Supervisees will vary in their exposure to testing and their experience working in clinical settings. They may or may not have had coursework, practical instruction, or supervised experience in neuropsychology. Even more advanced supervisees have gaps in their experience and benefit from training on additional tests. It is best not to assume that supervisees are competent in test administration and scoring without first observing and monitoring. Supervisors should implement a system to track competence with specific measures, until supervisees are independent to work with patients. Autonomy comes from instruction, prompt corrective feedback, and experience. Moreover, accurate and fluid test administration is only part of competent testing practices. Ultimately, supervisees must be able to administer tests correctly while concurrently observing a patient's behavior, altering the testing plan based on a patient's capabilities and deficiencies, and updating clinical hypotheses. As supervisees advance, they can learn to determine how and when to test limits and techniques for "bedside" testing of functions, when a patient cannot complete testing in a standardized way.

> **REMEMBER**
>
> Don't assume supervisees are competent in test administration and scoring!

Test Interpretation

When working with inexperienced supervisees, it is best to help them to understand what individual tests measure and to develop strategies to examine test data within and across cognitive and emotional domains. With guidance, they learn to identify patterns of behavior and relate them to the functioning of neural systems. Supervisors should encourage more experienced supervisees to think more deeply about the measures we employ and increase the sophistication of their interpretations. They should explore the multidimensional nature of our tests and identify common threads that underlie performance on seemingly disparate measures. Test scores need to be integrated with test-taking behavior. Supervisees need to be taught to determine when a behavioral observation is pathognomonic for impairment versus idiosyncratic versus normal. As advanced supervisees become competent, they should interpret test data within the context of psychometric issues, including reliability, validity, and normative characteristics for different clinical groups. The most advanced supervisees will integrate evidence-based practice into their test interpretation. This includes consideration of base rates/normal variability, predictive power, sensitivity/specificity, and reliable change. This is a lot to learn. Some of the knowledge can be acquired by reading—encourage supervisees to consult textbooks, testing manuals, and research articles to solidify their understanding of the measures. It also can be demonstrated through modeling (e.g., in sample reports) and direct teaching. The supervisees' responses and written reports provide insight into their level of understanding of issues salient to test interpretation. This is a great way to monitor their growth toward competency.

CONCEPTUALIZATION AND DIAGNOSIS

Neuropsychological formulation can be overwhelming to beginning and intermediate supervisees, as it requires the integration of many points of data, as well as a solid understanding of the meaning of test data, functional neuroanatomy, and cognitive symptoms. Supervisors need to provide their supervisees with a framework to analyze patterns in neuropsychological data and guide case conceptualization. I advocate a top-down approach to synthesizing test data. Supervisees can be taught to first describe a profile in terms of its general characteristics (e.g., abnormal versus normal, lateralized, systemic, focal), and then by overarching neurocognitive syndromes (e.g., amnesia, aphasia, delirium, dementia). Following that, supervisees can gradually increase the specificity with which they analyze and describe the nature of the impairment. The next steps are to (a) determine what the patterns of performance suggest about the functioning of various neurocognitive systems, (b) link neural system dysfunction with pathological processes, and (c) engage in differential diagnosis based on the onset, course, history, and other medical data. This kind of exercise provides supervisees with a structure from which to approach even the most complex cases. Practice can take place informally in supervision and can be reinforced through case conferences or fact-finding exercises. With experience, supervisees become more efficient at formulating cases with minimal guidance. At the point of competence, case conceptualizations are sophisticated and scientific evidence is integrated into the formulation.

Treatment Planning

The major work of the neuropsychologist is not characterized as intervention in a strict sense; however, multiple aspects of the clinical interaction have the potential for therapeutic benefit. In particular, neuropsychologists integrate historical information, medical data, test results, and clinical observations into a case formulation that is the springboard for thoughtful interventions. They provide psychoeducation. They teach patients strategies for cognitive and emotional remediation that provide a basis for behavior change.

≡ *Rapid Reference 8.7*

Top-Down Process for Integrating Neuropsychological Data

Step	Description	Example
1	Describe profile in terms of general characteristics	Abnormal, non-lateralized, focal
2	Describe profile in terms of overarching neuro-cognitive syndromes	Amnesia
3	Increase specificity of nature of impairment	Impairment in verbal and visual memory encoding and consolidation as demonstrated by limited learning of an auditory and a visual pattern and rapid forgetting of what was acquired
4	Determine what patterns of performance suggest about the functioning of various neurocognitive systems	Pattern of memory performance indicates bilateral mesial temporal lobe system dysfunction
5	Link neural system dysfunction with pathological processes	Bilateral mesial temporal sclerosis
6	Engage in differential diagnosis based on onset, course, history, and other medical data	Memory deficits related to ongoing complex partial seizures that originate in the bilateral mesial temporal lobes, consistent with event related. EEG showed independent seizure onsets in the right and left mesial temporal areas and MRI showing atrophy and increased signal in both hippocampi.

When working with less experienced supervisees, it is helpful to provide guidelines for the development of recommendations. Supervisors can structure supervisees' thinking by outlining general domains to consider when developing a treatment plan. Supervisees should explicitly consider the following treatment domains: psychiatric and medical treatments, cognitive interventions, recommendations for educational/vocational settings, recommendations to improve adaptive

⬟ Rapid Reference 8.8

Treatment Domains

- Psychiatric and medical treatments
- Cognitive interventions
- Recommendations for educational/vocational settings
- Recommendations to improve adaptive functioning
- Safety concerns
- Legal issues
- Lifestyle and health changes

functioning, safety concerns, legal issues, and lifestyle and health changes. This structure provides a framework that encourages comprehensive thinking.

Recommendations should be appropriate to the assessment context and consistent with evidence-based practice (Nelson et al., 2015). Supervisors need be cognizant of treatment outcome literature and familiar with empirically supported treatments for cognitive and emotional disorders, so that they can guide supervisees to formulate effective intervention plans through recommendations.

It is important to note that not all the domains of recommendations are relevant for every case. Recommendations need to be specific to the individual case. Teach supervisees to listen carefully to their patients, as this is the most important step in determining how best to help them. Work together with supervisees to adjust recommendations so as to be practical and achievable. When reviewing the case with a supervisee, ask critical questions to develop insights into the ways in which the evaluation can be meaningful for that individual. What are the patient's/family's primary concerns? Does the patient have limitations that will hinder his/her ability to follow up on recommendations (e.g., low insight, severe memory dysfunction, paralyzing anxiety)? What treatments will best help this patient meet his/her goals?

Contextual factors also influence the appropriateness of a given recommendation, as attitudes, beliefs, demographics, and cultural variables can influence a patient's openness to and access to differing types of treatments. As supervisees achieve competency, they recommend and implement interventions that are mindful of patient preferences, individual differences, and social-cultural issues that can impact treatment application or outcome (Nelson et al., 2015; Rey-Casserly et al., 2012).

Supervisees may benefit from sample recommendations that have been made for patients with similar profiles or from similar populations. Some supervisors provide resources, such as a "recommendations library" that consists of pre-written sample recommendations, to be used as a starting point. As supervisees become more advanced, encourage them to incorporate outcomes research to guide intervention planning and strengthen recommendations.

Report Writing

Supervision surrounding report writing in neuropsychology can be particularly intense, as the written report provides insight into the supervisee's thought processes and developmental level. The goal is to move the supervisee toward a clearly expressed, well integrated report that is appropriate to the referral source, purpose of the examination, and setting. Novice supervisees typically start by writing isolated sections of the reports (e.g., the history, the results) and progress to generating more comprehensive reports over time. Supervisors can provide supervisees with templates for report writing and/or sample reports. This provides a tangible model and maximizes the likelihood that a supervisee's product will be complete and professional in nature. When supervising reports, I recommend that supervisors try not to become too caught up in writing style. It is best to focus on clarity of expression, appropriateness of content, and context. As supervisees advance their skills, they learn to prioritize information effectively according to its relevance to the specific case. They construct the report to stress key elements of the case that are essential for differential diagnosis and formulation, while minimizing superfluous information. Excess detail about issues not pertinent to the case formulation detracts from the overall clarity of the report. For example,

> **WARNING**
> ....
> Supervising the report writing component of neuropsychological assessment can be fraught! Supervisees can have quite a bit of their ego wrapped up in their writing, and critical feedback on report drafts can be particularly difficult for supervisees and the supervisory relationship.

I have seen beginning and intermediate supervisees produce multiple paragraphs describing the childhood and educational background of a typically developed elderly individual referred for a dementia screen. In these cases, a simple statement regarding development would suffice (e.g., no history of developmental or learning disability) and allow the reader to focus on more germane details such as onset, course, and presenting symptoms.

As their skills evolve toward competency, supervisees develop autonomous writing style and generate reports that are clear, appropriate, and comprehensive. They become flexible in their writing styles and adapt their reports to the needs of specific audiences. For example, they can independently determine when the case merits a lengthy, detailed document versus a concise, targeted statement.

Provision of Feedback

Providing feedback to patients and families can be one of the most rewarding activities of the practicing neuropsychologist, but it is often the case that supervisees have limited experience delivering feedback prior to the internship year. Beginning and intermediate supervisees typically have the opportunity to observe feedback sessions, but few have had the opportunity to plan and lead sessions independently. This is a skill that needs to be closely mentored. Feedback sessions are more than simple oral deliveries of neuropsychological reports. They involve not only clear and effective communication, but also clinical acumen and flexibility. Supervisees learn to be sensitive to the needs of the patient, reflect compassion in the face of difficult conversations, motivate the patient for recommended interventions, thoughtfully consider and address questions, and, at times, rapidly adjust the approach based on a patient's response. Supervisors can help supervisees structure feedback sessions, monitor the effectiveness of their communications, and prepare for the often-needed flexibility. As supervisees become more competent, they set goals for the feedback sessions, tailor their approaches based on the individual patient's characteristics (e.g., cognitive level, insight, tolerance for frustration, emotional needs), and anticipate questions that may arise during the session. They integrate awareness of salient ethical issues (e.g., related to working with vulnerable populations, patient competence, and patient safety) into their approaches and can problem solve, make decisions, and display judgment when difficult situations arise.

CONCLUSION

The emerging literature on competency-based supervision is an excellent first step to guide neuropsychologists to conceptualize the goals of supervision and methods by which we achieve and monitor progress. Ensuring that these best practices are implemented in training and that they are flexibly adapted based on the level and strengths and weaknesses of the individual supervisee will likely lead to a rewarding, beneficial, and ultimately effective training experience.

TEST YOURSELF

1. **A supervisee who has solid experience, handles typical situations well, and requires supervision in complex situations is considered:**
   (a) Proficient
   (b) Advanced
   (c) Intermediate
   (d) Novice

2. **Effective methods in supervision include:**
   (a) Modeling
   (b) Practice exercises
   (c) Direct observation
   (d) All of the above

3. **Reflective practice, self-assessment, and ethical standards are examples of:**
   (a) Functional competencies
   (b) Goals of supervision
   (c) Foundational competencies
   (d) Top-down processing

4. **Training should include psychometric issues that influence test selection. These include:**
   (a) Reliability and validity
   (b) Multicollinearity
   (c) Appropriate normative groups
   (d) B and C
   (e) A and C

Answers: 1. b; 2. d; 3. c; 4. e.

REFERENCES

American Psychological Association (APA). (2010). Specialty in clinical neuropsychology. Retrieved from https://www.apa.org/ed/graduate/specialize/neuro.aspx

Board of Directors. (2007). American Academy of Clinical Neuropsychology (AACN) practice guidelines for neuropsychological assessment and consultation. *The Clinical Neuropsychologist*, 21(2), 209–231.

Hannay, H. J., Bieliauskas, L. A., Crosson, B. A., Hammeke, T. A., Hamsher, K. D. S., & Koffler, S. P. (1998). Proceedings: The Houston conference on specialty education and training in clinical neuropsychology. *Archives of Clinical Neuropsychology*, 13(2), 160–166.

Marcopulos, B. A. (2015). Supervising and mentoring in clinical neuropsychology. Paper presented to the Pacific Northwest Neuropsychology Society. Retrieved from https://pnns.org/archive-slides

Nelson, A. P., Roper, B. L., Slomine, B. S., Morrison, C., Greher, M. R., Janusz, J., … Wodusheck, T. R. (2015). Official position of the American Academy of Clinical Neuropsychology (AACN): Guidelines for practicum training in clinical neuropsychology. *The Clinical Neuropsychologist*, 29(7), 879–904.

Rey-Casserly, C., Roper, B. L., & Bauer, R. M. (2012). Application of a competency model to clinical neuropsychology. *Professional Psychology: Research and Practice*, 43(5), 422–431.

Rodolfa, E., Bent, R., Eisman, E., Nelson, P., Rehm, L., & Ritchie, P. (2005). A cube model for competency development: Implications for psychology educators and regulators. *Professional Psychology: Research and Practice*, 36(4), 347–354.

Shultz, L. A., Pedersen, H. A., Roper, B. L., & Rey-Casserly, C. (2014). Supervision in neuropsychological assessment: A survey of training practices and perspective of supervisors. *The Clinical Neuropsychologist*, 28, 907–925.

Stucky, K. J., Busch, S., & Donders, J. (2010). Providing effective supervision in clinical neuropsychology. *The Clinical Neuropsychologist*, 24, 737–758.

Nine

SUPERVISING THERAPEUTIC ASSESSMENT

Stephen E. Finn

WHAT IS THERAPEUTIC ASSESSMENT?

Therapeutic Assessment (TA) is a semi-structured form of collaborative psychological assessment developed in the 1990s by me and my colleagues at the Center for TA in Austin, TX (Finn, 2007). TA draws heavily from techniques and principles of collaborative psychological assessment (CPA) as described by Fischer (1985/1994), Handler (2006), and Purves (2002). A defining feature of TA is that clients are seen as essential contributors to the assessment process and are involved in every step, from defining individualized *assessment questions (AQs)* to be addressed by the assessment, interpreting their test responses and experiences during the *extended inquiry (EI)* of standardized testing, participating in targeted "experiments" during the *assessment intervention session (AIS)*, making sense of test findings and tying them to daily life in the *summary/discussion session*, and reviewing and commenting on any *written feedback*, often presented in the form of a *highly accessible letter*.

Essentials of Psychological Assessment Supervision, First Edition.
Edited by A. Jordan Wright
© 2020 John Wiley & Sons, Inc. Published 2020 by John Wiley & Sons, Inc.

≡ Rapid Reference 9.1

Collaborative Steps in TA

1. Defining Assessment Questions (AQs)
2. Interpreting test responses and experiences in the Extended Inquiry (EI)
3. Participating in targeted "experiments" in the Assessment Intervention Session (AIS)
4. Tying findings to daily life in the Summary/Discussion Session
5. Reviewing written feedback in the form of a highly accessible letter

This approach is different in major ways from the traditional forms of psychological assessment that are still dominant in clinical, counseling, and educational psychology (Finn & Tonsager, 1997). Although Collaborative/Therapeutic Assessment (CTA) has spread in recent years, traditional psychological assessment—which uses testing primarily for information gathering and where there is more power differential between assessor and patient—is still the model taught in most graduate training programs (Evans & Finn, 2017).

Research has demonstrated that TA and CTA are associated with substantial benefits in many different types of clients, including decreased symptomatology, increased self-esteem and self-awareness, and more motivation for and follow-through with subsequent treatment (see Kamphuis & Finn, 2018, for a recent summary of the efficacy of TA). This has led some experts to recommend that all psychologists receive training in TA (Poston & Hanson, 2010). In fact, my experience is that in recent years an increasing number of psychologists and graduate students are seeking training and supervision in Collaborative or Therapeutic Assessment (generically called "CTA").

To date, the only published references on doing supervision/consultation in TA are chapters by Finn (1998) and Handler (2008). However, there are a number of articles in which trainees describe their experiences of being supervised when learning TA (Dietrich-Maclean & Jackson, 2017; Haydel, Mercer, & Rosenblatt, 2011; Kelley, 2016; Peters, Handler, White, & Winkel, 2008). Further, there is an interesting qualitative study of the reactions of 10 graduate students being supervised on their first TAs as part of a graduate assessment course (Smith & Egan, 2017).

SUPERVISION VS. CONSULTATION

Before describing a supervision model I have developed, I first want to make an important distinction. I define *consultation* as the process of assisting *already licensed psychologists* in their practice of TA, especially when *the consultant has no institutional or legal responsibility for the psychologists' work* or for their clients. For example, Dr. Long, a licensed psychologist in Austin, may ask for my help with a difficult TA he is conducting in his private practice. We meet several times to discuss the assessment and review the client's test materials, but Dr. Long has the option of using my comments or not. In contrast, I use the term *supervision* for contexts in which one psychologist (presumably more expert) helps another psychologist or trainee in his or her practice of TA, and *the supervisor has a legal or institutional responsibility for the outcome of the supervisee's work.* This was the arrangement in the past when I supervised clinical psychology graduate students at the University of Texas doing TA with clients referred by clinicians in the Austin community (Finn, 1998). The student trainees were practicing "under my license," and I was ultimately responsible for the outcome of the TAs they conducted. Thus, I expected the students to do what I advised, as best they could.[1]

As the reader will see, I believe that *supervision* presents a number of dilemmas that are either absent or minimized in *consultation*.

≡ Rapid Reference 9.2

Consultation vs. Supervision

Consultation	Supervision
Assisting already trained (and licensed) clinicians in their TA work	Assisting clinicians in their TA work, whether licensed and/or trained or not
Consultant has no institutional or legal responsibility for the clinician's work	Supervisor has a legal or institutional responsibility for the clinician's work
Clinician can decide to use consultant's feedback or not	Clinician should use supervisor's feedback, as the supervisor is ultimately legally responsible for the work

GOALS OF SUPERVISION/CONSULTATION IN TA

In the model I describe here, the principal goal of supervision/consultation in TA is to *enhance the consultee's knowledge, skill, confidence, and professional identity* as regards TA. A secondary goal is to help the (consultee's) client and/or referring professional to have the best experience possible. As might be obvious, in situations where the supervisor has legal or institutional responsibility for the assessment conduct and outcome, this second goal is given almost equal weight as the first. In situations where the supervisor has no legal responsibility, the primary focus is on assisting the psychologist seeking help.

ISOMORPHY BETWEEN TA WITH CLIENTS AND SUPERVISION/ CONSULTATION OF TA

Another defining feature in both supervision and consultation of TA is that I demonstrate the same core values, principles, and techniques with consultees as I do with clients, with the result that there is isomorphy (i.e., an identical form and process) between the experience of consultees and that which I hope they will provide to their clients. This gives consultees an experience of what it is like to take part in a TA, which I believe in invaluable in helping them get "in their clients' shoes" (the title of my 2007 book). Let me now elaborate these parallels.

Collaborative Approach

Although expert consultation/supervision—like psychological assessment and psychotherapy—inherently involves a power imbalance between the two individuals involved, I aspire to take a collaborative approach throughout the process. For example, I make it clear from the beginning that although I might know more about certain tests or about TA than my consultees, it is they who are in the room with their clients. Hence, it is important that they feel free to question, disagree with, or modify any suggestions I might make. When their questions or ideas lead to a deepening of my understanding of the client, I explicitly underline this, which seems to give consultees more confidence that I am open to their input. In keeping with a collaborative model, when I am listening to accounts of client–assessor

> **REMEMBER**
>
> Each moment in consultation/supervision has the potential to be collaborative. Take every opportunity to be collaborative explicitly, as much and as often as possible in the consultative/supervisory relationship.

interactions, or reviewing a video of a session, I am more likely to ask questions than to make pronouncements; for example, "I wonder if your client went into shame there, right after you said what you did? Is that possible? If so, that might help explain why he suddenly became so quiet."

Centrality of the Consultant–Consultee Relationship

Just as the working alliance between assessor and client is central to the success of TA, so I consider the consultant–consultee relationship to be of the utmost importance in supervision/consultation. TA is an incredibly complex and difficult process to learn, and, as I have stressed, it is too difficult to practice in isolation (Finn, 2007). By creating an interpersonal environment in which consultees feel helped, supported, and contained, I aspire to create a "secure base" from which they can venture into deep explorations with their clients, knowing that I am there as an anchor, support, and advisor. I also pay attention to potential disruptions in my relationship with consultees, and I endeavor to make repairs when they seem warranted—either explicitly or simply by modifying my approach.

> **DON'T FORGET**
>
> Monitor the quality of the consultant-consultee relationship continuously throughout the work together, and work toward ensuring that consultees feel supported, contained, and safe to explore their TA work with their clients.

Attentiveness to Shame

In TA with clients, assessors pay special attention to shame; we attempt to avoid eliciting shame when possible and also to intervene when clients express or experience shame during an assessment (Aschieri, 2016). Likewise, I have come to believe that shame is an immensely important phenomenon in supervision/consultation. Research has shown that supervisees often experience shame but rarely speak about it directly; also, they often avoid shame by not telling supervisors important details about their interactions with clients (Ladany, Klinger, & Kulp, 2011; Yourman, 2003). In my experience, shame increases dramatically when I suggest that consultees and I watch videos of their TA sessions together. Many of my colleagues remember "traumatic" experiences of being shamed by supervisors during their training. As best I can reconstruct, this happens generally because of the following situations: (a) the supervisor empathizes with the client and wants the client to have the best experience possible; (b) the supervisor sees errors in the way the supervisee is working with the client; (c) the supervisor feels protective of the client and loses empathy for the supervisee; (d) the supervisor shows anger, exasperation, or impatience, or even calmly "talks down" to the supervisee; and (e) the supervisee goes into shame. Such interactions, when not acknowledged and repaired, make it less likely that supervisees will discuss places of insecurity or anxiety in supervision.

I attempt to address shame in three major ways, by: (a) cultivating a supervisory relationship in which I am humble, non-judgmental, affirming, and transparent; (b) maintaining my primary focus on the supervisee (while of course also paying attention to the client); and (c) using a number of specific shame interventions (described further below) that have been developed for TA with clients (Aschieri, Fantini, & Smith, 2016; Finn, 2007). Among these, I make frequent use of judicious self-disclosure, especially about my own mistakes in developing and practicing TA. I also help supervisees find a larger context for their own "missteps;" for example, I may hypothesize that they have been recruited into a process of projective identification with a client that has led to a therapeutic disruption.

SUPERVISION TECHNIQUES IN TA

Levels of Information

One of the essential methods in TA with clients is to give feedback/provide information throughout an assessment using a schema called "levels of information" (Finn, 2007). *Level 1* information is that closest to clients' current ways of thinking; *level 2* information is slightly discrepant from clients' existing views; and *level 3* information differs in significant ways from how clients currently think about themselves and the world. I have found this same framework to be valuable in working with consultees, and in my mind one of the most frequent ways consultants elicit shame in consultees is by providing level 3 feedback before paving the way for this information to be accepted.

≡ Rapid Reference 9.3

Levels of Information in TA

Level 1. Information closest to the client's (consultee's, supervisee's) current ways of thinking

Level 2. Information that is slightly discrepant from the client's (consultee's, supervisee's) existing views

Level 3. Information that differs significant in ways from how clients (consultees, supervisees) currently think about themselves and the world

This brings me to one of the most important aspects of distinguishing *consultation* from *supervision*. In consultation, where the consultant has no professional or legal responsibility for the consultee's work, it generally is not necessary to give level 3 information to the consultee. In supervision, where the supervisor is required to maintain certain standards and ensure than an assessment is being conducted competently, it may be impossible to avoid giving level 3 feedback. The latter situation increases the likelihood of disruptions in the supervisor–supervisee relationship and of the supervisee feeling shame in response to the supervisor's comments. One way to address this complication is for the supervisor to utilize two other techniques imported directly from TA with clients: *individualized questions* and *scaffolding*.

Individualized Consultation Questions

Whether I am engaged in consultation or supervision, I ask that the person help frame our work by giving me specific questions that he/she wants me to address in each meeting. These questions serve multiple purposes, just as individualized Assessment Questions (AQs) do in TA: (a) they signal where the consultee is open to input and ensure that I am attempting to meet his/her goals for the consultation; (b) they give me information about how the consultee is currently thinking about the client and the TA, which helps me gauge what is level 1, 2, and 3 information; and (c) they help me choose among the many things I could potentially comment on.

Just as clients may not be able to immediately offer up AQs for a TA, I find that consultees often need to "tell the story" of their experience with a client before they respond to my initial query of, "What questions do you have for me?" If so, I listen carefully, mirror back what I hear, and then eventually ask again, "Where do you most want my input today?" I help to reframe questions that are overly general; for example, to statements like "I want to know if I'm doing it right," I might ask, "What particular part do you feel most unsure of?" And if questions are too specific (e.g., "What should I do for the AIS?"), I try to broaden them (e.g., "Would it be helpful to talk through your case conceptualization first, and then to discuss what to target in the AIS?").

As stressed earlier, supervision is different from consultation in that there is an existing set of often implicit "background" questions that must be addressed whether supervisees actually pose them or not. Included in these are: "Does this TA meet basic standards of competence?" and "Am I as the supervisor comfortable that this TA will reflect well on me or on our institution?" I have found that it can be useful to make such questions explicit at the beginning of the supervision process, so that a supervisee is not surprised when I give feedback that goes beyond his/her level of curiosity. (This is parallel to how one would handle an involuntary assessment in CTA, by making it clear that there are questions from third parties that must be addressed in addition to any the client might pose.) In my 1998 chapter, I wrote about how this process of sharing implicit questions aided trust and learning in a required graduate assessment course in which I was required to grade and evaluate students learning TA.

There is one other special context in which consultants may end up giving level 3 feedback: when a consultee is attempting to qualify for certification in TA.[2] Again, an explicit consultation question is extremely useful, such as "When you watch this extended inquiry, do you think it demonstrates the competencies required for certification in this step?" In this way, the potentially distressing effects of any unanticipated comments are at least mitigated by the consultee's direct request for feedback. Also, the Therapeutic Assessment Institute (TAI) faculty members maintain a particular attitude about certification in any comments we make; that is, we do not assert that we know the "right" way to work with any particular client in a certain context. The certification criteria reflect the techniques and processes that we have found most useful to date and that have been supported by empirical research. We comment on whether an interaction is "on-model" or "off-model," rather than "right" or "wrong;" this helps reduce consultees' distress when we decide together that they do not yet meet the criteria for certification.

Scaffolding

Scaffolding is a term developed by Bruner (1978) and others to describe a process whereby learners are provided temporary active assistance to help them achieve goals that are just beyond their reach. Assessors learning TA are taught how to use "half-steps" and "bottom-up" learning to help clients modify their narratives and take in potentially threatening new information (Finn, 2007; Kamphuis & Finn, 2018). "Bottom-up" learning is where instructors provide direct experiences to learners and help them draw conclusions and insights (as opposed to "top-down" learning, in which conclusions are taught first, and then learners are exposed to examples [Sun & Zhang, 2004]). Again, the same approach is used in consultation. An important principle is to use Vygotsky's Zone of Proximal Development (ZPD) and for the consultant to give just enough help to allow the consultee to achieve his/her next step, but no more (Kamphuis & Finn, 2018). Half-steps can be used in many different learning contexts. For example, in assisting with test interpretation and case conceptualization, a consultant might at first give small "mini-lectures" about the meaning of a set of test scores, or recommend something for the consultee to read. When the same material is germane again, the consultant might ask, "Do you remember what we said before about this particular test configuration? I wonder whether that's relevant here also."

Scaffolding is extremely important when watching videos of assessment sessions (or live sessions) with consultees, as there are so many things one could comment on when a trainee is first learning TA, and commenting on many of them has the potential to be completely overwhelming and discouraging. Again, I try to work from consultees' questions and to identify potential "open doors" through which to send my comments. Below is an excerpt from a consultation with Tom, a mid-career licensed psychologist who had just started to incorporate TA in his work. Tom had asked me to watch a video of an extended inquiry he had done with a young adult client about his Rorschach responses. At a previous consultation, we had discussed a video of the initial TA session Tom did with this same client.

AN EXAMPLE OF SCAFFOLDING IN TA CONSULTATION

Tom: *So please watch this clip and let me know if it's any good.*

Finn: *Is there something in particular you want me to look for?*

T: *Well, I'm not sure if I'm getting this half-step thing, and there's one place where I felt really stuck.*

SF: *OK, before we watch the extended inquiry, were there any things you noticed when administering the Rorschach?*

T: *(Shows sequence of scores) Yes. Look at all these Aggressive Content scores.*

SF: *Wow, I see that. And it looks like they are really frequent on Cards VIII, IX, and X.*

T: *I hadn't noticed that. You're right.*

SF: *Any theories?*

T: *Well, this is the guy who asked, "Why do I get so angry at times?"*

SF: *Thanks for reminding me. What are you thinking?*

T: *That maybe when he gets emotionally aroused, the anger starts showing up?*

SF: *That seems possible. Is that what you targeted in the EI?*

T: *Not quite, but you'll see.*

Tom and Finn then watch a 10-minute section of video, in which Tom tried to explore the client's AGC responses with him.

T: *So what do you think?*

SF: *I think there are some lovely moments. I was really happy about the client's statement at the end, "Maybe I'm angrier than I realize!"*

T: *Me too. That was good, right?*

SF: *Really good! That growing awareness could help him solve a lot of the puzzles he has about himself, don't you think?*

T: *Yes. But I wasn't sure I was going to get there at first.*

SF: *OK. During which part?*

T: *I felt really stuck at the beginning when I tried to point out all the aggressive things he had seen.*

SF: *Right, he balked at that, didn't he? Is that the place where you were wondering about the half-steps?*

T: *Yes. Exactly. I guess I tried to go too fast there. . . . What would be a half step?*

SF: *I'm not sure, but I wonder about saying something like, "I want to read you some of your responses and see if anything stands out for you." Then you could pick out all the AGC responses and read them and see what the client says.*

T: *I see. So try to help him see the pattern I see.*

SF: *Right, then if the information is Level 3, the client doesn't have to disagree with you. You can stay on the same side as he is.*

T: *And if he doesn't notice the pattern?*

SF: *Good question. Any ideas?*

T: *I guess I could say, "Well, I was thinking these all seem like aggressive things. What do you think?"*

SF: *Perfect! You ask the client for confirmation. And if you really think the observation is threatening, you can go even more one-down when you bring it up, like, "I'm not sure what this means, but I wonder if some people might think these things were angry or aggressive. Do they seem like that to you?"*

T: *I see. I did go too fast.*

SF: *I know how that is. It's really hard sometimes to contain and take half steps when we see something important in a client's test responses. But let's be clear, what you did didn't completely derail things. I saw you back up, and then you and the client got there together by the end.*

T: *That's right. We did. Didn't we?*

SF: *It's impossible to be perfectly attuned in an extended inquiry. We try to be, and to watch the client. But inevitably we over- and undershoot and then have to make adjustments. That is how we get in the client's shoes.*

T: *Wow. So no one can get it right all the time.*

SF: *I sure don't! And I get frustrated with myself sometimes. But I am getting better at noticing when I go too fast, and then making a shift. That helps the client feel seen and understood, because I'm adjusting myself to be more in-synch with him. . . .*

I provide this lengthy excerpt because it illustrates many of the principles and techniques of consultation in TA. One major goal was for me to practice the exact kind of containment and scaffolding with Tom that he was trying to implement with his client. My comments and suggestions were connected to Tom's supervision questions, instead of being my own non-contextualized thoughts and opinions. And whenever possible, I invited Tom to give his thoughts before offering mine, although I was willing to provide direct and specific feedback. Further, I tried to hold in mind the vulnerability any of us would feel when showing a videotape of our work to a consultant, and to use specific shame interventions developed for work with clients in TA (Aschieri et al., 2016): (a) I genuinely mirrored the positive things I saw in Tom's interactions with his client ("I think there are some lovely moments…"); (b) I contextualized the struggles he was having ("It is really hard sometimes to contain and take half-steps…"); and (c) I self-disclosed about similar struggles ("I sure don't [get it right all the time]! And I get frustrated with myself sometimes."). My hope was that by doing all these things, I would provide a bottom-up learning experience for Tom that would help him "feel his way" into the collaborative stance of an assessor doing TA. In fact, in the next session Tom and I reviewed on video, he was more collaborative with the client and more skilled in his attempts to scaffold new understandings.

≋ Rapid Reference 9.4

Managing Shame in TA Consultation/Supervision

Shame is an extremely painful emotional state that arises when we are aware that we have fallen short of our own or an important other's expectations. Research has shown that trainees often feel shame in psychotherapy supervision and that they avoid shame by not telling supervisors important information they fear will be judged. Supervisors can minimize and address shame in a variety of ways:

1. Invite supervisees to pose questions they wish to have answered during the supervision; this way they feel some control over where they will be exposed.
2. If possible, focus your comments and feedback on addressing those questions. If you must address things the supervisee has not asked about, make it clear why you must do so; e.g., "Since I am legally responsible for your work, I also need to make sure that your work meets our basic standards."
3. Use role plays, videos, and other experiential learning methods that help supervisees arrive at understandings on their own, without your having to tell them.
4. Notice and comment on things supervisees do well or points where you can see them trying. Many new things can be taught by progressively rewarding positive steps.

5. Be aware that TA is difficult to learn and that various factors can impede supervisees' learning. Be curious about supervisees' dilemmas of change in learning TA.

6. When trainees feel ashamed or embarrassed, acknowledge that such feelings are human when trying new things, common in supervision, and do not reflect some personal shortcoming of the supervisee.

7. Help supervisees find the larger context for any missteps or mistakes; e.g., special challenges posed by the client, systemic or cultural factors that are at play, or a lack of experience dealing with the client's issues.

8. Self-disclose in a judicious way about times when you've made similar mistakes.

SUPERVISION CHALLENGES IN TA

Dilemmas of Change

A central goal in TA with clients is that of identifying their *dilemmas of change*. These are areas where clients' growth, learning, and development are blocked by restraining forces connected to past traumas, biological factors, economic limitations, or their cultural/familial context (Finn, 2007). For example, an adult woman might be referred for a TA by her therapist, who is impatient with her inability to stand up for herself even after a great deal of assertiveness coaching. The TA assessor and client might come to understand that her assertiveness is blocked in part by shame about childhood sexual abuse by her father. Resolving this shame is not so easy because (a) the client feels a great deal of loyalty to her parents and is financially dependent on them, (b) in her familial/cultural group, women and girls are seen as responsible for their sexual abuse, and (c) blaming herself keeps the client from acknowledging she was not in control, which results in a great deal of fear about her current life. By appreciating this dilemma of change, the client, assessor, and referring therapist can find more compassion about her lack of assertiveness and discuss ways to address the underlying dilemma.

Similarly, in supervision/consultation in TA, various factors may interfere with a consultee's ability to learn and practice TA, and curiosity about such restraining forces is essential to keep both consultant and consultee from becoming discouraged or frustrated. Let me briefly highlight some of these potential blocks to practicing TA:

Previous Training in Traditional, Non-collaborative Assessment

Psychologists and graduate students who have previous training in traditional information-gathering assessment sometimes experience quite a lot of turmoil when beginning to learn CTA because its practices and philosophy are so different from what they learned in their initial training (Finn & Tonsager, 1997). For example, I remember one mid-career psychologist who was quite drawn to TA, but who struggled with the idea of doing extended inquiries of standardized tests. Initially, he voiced concerns in consultation about whether an EI might invalidate future scores if a client were retested. As we spoke further, he acknowledged that it was very unlikely most of his clients would ever be tested again. He then realized that he "winced" at the idea of using tests in other than strict, standardized ways (even if he had first done a standardized administration) because his early training had so emphasized the importance of standardized procedures. Practicing TA required him to manage the cautionary voices of past supervisors that he still heard in his mind when working with clients ("Don't deviate from standardized procedures!"). I suggested he read a number of case examples in the CTA casebook (Finn, Fischer, & Handler, 2012), and this helped him feel more comfortable with extended inquiries. It seemed clear that the fact I could understand and accept his internal struggle, rooted in his previous training in traditional assessment, was crucial to his being able to move forward in practicing TA.

Investment in Being Viewed as an Expert

We all become psychologists for varied reasons, and it is not uncommon that we find comfort, solace, and self-esteem in a role where we are viewed as authorities or respected test "experts." The collaborative stance of TA requires assessors to acknowledge that clients are "experts on themselves" and that clients' input is essential for understanding any test score. Some trainees seem relieved by this point of view, but others find it extremely uncomfortable. As one mid-career consultee once told me, "It's pretty breezy out there when I take off my 'white coat'!"

Anxiety About Speaking Honestly/Making Mistakes/Hurting Clients

Not surprisingly, when we step out of the role of wise, all-knowing experts whose assessment tools tell the "Truth" about clients, many of us experience anxiety about the daunting task we are undertaking in psychological assessment: to use our fallible psychological instruments and imperfect selves to help people who are in great pain and confusion about how to move forward in their lives. As Handler (2008) wrote, a fear expressed by many graduate students learning TA is that they will not be able to answer clients' assessment questions, or that the responses they give will fall flat or, worse, do harm. I have found that many trainees are confused about the distinction between Level 3 information (which might be difficult for a client to hear) and test results that are Level 1 but perhaps socially undesirable, such as, "From your Rorschach responses, it seems that your thinking is sometimes quite confused, and it might be hard for others to understand you. Is that right?" Again, in traditional assessment, assessors might never give such feedback directly to clients; thus, they never learn that many clients are relieved by the fact that someone has understood their experience and shown that it is not too terrible to discuss.

Difficulties Being Spontaneous

Another block discussed by Handler (2008) is the difficulty many trainees have learning to use themselves creatively and reacting in-the-moment to important events that arise in testing sessions without warning. Again, traditional assessment emphasizes following structured procedures and, to some degree, being circumspect with clients about one's observations. In TA, we aspire to invite clients "up on the observation deck" to witness and discuss experiences and behaviors that are relevant to their problems in living. This requires an ability to think on one's feet and to participate actively while also observing. Some trainees are able to do this more easily than others.

Lack of Deep Knowledge About Tests

Because TA is a brief therapeutic intervention, some aspiring trainees are attracted by the psychotherapeutic aspects, but lack much knowledge of psychological tests. These clinicians are sometimes quite disappointed to find out that to be skilled at TA, they need a deep grounding in standardized tests, and this can take years to acquire. Also, as assessment training declines in psychology graduate programs (Evans & Finn, 2017), I find that much of my consultation time is spent helping people with test interpretation and case conceptualization. I find that consultees often learn tests more quickly when they are actually using them with clients, as opposed to reading about them in a book or hearing lectures in a classroom.

Personal Blind Spots

Because assessors in TA aspire to get "in their clients' shoes," we are also continually challenged to "find our own version" of clients' struggles in order to empathize with them. As a result, as a consultant I am often called upon to help consultees with personal blind spots that are impeding their ability to understand and have compassion for certain clients. I have previously shared an example from my own training in which a skilled supervisor, Dr. Ken Hampton, helped me face an area of my personality I was previously unaware of (Finn, 2005). I was a 26-year-old psychology intern working on the inpatient psychiatric unit of a large county hospital, and I had been asked to assess a man, John, about my same age, who had prominent narcissistic features. John had alienated a lot of the hospital staff with his depreciating manner, and he openly put me down, telling me he could learn nothing from an inexperienced trainee. John's Rorschach was full of his dissociated shame and anxiety, but I was furious at his demeaning treatment of me and had no empathy for how his grandiose character defenses protected him from intolerable shame. One day in supervision I asked, "But why doesn't John just admit to his pain and let us help him?" Dr. Hampton then asked me if I could understand how a person "might rather hide his pain and insecurity with an air of competence and self-sufficiency rather than face the shame of admitting that he needed help" (Finn, 2005, p. 30). Suddenly, I could, and I understood not only John, but also myself in a new way. Dr. Hampton's intervention allowed me to talk to John about his assessment results in clear, kind language that proved helpful to him, explain his obnoxious behavior to the hospital staff so that they had more compassion, and reflect on some of my own relational challenges. The supervision helped identify a blind spot in me that interfered with my work with John, and that also was impacting my personal life.

> **DON'T FORGET**
>
> Find empathy for the "blocks" in assessors learning and applying TA. Think of your own development, stumbles, and challenges when learning TA. Remember that you too struggled with:
> 1. Previous training in traditional, non-collaborative assessment
> 2. Investment in being viewed as an expert
> 3. Anxiety about speaking honestly, making mistakes, and hurting clients
> 4. Difficulty being spontaneous
> 5. Personal blind spots
>
> Also, remember how difficult it can be to learn and truly understand in a deep way the tests and methods we use in assessment. Being an assessor is a huge investment and can be a steep climb.

PERSONAL TRANSFORMATION IN LEARNING TA

This leads to a point I have written about before (Finn, 2005), that practicing TA at a high level challenges clinicians to face aspects of themselves and the world they might otherwise not have encountered, and this requires, among other things, a commitment to becoming increasingly self-aware. In thinking back, I now see that all the psychologists I have supervised to the point of their being certified in TA have undergone some significant personal transformation as a result of their work with TA. I have been humbled and honored to see them engage in this kind of growth. Of course, similar changes arise when learning and doing psychotherapy, but I think such transformations may be more intense in TA, because the clients we tend to see have baffled and challenged other good psychiatrists and psychotherapists (suggesting they are not that easy to comprehend), and our tests give us a window into clients' inner worlds in a way that breaks through our defenses and coping mechanisms. Traditional assessment provides some "protection" to assessors because of its more distant interpersonal stance and its view of tests as objective instruments. When we use tests as "empathy magnifiers" to get "in our clients' shoes" (Finn, 2007), we are often stretched in ways that are personally uncomfortable.

I remember one supervisee working with a client who had a history of torturing animals. The supervisee (an animal lover, as it turned out) was repulsed by the client at first and reported feeling intense nausea during the administration of the Rorschach, which was full of sadistic and gory images. It was only through our joint discussion of the Rorschach that the supervisee came to understand that the client used sadism as a way to cope with intense feelings of powerlessness and fear related to his traumatic past. This helped him understand behavior that had previously disgusted him. Several months later, the supervisee told me our work had a major impact on him, and that he now realized he too sometimes wanted to hurt others when he felt powerless.

Using Recordings in Supervision

I have already mentioned the importance of watching videotapes of trainees working with clients as part of TA supervision, and videos present rich opportunities for personal growth in assessors. When I watch videos of my own or others' work with clients, my attention is on moment-to-moment interactions between assessor and client. I pay special attention to therapeutic disruptions and clients' shame; therefore, it is not hard to notice interactions where assessors are misattuned with clients and to follow those moments of misattunement back to assessors' own unintegrated parts of self.

Of course, this can be challenging for all of us, but my experience is that after awhile of practicing TA and watching videotapes, the shame of discovering our blind spots decreases, and curiosity and excitement predominate. Currently, as I watch my own work, I find myself more and more compassionate about my humanness. I think this attitude also shapes my interactions with consultees and helps them have more compassion for themselves.

Supervision/Consultation vs. Psychotherapy

One question that arises frequently when I am training supervisors of TA is: "What is the boundary between supervision/consultation and psychotherapy?"

This topic is highly relevant because assessors are asked to engage personally with clients during TA; thus, as already described, personal blocks that are impacting consultees' work easily come into view during TA supervision. How should one work with these? My approach is to help consultees identify and name these blocks and to work with these issues in the context of their assessments, for example, by doing role plays or watching a video in which they felt stuck and imagining other possibilities. If consultees begin to make links to their personal histories during consultation sessions (e.g., "I just realized this client is so hard for me because she reminds me of my mother"), I encourage such reflections and am happy to listen and help name dilemmas of change (e.g., "How helpful to know that! So your personal work is to remember that the client is not your mother and to find ways to respond that would have been impossible for you when you were a child"). Then the discipline of addressing consultation questions is very helpful: if a consultee asks, "What is the best way to work on this personal issue?" I might recommend psychotherapy. Otherwise, I typically wait until this question is asked. By containing discussions in our consultation sessions mainly to the consultees' interactions with clients—not friends and family—I also help them realize that if they want to work further on their personal contexts, they can do this best in psychotherapy.

Sometimes, a consultee may ask whether he/she can see me for individual psychotherapy. My policy, based on my interpretation of the ethical guidelines of the American Psychological Association (APA, 2010), is "once a client, always a client." That is, if a consultee transitions to becoming a therapy client, he/she will no longer be able to seek regular assessment consultation with me in the future. (This does not mean that client issues are off limits when I see a psychologist in psychotherapy.) In this way, I protect myself and the client from confusing dual relationships.

Personal Growth in TA Supervisors

Finally, let me speak briefly about the personal and professional challenges in doing TA consultation/supervision that create opportunities for personal growth in supervisors. Because TA consultation/supervision focuses mainly on the experience of assessors, and secondarily on the experience of clients, supervisors are very frequently asked to get in the *supervisee's* shoes. This requires us as supervisors to be empathic with the challenges of learning TA and to find compassion for earlier versions of ourselves during our training. Also, when I find myself feeling frustrated, impatient, or critical of a supervisee, I ask myself, "What is personally at stake for me in this situation?" I then typically locate either: (a) an important reality variable (e.g., the supervisee is behaving in an irresponsible way that puts me at legal risk); (b) a personal block I have not yet faced (e.g., there is some way I am over-identifying with the client and angry at the assessor for not being more attuned); and/or (c) some way where I am overly invested in the supervisee's performance (e.g., I am intent on impressing a demanding referring professional and am concerned that the supervisee is not doing a good enough job to allow this to happen). Once I am aware of the source of my impatience, I usually find it easier to support the assessor in the way that is most helpful to him/her.

CONCLUSION

Consultation/supervision in TA is a complex and demanding process, but it is simplified by the goal of applying the same core values and techniques with supervisees that we use in TA with clients. Current research suggests that supervision/training conducted in this way is valuable to supervisees and can build interest in psychological assessment in trainees who previously had strong reservations about practicing assessment (Smith & Egan, 2015). With its emphasis on reducing shame and addressing personal blocks in clinicians, supervision in TA may also be a potent way of helping assessors at many different levels of training reach a high level of clinical competence and further their personal development.

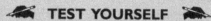

TEST YOURSELF

Choose the best answer for each item below:

1. **Which is *not* characteristic of Therapeutic Assessment with clients?**
   (a) The client is treated as an essential collaborator.
   (b) The client is not given feedback about the assessment results.
   (c) The client is asked to pose questions to be answered via the assessment.
   (d) The assessor never says anything that might challenge the client.

2. **How does Finn distinguish supervision from consultation?**
   (a) The consultant is legally responsible for the assessor's work, while in supervision this is not true.
   (b) The supervisor is legally responsible for the assessor's work, while in consultation this is not true.
   (c) The expert is paid for supervision, but not for consultation.
   (d) There is no difference between the two situations.

3. **Which of the following can be impediments to a trainee learning TA?**
   (a) Previous training in non-collaborative assessment
   (b) An investment in maintaining an expert stance with clients
   (c) Personal blind spots
   (d) All of the above
4. **How does Finn contrast supervision and psychotherapy?**
   (a) Psychotherapy leads to personal growth, but this is not true for supervision.
   (b) All supervisees should also undergo personal psychotherapy.
   (c) Supervision focuses on how personal issues influence work with clients, not on how they come into play in personal contexts.
   (d) There really is no distinction.

Answers: 1. d; 2. b; 3. d; 4. c

NOTES

1. In the remainder of this chapter, I will use the terms "consultation," "consultant," and "consultee" when making points that are general to supervision/consultation, and "supervision," "supervisor," and "supervisee" for those situations where there is a formal training or legal relationship between the two parties.
2. The Therapeutic Assessment Institute offers a certification process for psychologists who wish to know whether they are practicing TA in the way we have found most useful (Therapeutic Assessment Institute, 2018).

REFERENCES

American Psychological Association (APA). (2010). Ethical principles of psychologists and code of conduct including 2010 amendments. Retrieved from http://www.apa.org/ethics/code/index.aspx

Aschieri, F. (2016). Shame as a cultural artifact: A call for reflexivity and self-awareness in personality assessment. *Journal of Personality Assessment, 98*(6), 567–575. https://doi.org/10.1080/00223891.2016.1146289

Aschieri, F., Fantini, F., & Smith, J. D. (2016). Collaborative/Therapeutic Assessment: Procedures to enhance client outcomes. In S. Maltzmann (Ed.), *Oxford handbook of treatment processes and outcomes in counseling psychology* (pp. 241–269). New York, NY: Oxford University Press.

Bruner, J. S. (1978). The role of dialogue in language acquisition. In A. Sinclair, R. J. Jarvelle, & W. J. M. Levelt (Eds.), *The child's concept of language* (pp. 241–256). New York, NY: Springer-Verlag.

Dietrich-MacLean, G., & Jackson, P. (2017). Using advanced training to build collegial relationships in therapeutic assessment practice. *The TA Connection*, 5(1), 8–12.

Evans, F. B., & Finn, S. E. (2017). Training and consultation in psychological assessment with professional psychologists: Suggestions for enhancing the profession and individual practices. *Journal of Personality Assessment*, 99(2), 175–185. https://doi.org/10.1080/00223891.2016.1187156

Finn, S. E. (1998). Teaching Therapeutic Assessment in a required graduate course. In L. Handler & M. Hilsenroth (Eds.), *Teaching and learning personality assessment* (pp. 359–373). Mahwah, NJ: Erlbaum.

Finn, S. E. (2005). How psychological assessment taught me compassion and firmness. *Journal of Personality Assessment*, 84, 27–30.

Finn, S. E. (2007). *In our clients' shoes: Theory and techniques of Therapeutic Assessment*. Mawah, NJ: Erlbaum.

Finn, S. E., Fischer, C. T., & Handler, L. (2012). *Collaborative/Therapeutic Assessment: A casebook and guide*. Hoboken, NJ: Wiley.

Finn, S. E., & Tonsager, M. E. (1997). Information-gathering and therapeutic models of assessment: Complementary paradigms. *Psychological Assessment*, 9, 374–385.

Fischer, C. T. (1985/1994). *Individualizing psychological assessment*. Mawah, NJ: Routledge.

Handler, L. (2006). The use of Therapeutic Assessment with children and adolescents. In S. Smith & L. Handler (Eds.), *Clinical assessment of children and adolescents: A practitioner's guide* (pp. 53–72). Mawah, NJ: Erlbaum.

Handler, L. (2008). Supervision in therapeutic and collaborative assessment. In A. Hess, K. Hess, & T. Hess (Eds.), *Psychotherapy supervision: Theory, research, and practice* (Vol. 2, pp. 200–222). Hoboken, NJ: Wiley.

Haydel, M. E., Mercer, B. L., & Rosenblatt, E. (2011). Training assessors in therapeutic assessment. *Journal of Personality Assessment*, 93(1), 16–22.

Kamphuis, J. H., & Finn, S. E. (2018). Therapeutic Assessment in personality disorders: Toward the restoration of epistemic trust. *Journal of Personality Assessment*. https://doi.org/10.1080/00223891.2018.1476360

Kelley, D. (2016). Therapeutic Assessment: An experience with consultation. *The TA Connection*, 4(1), 14–18.

Ladany, N., Klinger, R., & Kulp, L. (2011). Therapist shame: Implications for therapy and supervision. In R. L. Dearing & J. P. Tagney (Eds.), *Shame in the therapy hour* (pp. 307–322). Washington, DC: American Psychological Association.

Peters, E. J., Handler, L., White, K. G., & Winkel, J. D. (2008). "Am I going crazy, doc?": A self psychology approach to Therapeutic Assessment. *Journal of Personality Assessment*, 90, 421–434.

Poston, J. M., & Hanson, W. M. (2010). Meta-analysis of psychological assessment as a therapeutic intervention. *Psychological Assessment*, 22, 203–212.

Purves, C. (2002). Collaborative assessment with involuntary populations: Foster children and their mothers. *The Humanistic Psychologist*, 30, 164–174.

Smith, J. D., & Egan, K. N. (2015). Trainee and client experiences of Therapeutic Assessment in a required graduate course: A qualitative analysis. *Journal of Personality Assessment*, 99(2), 126–135.

Smith, J. D., & Egan, K. N. (2017). Trainee and client experiences of Therapeutic Assessment in a required graduate course: A qualitative analysis. *Journal of personality assessment*, 99(2), 126–135.

Sun, R., & Zhang, X. (2004). Top-down versus bottom-up learning in cognitive skill acquisition. *Cognitive Systems Research*, 5, 63–89.

Therapeutic Assessment Institute (2018). Certification in Therapeutic Assessment. Retrieved from www.therapeuticassessment.com

Yourman, D. B. (2003). Trainee disclosure in psychotherapy supervision: The impact of shame. *Journal of Clinical Psychology*, 59(5), 601–609.

Ten

SUPERVISING PSYCHOLOGICAL ASSESSMENT REPORT WRITING

A. Jordan Wright
Hadas Pade

Perhaps one of the toughest and most frustrating aspects of supervision during the assessment process is the actual overseeing of report writing. One reason for this difficulty and frustration is because the style of writing for assessment reports is unlike the style for any other discipline, and it is unlikely that assessment report writing style aligns all that well with any other type of writing training any individual has ever received. Another primary reason for difficulty and frustration is that there are probably as many different styles and idiosyncrasies in assessment report writing as there are assessment supervisors in the world. That is, each of us has our own unique style, requirements, and ultimate expectations for the way supervisees write reports. A third reason, and one that should not be overlooked, is that students are often simply not trained well enough in writing good reports. There may be good reasons for this (including needing the classroom time to ensure reliable and valid test administration, scoring, and interpretation, as well as understanding that report writing varies so widely in the field), but Ready, Santorelli, Lundquist, and Romano (2016) found that, when evaluating the quality of students' assessment skills, "report writing was the skill that needed the most improvement according to internship directors" (p. 330). This is not limited to students either; Evans and Finn (2016) noted important concerns about the quality of assessment reports in the field in

Essentials of Psychological Assessment Supervision, First Edition.
Edited by A. Jordan Wright.
© 2020 John Wiley & Sons, Inc. Published 2020 by John Wiley & Sons, Inc.

general. This chapter cannot encompass all the specific details on report writing that may be unique to each supervisor; rather, this chapter will focus on some broad recommendations when supervising the writing of assessment reports.

REPORT EXPECTATIONS

Supervisors vary in how rigid they are about what final psychological assessment reports look like. Knowing and understanding how rigid or flexible you are as a supervisor in what you expect to see at the end can help determine how to make your expectations for the report itself explicit to supervisees. In general, the more structured you are in what you expect the end product to be, the more helpful it can be to provide specific written sample reports to your supervisees. Of course, providing written examples presents pros and cons; supervisees may simply adapt report examples with their own findings, without developing their own style, their own voice, or even (at its worst) working to understand the data more deeply. On the other hand, making a supervisee "guess" as to what you as a supervisor want to see, when that is pretty structured and inflexible, sets both up for a great deal of frustration. One compromise that works for some is to provide a template only, rather than full example reports. This is especially useful for those supervisors who are less concerned with specific structure, particular wording within sections, or other such details, but rather care more that supervisees are communicating (however they are writing the information) clearly. Supervisees often come to us with habits though, both good and bad, learned from their training and previous supervisors. Determine for yourself, as a supervisor, how flexible you are willing to be with wording. (A middle ground may be a template with clear guidance within each section about what is expected.)

Full disclosure: the first author on this chapter tends to give a great number of sample reports (such as those presented in Wright, 2010, and Groth-Marnat & Wright, 2016), not feeling the need for each supervisee to "reinvent the wheel" and encouraging each of them to "plagiarize" freely. For example, if there is a clear description of a specific subtest on the WISC-V, there is no need to tailor the language any differently than it has been presented in any of those examples; supervisees need not "make it their own" in any way.

Supervisors should not underestimate just how many errors make it into written reports, even by fully independent professionals (for examples of just cognitive score data errors, see Belk, LoBello, Ray, & Zachar, 2002; Erdodi, Richard, & Hopwood, 2009; Kuentzel, Hetterscheidt, & Barnett, 2011; Loe, Kadlubek, & Marks, 2007; Oak, Viezel, Dumont, & Willis, 2018; Styck & Walsh, 2016). Even the more hands-off supervisors should be vigilant about the accuracy of information that is included in the final reports. It is recommended that at some point in the writing process (often the best time is when a supervisee submits a first draft), the supervisor comb through the report and the raw data to ensure that all data are aligned and accurate throughout. This is tedious. There is simply no way around it, though. Some supervisors use intermediate supervisors (such as post-docs) to do this process for them. As long as the supervisor is confident that all the information in the final report is at least accurate, even a report that is not optimally written will at least be defensible.

> **REMEMBER**
>
> Mistakes find their way into reports too often. Do not take shortcuts when supervising this aspect of report writing. Ensure that all data included in the report are accurate.

While *accuracy* is the foundation of any quality assessment report, the two other most important qualities for a report are *clarity* and *meaningfulness* (Pade, Summer 2018b; Pade, Winter 2018a). Supervisors can use the "MAC" (meaningful, accurate, and clear) report framework (or "CAM" report framework, depending on which author of this chapter you ask) to orient their supervisees to what they expect in terms of overall qualities of a report (beyond the structure). Supervisees should be guided by their supervisors to ensure that all of their (valid) findings and assertions are presented as clearly as possible, with the supervisee having "clarif[ied] their thinking and crystalize[d] their interpretations" (Groth-Marnat & Wright, 2016, p. 32). Supervision may include helping supervisees pare down their jargon-filled language, disentangle words from computer-generated test reports, simplify interpretations, and condense data to enhance clarity.

Meaningfulness may be the most difficult of the three to achieve in an assessment report, partly because we spend so much time training and supervising accuracy, and to a lesser extent clarity. Many have written about how important it is for reports to be specifically useful to the particular stakeholders (e.g., Bram & Peebles, 2014; Groth-Marnat & Wright, 2016; Schneider, Lichtenberger, Mather, & Kaufman, 2018). Schneider et al. (2018), for example, discuss three levels of test interpretation and related writing, including *concrete* (describing test scores with no interpretation), *mechanical* (describing differences in test scores with limited interpretation), and *individualized* (integrating data and offering person-oriented interpretations), with the last type being the most useful to consumers. On a larger scale, conclusions should be as meaningful, and recommendations as useful, as possible (see the chapter in this text on supervising recommendations). Supervisors often need to help supervisees understand how

DON'T FORGET

Evaluate yourself as a supervisor and how structured versus flexible you are in what you expect final reports to look like. The more structured you are, the more helpful it is to provide supervisees with sample reports they can model even specific sentences on.

to make information, interpretations, assertions, and ultimately conclusions and recommendations more meaningful to those who will be reading the report.

A final note is about editing of assessment reports. Supervisors will differ, and indeed may vary depending on the developmental level of the supervisee, in how much they will offer feedback versus directly edit assessment reports. While it is common for supervisors to edit reports, especially earlier in supervisees' training, the extent to which they do so warrants attention. That is, while the ultimate goal and responsibility is a helpful, adequate product for whoever the client or stakeholder is, supervisors need to note that heavily editing reports may render them less reflective of the supervisee's actual work. This may or may not be important, depending on how the reports may be used; for example, a graduate student may redact a report and submit it for an application to internship, in which case the actual authorship of the report is critical. On the other hand, there are certainly examples, such as in forensic work, in which a supervisor may need to increase his or her level of editing for the benefit of the client. Rather than recommending how much direct editing should occur within the report writing process, we simply recommend that the supervisory dyad be cognizant of this issue throughout their work.

SUPERVISION EXPECTATIONS

While every stage in assessment supervision entails some negotiation between supervisor and supervisee about how they will interact, the stage of report writing may include the greatest need for clarity on the part of the supervisor. Some supervisors are extremely hands-on, detail-oriented, and (dare we say) even nitpicky when it comes to written reports (note that this is not meant to be pejorative in any way—many supervisors are nitpicky because they *have to be* nitpicky, both in order to produce quality reports and to cover their own ... selves ... in case these reports end up in court at some point, for example). Other supervisors are quite hands-off and review a final draft of a report, making minor edits or comments. Many supervisors fall in between these two extremes. Supervisees should know ahead of time what kind of supervisor they will have at this stage of the process (which may be starkly different than the type of supervisor they had during the rest of the process, despite it being the same person!). Supervisees are less likely to be anxious, to procrastinate, or to be frustrated if they have a clear picture of how involved their supervisor will be in the writing process.

Additionally, supervisors should be explicit about their expectations related to timeliness of report writing. Many supervisors ask their supervisees to complete sections of reports as they can; for example, the presenting problem and relevant background information sections can often be completed after a clinical interview, well before the actual testing has occurred. If the supervisor wants that section drafted for review as soon as possible, he or she should make this explicit at the beginning of the supervisory relationship. Alternatively, if the supervisor expects a full draft of the report once all data have been collected and discussed in supervision, this should be made clear as early in the supervisory relationship as possible as well. There is a theme in the supervision of report writing, and it is *clarity*. Supervisors need to take great care to be as clear as possible about all expectations throughout the process of writing up assessment reports. This can provide not only realistic goals for supervisees to meet, but also a context within which to evaluate the progress of supervisees in their report-writing work.

> **REMEMBER**
>
> Make all expectations as *clear* as possible! That includes expectations for timeliness, style, content of reports, and the type of interaction and collaboration between supervisor and supervisee during the process.

SPECIFIC SUPERVISION STRATEGIES

Thinking Developmentally About Supervision

As with other areas of the assessment process, it can be extremely useful and supportive to frame report writing within a developmental context. For example, as part of National Council of Schools and Programs in Professional Psychology (NCSPP)'s Competency Developmental Achievement Levels (2007), within the assessment competency, report writing comes up first within the developmental level of beginning internship, at which point they recommend that students should be able to communicate findings in written form (presumably decently well or clearly), then at the point of graduation from a doctoral program, at which point they recommend that students should have the ability to communicate their findings in writing *appropriately*, to relevant audiences. Based on these expectations, if you are supervising someone during his or her doctoral program, it would be unrealistic to expect a fully "appropriate" report as a first draft. In practice, even when supervising a licensed, doctoral-level psychologist on assessment report writing, we find that first drafts are often not fully adequate! But supervisors need to be okay with less-than-fully-skilled drafts of reports, not becoming frustrated, understanding that supervisees are in supervision for a reason (whether legal/ethical, because they are not yet licensed, or simply to learn and grow). Having this developmental attitude can decrease supervisors' frustration and convey a growth mindset to supervisees, which can be extremely empowering.

As part of the developmental framework, as discussed in the Introduction of this book, supervisors are encouraged to evaluate previous written reports at the beginning of the supervisory relationship, in order to assess already existing writing habits, strengths, and areas of growth. Doing this kind of first evaluation can help supervisors set realistic goals and benchmarks with supervisees, determining whether supervisees are "ready" to write an entire report draft independently to begin with, whether certain component parts or aspects of reports will need more explicit guidance, and whether concrete guidance or examples will be necessary to write a report the way you as a supervisor want it written. From a developmental perspective, consider Vygotsky's (1980) zone of proximal development; supervisors should think about which components of writing a report are fully within a supervisee's skill set and which supervisees cannot complete on their own, but can with specific assistance. Supervisors should provide an appropriate environment for supervisees to complete difficult components of report writing, and they should ultimately figure out exactly what supports are needed for supervisees to complete the most difficult aspects of report writing (Wass & Golding, 2014).

Determining appropriate supports may require a trial and error approach with each individual supervisee, and it may require some renegotiation as the process unfolds. It may also require supervisors to check in regularly and repeatedly with supervisees to determine what supervisees understand and do not understand, can do and cannot do, and even what they feel is helpful and not in the supervision process. An example of a strategy for scaffolding their writing skills learning is taking something that they have written and transforming it deliberately and explicitly in front of them, literally saying aloud your thought process as you do so. This can be extremely effective, for example, when supervisees are writing about specific test scores that need to become more meaningful in a report. Going through this process once or twice in supervision can help supervisees gain that next level of skill and apply it throughout the rest of their reports.

When thinking developmentally about writing assessment reports, supervisors should always remember that, regardless of how…in process…first drafts are, supervisees have strengths that they are bringing to the process. Supervisors need to positively reinforce any and every aspect possible of their supervisees' report writing skills (e.g., Thow & Murray, 2001). This cannot be understated. Supervisees need to hear and know that they are doing well, even when we give them constructive feedback on their work. This is at the heart of a developmental perspective. While their work will not yet be perfect, they are doing the best they can at their current developmental level, and this fact should not go unacknowledged.

> **DON'T FORGET**
> ....
> Be supportive! Offer praise and positive reinforcement for aspects of the report writing process that the supervisee is doing well, whatever it is.

SPA Framework

Without reiterating how supervision can effectively use the Society for Personality Assessment [SPA] (2015) framework's report review form (rubric) from the first chapter in this book on using guidelines, it is important to note that the rubric is meant to be applied to assessment reports (and drafts). While there is no one best way to use the rubric in supervision, some supervisors have used it as is or adapted it for use as a formative evaluation tool in supervision (Pade, Stolberg, Baum, Clemence, & Wright, 2018). Supervisees can rate their own report drafts throughout the writing process to determine how strong the drafts are—the rubric provides a concrete, tangible breakdown of the major components of "good" assessment reports, which are generally applicable across setting, type of assessment, and circumstance. Other supervisors use the rubric as a more formal evaluation tool in supervision, rather than a self-evaluation. However it is used, the rubric can provide a more structured, objective way to evaluate component parts, aspects, and qualities of supervisees' reports.

Diversity

Critical at every stage of the assessment process, regardless of type of assessment, setting, or context, be especially mindful of diversity during the process of supervising report writing (e.g., Yalof, 2018). Diversity issues within the relationship between supervisor and supervisee can emerge as important during the process, as will diversity issues related to the client being assessed. Language is important (for a fascinating, though dense, seminal essay on the topic, see Olson, 1977), and supervisors need to evaluate report drafts for any evidence of possible biased (culturally or otherwise) language. An area that often needs close attention is the language around cultural identifiers. While it is often beneficial to use clients' own language around how they culturally self-identify, there are many debates in the literature about different cultural identifiers. For example, there is debate about using person-first or identity-first language when writing about people with disabilities (or disabled people, if using identity-first language; Dunn & Andrews, 2015). Another example is the term "Latinx," which is also debated in the literature, as some find it progressive, while others argue that it is elitist and unnecessarily gender-neutral, leading to genderblind sexism (Trujillo-Pagán, 2018; Vidal-Ortiz & Martínez, 2018). Supervisors need to be aware of current trends in these areas, and report drafts should be scanned for both bias and inappropriate cultural identifiers.

One specific topic that merits noting is the provision of report writing supervision to supervisees who are English language learners (ELL) or use English as a second language (ESL; the remainder of this section will use the term ELL). While not much is written specifically around supervising psychological assessment report writing with ELL supervisees, supervisors need to be aware when working with these supervisees that they will have different, specific needs from most other supervisees. Even strong clinical competence and skill in the entire assessment process can easily be overshadowed by writing errors that are typical of ELL supervisees (Pade, 2016a). Typical writing errors can include the misuse of adverbs, adjectives, tense, plural possessives, and overall poor or problematic sentence structure (Folse, 2009). Supervisors need to differentiate clearly whether problems in the report are related to weak psychological assessment skills, such as interpreting or explaining test results; weak writing that is independent of ELL status, such as poor organization or uneven amounts of details; or more surface writing errors that are typical of ELL writers, such as awkward sentence structure and misuse of tense (Pade, 2016a). Supervisors should also be aware that problems in writing could be some combination of these three factors.

When working with ELL supervisees, supervisors need to make reasonable accommodations and offer extra supports throughout the report writing process. When possible (and not clinically contraindicated), non-native speakers need more time than is typical to draft reports, which is a challenge on its own, as supervisees' schedules are often overwhelming (Pade, 2016a). Nilsson and Anderson (2004) noted that "compared with U.S. students, international students may need to depend more on their supervisors for advice, support, training, and validation" (p. 310). Aligned with this, supervisors may consider writing collaboratively during supervision with their ELL supervisees, in order to effectively communicate on paper the concepts that the supervisee articulates.

≡ Rapid Reference 10.1

Working with ELL Supervisees

When working with supervisees who are ELL or use English as a second language, supervisors need to evaluate whether report writing problems reflect:

1. Weak psychological assessment skills, such as interpreting or explaining test results
2. Weak writing that is independent of language-status, such as general organization or uneven amounts of details
3. Writing errors typical of ELL, such as awkward sentence structure or misuse of tense
4. Some combination of the above

Thinking About Varied Audiences

A referral for a psychological assessment can come from a variety of sources, addressing a multitude of referral questions, and thus the written report may be shared with multiple individuals, each constituting a different *audience*. Bram and Peebles (2014) discuss the notion "that many non-testing clinicians have come to believe that psychological testing offers little in terms of therapy guidelines beyond what a good clinical interview provides" (p. 3). This attitude belies a deep problem with the reports that emerge from assessments, and it is undoubtedly shared not just by treating clinicians about therapy, but by many other potential referral sources about their own needs and wants. These attitudes can be traced back to the written report, and part of the issue includes a limited understanding or recognition of writing specifically to meet the needs of the report's audience.

Writing a report for the client directly may differ in some ways from one written for a school or licensing board, for a third-party provider, or for the court. While some of the underlying components for an effective and meaningful report will stay the same (e.g., presenting accurate data, justifying diagnostic impressions), the length, tone, attitude, wording, format, and inclusion of data may vary significantly. Supervisors should make explicit the questions about report audience. Bram and Peebles (2014), Flower and Hayes (1981), and Allyn (2012) offer helpful guidance for framing questions to supervisees about how to frame a report. For example, some questions may include, "Do we know who our primary audience is, as well as potential secondary audiences?" (It is always important to consider that any report may end up in court, for any number of reasons.) Others may include, "What does our reader really need from this assessment/report?"; "What are the take-home messages our readers need in order to be most helpful to the client?"; "How might the reader use the information presented in this report?"; and "How might someone *misuse* this report in a way that could potentially be harmful to the client or others?" Asking these questions explicitly of supervisees earlier in their training, then perhaps posing them as explicit thought questions for supervisees later in their learning, can help them think critically about how they are framing their reports.

While accuracy in reports is obviously critical, so are tone and choice of language. Supervisors should address these issues both before the writing process

≡ Rapid Reference 10.2

Understanding the Report Audience

Some questions to pose to supervisees about the report audience *before writing*:

1. Who is our primary audience/reader?
2. Who are potential secondary audiences/readers (including a court)?
3. What does our reader really need from this assessment/report?
4. What are the take-home messages our readers need in order for this report to be as helpful as possible?
5. How might the reader use the information presented in this report?
6. How might someone *misuse* this report in a way that could potentially harm the client or someone else?

Some questions to pose to supervisees about the report audience *after drafting*:

1. Are the structure, language used, and overall tone appropriate for our identified primary audience?
2. Are the structure, language used, and overall tone appropriate for our identified potential secondary audiences?
3. Did we clearly, succinctly, and comprehensively address the identified needs of the reader of this report?
4. Are the take-home messages from the report that we intended to get across easily identifiable and clear enough not to be easily misinterpreted?
5. Did we write in a way that makes clear the new understanding we want the reader to gain about the client?
6. Did we take steps to prevent any reader from being able to misinterpret our writing, conclusions, and recommendations?

begins and after a report has been drafted, in order to set goals and expectations, then see whether the supervisee was successful in meeting them. Supervisees (especially earlier in their training) often believe that formal and professional writing means using "fancy" words and jargon-based terminology; this is a misconception that should be evaluated and stamped out as early as possible by supervisors. Similarly, supervisors need to help supervisees "remember" what certain words mean to those not in a mental health profession. For example, the word "trauma" means something specific to those savvy about the DSM-5, requiring "[e]xposure to actual or threatened death, serious injury, or sexual violence" (American Psychiatric Association, 2013, p. 271), whereas the same word to others has a much broader and less specific meaning (usually related to negative events). Choosing language very deliberately is important in writing strong and useful assessment reports, and understanding the potential audiences/readers is key in this task.

Schneider et al. (2018) emphasize that understanding who the audience of a report will be can help guide the supervisee to write empathically, attentive to the needs of the reader, and to adopt "a style that best communicates what is useful and true" (p. 40). They identify one of the primary goals of any report as helping "guide the reader to a new understanding of the examinee's difficulties" (p. ix); this requires understanding who the reader is and what the reader's new understanding should be from the report. Ultimately, evaluating whether or not a report has clearly led the primary audience/reader to this new understanding is critical. Supervisors can remind supervisees of these goals, and the supervisory dyad should always ask themselves at the drafting stage of the process whether or not they are meeting them.

Supervisee Procrastination

Procrastination of academic tasks is a complex, often multiply determined behavior that involves both cognitive and emotional components (Beswick, Rothblum, & Mann, 1988; Brownlow & Reasinger, 2000; Chun Chu & Choi, 2005; Visser, Korthagen, & Schoonenboom, 2018). Despite a great deal of empirical inquiry, there is still no widespread agreement as to why individuals do it (Katz, Eilot, & Nevo, 2014; Klingsieck, Grund, Schmid, & Fries, 2013; Steel, 2007; Visser et al., 2018). Supervisors need to remember that writing reports is complex, time-consuming, and tedious, and it can be intimidating and overwhelming to supervisees (and even the best of us!). Other factors that may contribute to procrastination include supervisees idealizing their supervisors and feeling generally inadequate (Handler & Hilsenroth, 2013; Yalof, 1996); report writing simply not being enjoyable to supervisees (Visser et al., 2018); or even some supervisees thriving on the time pressure related to putting off tasks (Chun Chu & Choi, 2005). Regarding the latter, Chun Chu and Choi (2005) identified two different "types" of procrastinators: *passive* procrastinators, who postpone work because of psychological and other roadblocks that impede their ability to work in a timely fashion, and *active* procrastinators, who purposely delay tasks because they prefer and thrive off of time pressure, and ultimately complete tasks successfully and on time. Taken together, there may be many reasons—logistic, practical, emotional, psychological, and even relational (resistance toward supervisors is not unheard of!)—that contribute to procrastination.

Here we are offering some guidance for dealing with supervisee procrastination on writing reports. The first step is to evaluate what kind of procrastination is occurring. If it is active procrastination, then breaking the overarching task of writing a whole report into component parts and providing concrete deadlines for each of those component parts can facilitate the supervisee's completion of the work. There is not a true measure or reliable way to assess whether the supervisee is an active procrastinator, so we recommend that you engage in a conversation to determine if this is the case. Ask about previous experiences with procrastination (sometimes testing a deadline for a component of the writing process can help with the determination). If the procrastination is passive, then it is important to next evaluate what phase of procrastination the supervisee is engaged in.

Visser et al. (2018) suggested that there are three phases of procrastination: the first phase, which they termed the *forethought and planning phase*, occurs before any work on the report has begun. This phase is often where supervisees get stuck, unable to sit down and simply start writing. The second phase, which they termed the *monitoring performance and motivation phase,* occurs during the writing process, once the supervisee has already begun the task of working on the report. The *third phase, after the work has been completed,* is not as important for the current discussion. So the supervisor's task is to determine whether the supervisee is having difficulty actually starting or whether he or she is writing and it is going slowly or is difficult, or there is some other reason the supervisee cannot write a specific component. If the supervisee has begun writing and is having difficulty with certain sections, then the

> ### **DON'T FORGET**
> ....
> Writing reports is time-consuming, and not just for supervisees! Make sure you are realistic about how much time you will spend supervising the process and editing reports, and try not to get too frustrated when you yourself procrastinate!

supervisor should offer straightforward, concrete supports to help him or her continue to write. These may include samples, resources (such as books that help with certain sections), or even writing sections together.

If the supervisee is having difficulty with initiating writing, the supervisor should work with the supervisee to determine some of the underlying reasons. Remember that there may be multiple reasons for procrastination, all occurring at the same time, some logistical, some cognitive, and some emotional. Always consider psychological processes like self-efficacy, feelings of intimidation or being overwhelmed, and lack of enjoyment in the writing process. For this last problem, supervisors can simply empathize, commiserate, and potentially cheer-lead the writing process. It can be very gratifying and validating for a supervisee to hear from a supervisor that the writing process can indeed be tedious, boring, and frustrating. However, it can also be energizing to encourage supervisees to—for the time being—skip to the "more fun" parts of writing, such as the case formulation/conceptualization (often the most intimidating section, but also the most interesting and exciting to work on). When confidence is an issue, Handler and Hilsenroth (2013) recommend providing "carefully orchestrated success experiences" (p. 447) in supervision. These may include very unambitious writing expectations (like completing a mental status evaluation before the next in-person supervision session) that are easy for a supervisee to complete and receive positive reinforcement for. Some supervisees may just need emotional encouragement, and others may need specific positive reinforcement for what has already been done, whether part of the present assessment (such as having done a great job interpreting tests or organizing the background information) or evaluation of previous work (such as reinforcing previous work on a report, even if it is one that was submitted early in the supervisory relationship for developmental evaluation and has nothing to do with the work you are currently doing).

When supervisees are overwhelmed with the task of writing an assessment report, concrete resources can be extremely helpful. These can include specific structure, such as helping supervisees break the task into multiple component parts or offering specific deadlines for parts of the report. Additionally, some supervisees benefit from more sample reports or resources that can help with the writing, such as texts with sample reports or guidance on specific sections of reports. Finally, when inertia is the supervisee's enemy, sitting down together and starting to write some sections collaboratively can be a powerful tool in helping with momentum. Of course there will be times when a supervisee simply does not follow through on work, at which point a supervisor will need to give clear feedback on any more formal evaluation forms.

⇌ Rapid Reference 10.3

Guidance on Dealing with Supervisee Procrastination

1. Evaluate what type of procrastination is likely occurring.
   a. If *passive*, go to Step 2.
   b. If *active*, give concrete deadlines for component parts of the writing process.
2. Determine what phase of procrastination the supervisee is in.
   a. If the forethought/planning phase, go to Step 3.
   b. If the monitoring performance/motivation phase, go to Step 4.
3. Identify potential underlying reasons (including evaluating previous reports to help understand supervisee's skill level). Consider:
   a. Low confidence/feelings of inadequacy
   b. Logistical barriers, such as time management and competing demands
   c. Feelings of intimidation and being overwhelmed
   d. Lack of enjoyment of the process
4. Offer specific guidance (including concrete advice, skills, and resources) and support (including building the supervisee's confidence).

Potential types of support:

If *confidence* is an issue:
- Offer "carefully orchestrated success experiences" (Handler & Hilsenroth, 2013, p. 447) in supervision.
- Offer active emotional support and encouragement.
- Offer positive feedback about what has been done so far (either in the current process, or about previous reports).

If the supervisee is *overwhelmed*:
- Offer more structure.
- Offer more sample reports.
- Meet face-to-face, and even consider writing some components together.

Supervision Problems

There will be moments in every supervisor's professional life when supervision does not go as planned, or go well at all. This is certainly the case when supervising report writing, which can be fraught with landmines to navigate. While not specific to supervising writing of assessment reports or to supervising the assessment process, supervisors need to know how to handle relationship difficulties between themselves and their supervisees, when and if they arise. Grant, Schofield, and Crawford (2012) offer a framework for handling difficulties within the supervisory relationship. They recommend *relational strategies*, including empathizing, validating, and modeling, to shore up the supervisory alliance and ensure that supervisees are in an emotional space to "hear" feedback. Further, they recommend *reflective strategies*, such as ongoing monitoring, being patient, and trying to contextualize supervisees' behavior and work products, when the problems relate to actual clinical material, which is often the case with report writing. Finally, they recommend *confrontive strategies*, such as becoming directive, confronting problems directly, referring for personal therapy or remediation, and taking formal action, when the problems relate to problematic supervisee behavior (such as ethical breaches), competence problems (such as not adhering to deadlines in the report writing process), and other supervision-impeding behaviors.

We further suggest that supervisors not be shy about consulting with colleagues, peers, or their own mentors when trying to deal with supervisory problems. Gaining another perspective on what may be going on in the supervisory relationship can be invaluable in helping to rectify problems. As psychologists are lifelong learners (Taylor & Neimeyer, 2015; Webster, 1971), we always need to be open to receiving feedback on our work, no matter how "expert" we are.

> **REMEMBER**
>
> When facing problems in the supervisory relationship, which can emerge during the negotiation of report writing, be relational (empathize and validate) and reflective (continue to monitor and assess the nature of the problem). Then confront the problem, as appropriate, and consult colleagues, peers, or mentors, as needed!

CONCLUSION

Writing psychological assessment reports is complex, and supervising this process requires flexibility, savvy, and grace on the part of the supervisor. The same "problem" of a weak first draft (or even a missing one) can have a myriad of underlying causes, sometimes making the supervisor long for a psychological assessment of the supervisee! The relationship between supervisor and supervisee during the report writing process requires a delicate balance of support, direct (and often critical) feedback, and humility on both sides. Supervisors need to be more developmental in their approach than uniformly critical, which goes not only for their supervisees' process and work product, but also for their own work as supervisors. They should lean on colleagues, peers, and mentors whenever they encounter a supervisory problem that frustrates them. Every supervisory dyad is different, and the process of supervising psychological assessment reports is often quite difficult to navigate. Supervisors must realize the complexity of this process, allow themselves to mess up and repair, and ask for help when needed.

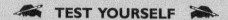

TEST YOURSELF

1. **The three overarching and critical components to consider for an effective assessment report include:**
   (a) Accuracy, clarity, and meaningfulness
   (b) Length, organization, and clarity
   (c) Language, data, and recommendations
   (d) Format, jargon, and meaningfulness

2. **What are the two types of procrastination that may interfere with a supervisee's report writing progress:**
   (a) Initiative and responsive
   (b) Passive and active
   (c) Responsive and proactive
   (d) Passive and purposeful

3. **Which of the following are important aspects of report writing supervision when working with a supervisee whose English is a second language?**
   (a) Recognize they will need/take more time with report writing and plan accordingly.
   (b) Identify whether their writing difficulties stem from ESL issues specifically or not.
   (c) Do not assume they have weak clinical skills based on poor writing.
   (d) All of the above.

4. **All of the following statements are true about report writing supervision except:**
   (a) Understanding type and phase of supervisee procrastination can inform effective interventions.
   (b) Making the supervisor's report writing expectations clear from the beginning is crucial.
   (c) Providing positive feedback on a weak draft report is not helpful.
   (d) Providing ongoing encouragement to the supervisee regardless of skill can build his or her confidence and potentially reduce procrastination.

5. **Providing sample reports is most recommended for supervisors who are:**
   (a) Flexible with format and wording
   (b) Rigid with report expectations
   (c) Hands on with the report writing supervision and break down the process
   (d) None of the above

6. **Considering the audience(s)/reader(s) for the report is important and can help guide the process. All of the following are recommended except:**
   (a) Consider who the primary audience is for the report as well as potential secondary audiences.
   (b) Ask yourself how the reader might use or misuse the information presented in this report.
   (c) Unless you are in a forensic setting, you do not need to consider the court as a potential audience.
   (d) Make sure to clearly, succinctly, and comprehensively address the identified needs of the reader of this report.

Answers: 1. a; 2. b; 3. d; 4. c; 5. b; 6. c.

REFERENCES

Allyn, J. B. (2012). *Writing to clients and referring professionals about psychological assessment results: A handbook of style and grammar.* New York, NY: Routledge.

American Psychiatric Association (APA). (2013). *Diagnostic and statistical manual of mental disorders (5; DSM-5).* Arlington, VA: Author.

Belk, M. S., LoBello, S. G., Ray, G. E., & Zachar, P. (2002). WISC-III administration, clerical, and scoring errors made by student examiners. *Journal of Psychoeducational Assessment, 20*(3), 290–300. https://doi.org/10.1177/073428290202000305

Beswick, G., Rothblum, E. D., & Mann, L. (1988). Psychological antecedents of student procrastination. *Australian Psychologist, 23*(2), 207–217.

Bram, A., & Peebles, M. (2014). *Psychological testing that matters: Creating a road map for effective treatment.* Washington, DC: American Psychological Association.

Brownlow, S., & Reasinger, R. D. (2000). Putting off until tomorrow what is better done today: Academic procrastination as a function of motivation toward college work. *Journal of Social Behavior and Personality, 15*(5; SPI), 15–34.

Chun Chu, A. H., & Choi, J. N. (2005). Rethinking procrastination: Positive effects of "active" procrastination behavior on attitudes and performance. *The Journal of Social Psychology, 145*(3), 245–264.

Dunn, D. S., & Andrews, E. E. (2015). Person-first and identity-first language: Developing psychologists' cultural competence using disability language. *American Psychologist, 70*(3), 255–264. https://doi.org/10.1037/a0038636

Erdodi, L. A., Richard, D. S., & Hopwood, C. (2009). The importance of relying on the manual: Scoring error variance in the WISC-IV Vocabulary subtest. *Journal of Psychoeducational Assessment, 27*(5), 374–385. https://doi.org/10.1177/0734282909332913

Evans, B. F., & Finn, S. E. (2016). Training and consultation in psychological assessment with professional psychologists: Suggestions for enhancing the profession and individual practices. *Journal of Personality Assessment, 98*, 1–11. https://doi.org/10.1080/00223891.2016.1187156

Flower, L., & Hayes, J. R. (1981). A cognitive process theory of writing. *College Composition and Communication, 32*(4), 365–387.

Folse, K. (2009). *Keys to teaching grammar to English language learners: A practical handbook.* Ann Arbor, MI: University of Michigan Press.

Grant, J., Schofield, M. J., & Crawford, S. (2012). Managing difficulties in supervision: Supervisors' perspectives. *Journal of Counseling Psychology, 59*(4), 528–541.

Groth-Marnat, G., & Wright, A. J. (2016). *Handbook of psychological assessment (6).* Hoboken, NJ: Wiley.

Handler, L., & Hilsenroth, M. J. (Eds.) (2013). *Teaching and learning personality assessment.* Mahwah, NJ: Earlbaum.

Katz, I., Eilot, K., & Nevo, N. (2014). "I'll do it later." Type of motivation, self-efficacy and homework procrastination. *Motivation and Emotion, 38*(1), 111–119.

Klingsieck, K. B., Grund, A., Schmid, S., & Fries, S. (2013). Why students procrastinate: A qualitative approach. *Journal of College Student Development, 54*(4), 397–412.

Kuentzel, J. G., Hetterscheidt, L. A., & Barnett, D. (2011). Testing intelligently includes double-checking Wechsler IQ scores. *Journal of Psychoeducational Assessment, 29*(1), 290–300. https://doi.org/10.1177/0734282910362048

Loe, S. A., Kadlubek, R. M., & Marks, W. J. (2007). Administration and scoring errors on the WISC-IV among graduate student examiners. *Journal of Psychoeducational Assessment, 25*, 237–247. https://doi.org/10.1177/0734282906296505

National Council of Schools and Programs in Professional Psychology (NCSPP). (2007). Competency Developmental Achievement Levels. Retrieved from http://ncspp.net/wp-content/uploads/2017/08/DALof-NCSPP-9-21-07.pdf

Nilsson, J., & Anderson, M. (2004). Supervising international students: The role of acculturation, role ambiguity, and multicultural discussions. *Professional Psychology: Research and Practice*, 35(3), 306–312.

Oak, E., Viezel, K. D., Dumont, R., & Willis, J. (2018). Wechsler administration and scoring errors made by graduate students and school psychologists. *Journal of Psychoeducational Assessment*. Retrieved from https://doi.org/10.1177/0734282918786355

Olson, D. (1977). From utterance to text: The bias of language in speech and writing. *Harvard Educational Review*, 47(3), 257–281.

Pade, H. (2016a). On the other side of the table: Examiner accessibility and digital assessment platforms. In M. Carlos & J. Reesman (Chairs), Addressing Training Needs of Psychologists with Disabilities in Psychological Testing and Assessment. A symposium conducted at the annual convention of the American Psychological Association, Denver, Colorado.

Pade, H. (Winter 2016b). Teaching and supervising assessment students and trainees with English as a second language (ESL). *SPA Exchange*, 28(1), 6–16.

Pade, H. (Winter 2018a). The MAC report: Components of proficient report writing: Part I. *SPA Exchange*, 30(1), 6–8.

Pade, H. (Summer 2018b). The MAC report: Components of proficient report writing: Part II. *SPA Exchange*, 30(2), 5–8.

Pade, H., Stolberg, R., Baum, L., Clemence, A. J., & Wright, A. J. (2018). Utility of the proficiency report review form in assessment coursework and clinical training. Roundtable discussion conducted at the annual meeting of the Society for Personality Assessment, Washington, D.C.

Ready, R. E., Santorelli, G. D., Lundquist, T. S., & Romano, F. M. (2016). Psychology internship directors' perceptions of pre-internship training preparation in assessment. *North American Journal of Psychology*, 18, 317–334.

Schneider, W. J., Lichtenberger, E. O., Mather, N., & Kaufman, N. L. (2018). *Essentials of assessment report writing (2)*. Hoboken, NJ: Wiley.

Society for Personality Assessment (SPA). (2015). Personality Assessment Proficiency: Report Review Form. Retrieved from http://storage.jason-mohr.com/www.personality.org/General/pdf/Proficiency%20Report%20Review%20Form%202015.pdf

Steel, P. (2007). The nature of procrastination: A meta-analytic and theoretical review of quintessential self-regulatory failure. *Psychological Bulletin*, 133(1), 65–94.

Styck, K. M., & Walsh, S. M. (2016). Evaluating the prevalence and impact of examiner errors on the Wechsler scales of intelligence: A meta-analysis. *Psychological Assessment, 28*, 3–17. https://doi.org/10.1037/pas0000157

Taylor, J. M., & Neimeyer, G. J. (2015). The assessment of lifelong learning in psychologists. *Professional Psychology: Research and Practice, 46*(6), 385–391.

Thow, M. K., & Murray, R. (2001). Facilitating student writing during project supervision: A practical approach. *Physiotherapy, 87*(3), 134–139.

Trujillo-Pagán, N. (2018). Crossed out by LatinX: Gender neutrality and genderblind sexism. *Latino Studies, 16*(3), 396–406.

Vidal-Ortiz, S., & Martínez, J. (2018). Latinx thoughts: Latinidad with an X. *Latino Studies, 16*(3), 384–395.

Visser, L., Korthagen, F. A., & Schoonenboom, J. (2018). Differences in learning characteristics between students with high, average, and low levels of academic procrastination: Students' views on factors influencing their learning. *Frontiers in Psychology, 9*, 808.

Vygotsky, L. S. (1980). *Mind in society: The development of higher psychological processes.* Cambridge, MA: Harvard University Press.

Wass, R., & Golding, C. (2014). Sharpening a tool for teaching: The zone of proximal development. *Teaching in Higher Education, 19*(6), 671–684.

Webster, T. G. (1971). National priorities for the continuing education of psychologists. *American Psychologist, 26*, 1016–1019.

Wright, A. J. (2010). *Conducting psychological assessment: A guide for practitioners.* Hoboken, NJ: Wiley.

Yalof, J. (2018). Supervision and training of personality assessment with multicultural and diverse clients. In R. Krishnamurthy & S. Smith (Eds.), *Diversity sensitive personality assessment* (pp. 349–372). New York, NY: Routledge.

Yalof, J. (1996). Teaching psychological testing in a diagnostic seminar: Psychodynamics of three teacher tasks. *Bulletin of the Menninger Clinic, 60*(3), 366–376.

Subject Index

Essentials of Psychological Assessment Supervision, First Edition.
Edited by A. Jordan Wright
© 2020 John Wiley & Sons, Inc. Published 2020 by John Wiley & Sons, Inc.